REA's Test Prep Books Are The Best!

(a sample of the <u>hundreds of letters</u> REA receives each year)

" I did well because of your wonderful prep books... I just wanted to thank you for helping me prepare for these tests. "

Student, San Diego, CA

" My students report your chapters of review as the most valuable single resource they used for review and preparation. "

Teacher, American Fork, UT

" Your book was such a better value and was so much more complete than anything your competition has produced — and I have them all! "

Teacher, Virginia Beach, VA

" Compared to the other books that my fellow students had, your book was the most useful in helping me get a great score. "

Student, North Hollywood, CA

" Your book was responsible for my success on the exam, which helped me get into the college of my choice... I will look for REA the next time I need help. "

Student, Chesterfield, MO

" Just a short note to say thanks for the great support your book gave me in helping me pass the test... I'm on my way to a B.S. degree because of you! "

Student, Orlando, FL

(more on next page)

(continued from front page)

" I just wanted to thank you for helping me get a great score
on the AP U.S. History exam... Thank you for making great test preps! "
Student, Los Angeles, CA

" Your *Fundamentals of Engineering Exam* book was the absolute best
preparation I could have had for the exam, and it is one of the major
reasons I did so well and passed the FE on my first try. "
Student, Sweetwater, TN

" I used your book to prepare for the test and found that the advice and the
sample tests were highly relevant... Without using any other material, I earned
very high scores and will be going to the graduate school of my choice. "
Student, New Orleans, LA

" What I found in your book was a wealth of information sufficient to shore up
my basic skills in math and verbal... The section on analytical ability was
excellent. The practice tests were challenging and the answer explanations most
helpful. It certainly is the *Best Test Prep for the GRE*! "
Student, Pullman, WA

" I really appreciate the help from your excellent book. Please keep up
the great work. "
Student, Albuquerque, NM

" I am writing to thank you for your test preparation... your book helped me
immeasurably and I have nothing but praise for your *GRE* preparation."
Student, Benton Harbor, MI

(more on back page)

REA's VERBAL BUILDER

for Admission & Standardized Tests

Book plus Software Games with CD-ROM for both Windows and Macintosh

by the staff of
Research & Education Association

Research & Education Association
61 Ethel Road West • Piscataway, New Jersey 08854

REA's VERBAL BUILDER
for Admission & Standardized Tests
with REA's Verbal Builder Software Games for
both Windows & Macintosh

Printed in the United States of America

Library of Congress Catalog Card Number 99-75133

International Standard Book Number 0-87891-172-3

Research & Education Association
61 Ethel Road West
Piscataway, New Jersey 08854

CONTENTS

ACKNOWLEDGMENTS

We thank the following contributors for their work on the Verbal Builder:

Earvin Berlin Aaron, Ed.D.
Chairperson, Department of Curriculum and Instruction
Texas Southern University, Houston, TX

Pauline Alexander-Travis, Ph.D
Assistant Professor of Reading
Southwestern Oklahoma State University
Weatherford, OK

Suzanne Coffield, M.A.
English Instructor
Northern Illinois University, DeKalb, IL

Ellen Davis Conner, M.A.
English Instructor
Clearlake High School, Houston, TX

Anita Price Davis, Ed.D.
Chairperson, Education Department
Converse College, Spartanburg, SC

Connie Gillespie, M.A.
English Instructor
Connersville High School, Connersville, IN

Gary F. Greif, Ph.D.
Chairperson, Philosophy Department
University of Wisconsin-Green Bay, Green Bay, WI

Ellen Thompson Little, M.A.
Former Teacher of English
East High School, Columbus, OH

Sharon Yunker, M.Ed.
English Instructor, St. Bernard - Elmwood Place High School
St. Bernard, OH

• • •

We also extend our appreciation to the following:

Dr. Max Fogiel, President, for his overall guidance which has brought this
publication to completion;

John Paul Cording, Manager of Educational Software Publishing, for his editorial
contributions;

Larry B. Kling, Quality Control Manager of Books in Print, for his supervision of
revisions;

Kristin M. Rutkowski, Project Manager, for coordinating revisions;

Chad Holland, Editorial Assistant, for his editorial contributions; and

Marty Perzan for typesetting the manuscript.

ABOUT RESEARCH & EDUCATION ASSOCIATION

Research & Education Association (REA) is an organization of educators, scientists, and engineers specializing in various academic fields. Founded in 1959 with the purpose of disseminating the most recently developed scientific information to groups in industry, government, high schools, and universities, REA has since become a successful and highly respected publisher of study aids, test preps, handbooks, and reference works.

REA's Test Preparation series includes study guides for all academic levels in almost all disciplines. Research & Education Association publishes test preps for students who have not yet completed high school, as well as high school students preparing to enter college. Students from countries around the world seeking to attend college in the United States will find the assistance they need in REA's publications. For college students seeking advanced degrees, REA publishes test preps for many major graduate school admission examinations in a wide variety of disciplines, including engineering, law, and medicine. Students at every level, in every field, with every ambition can find what they are looking for among REA's publications.

While most test preparation books present practice tests that bear little resemblance to the actual exams, REA's series presents tests that accurately depict the official exams in both degree of difficulty and types of questions. REA's practice tests are always based upon the most recently administered exams, and include every type of question that can be expected on the actual exams.

REA's publications and educational materials are highly regarded and continually receive an unprecedented amount of praise from professionals, instructors, librarians, parents, and students. Our authors are as diverse as the fields represented in the books we publish. They are well-known in their respective disciplines and serve on the faculties of prestigious high schools, colleges, and universities throughout the United States and Canada.

CHAPTER 1

About the
Verbal Builder

About this Book

REA's staff of authors and educators has prepared material, exercises, and tests based on each of the major standardized exams, including the CLEP, GRE, GMAT, LSAT, SAT I, PSAT, CLAST, ACT, PRAXIS II, MCAT, CBEST, PPST, and other teacher certification tests. The types of questions represented on these standardized exams have been analyzed in order to produce the most comprehensive preparatory material possible. You will find review material, helpful strategies, and exercises geared to your level of studying.

How to Use this Book

If you are preparing to take the CLEP, GRE, GMAT, LSAT, SAT I, PSAT, CLAST, ACT, PRAXIS II, MCAT, CBEST, PPST or any teacher certification exam, you will be taking a test requiring excellent verbal ability. CLEP examinees should be aware that because there are two versions of the CLEP Examination in English Composition, your need to take the essay version will be determined by your college or university. Similarly, in the case of the four CLEP Subject Examinations in Composition and Literature, your school may require the optional essay portion of the test. This book comprises a comprehensive verbal review which can be tailored to your specific test preparation needs.

This book will help you prepare for your test since it includes different types of questions and drills that are representative of your specific test. The book also includes diagnostic tests so that you can determine your strengths and weaknesses within each subject. The explanations are clear and comprehensive, and not only explain why the answer is correct, but also why the remaining answers are incorrect. The Verbal Review gives you practice within a wide range of categories and question types.

The **Grammar and Usage** chapter will prepare students for such questions on the CLEP, GRE, SAT I, PSAT, CLAST, ACT, PRAXIS II, and PPST. But even if you are not planning to take an exam in which grammar is tested, this chapter will still be extremely helpful in enhancing your writing skills.

The **Verbal Ability** chapter includes a comprehensive vocabulary list with drills, as well as material on synonyms, antonyms, analogies, and sentence correction. CLEP, GRE, GMAT, SAT I, PSAT, and ACT examinees see most of these types of questions on their tests. If your exam does not test these areas, you will still benefit from studying the Comprehensive Vocabulary Review, since a strong vocabulary will always aid you in your verbal tests.

Reading Comprehension is included on most standardized tests, including the CLEP, CLAST, PRAXIS II, CBEST, and PPST. As you study this section, you will find practical suggestions to follow, and you will be alerted to the most commonly asked questions. Finally, you will have the opportunity to actually practice the skills you have just strengthened. Although almost every test offers Reading Comprehension, the difficulty level of the vocabulary and the types of questions will vary from test to test. The most simple reading comprehension questions would primarily be found in the ACT exam; the next most challenging questions would be found in graduate-level tests, such as the GRE; the most difficult or challenging questions would be found on a professional-level test, such as the GMAT, LSAT, or the MCAT.

	Grammar and Usage* Chapter 2 Pages 9–86	Verbal Ability† Chapter 3 Pages 89–189 Specifically Pages 89–138	Reading Comprehension Chapter 4 Pages 193–215	Critical Reading Chapter 5 Pages 219–269	Exam Essay Writing Chapter 6 Pages 273–291	Application Essay Writing Chapter 6 Pages 295–299
GMAT		X	X			X
MCAT			X		X	X
GRE	X	X	X			X
SAT I	X	X		X		X
PSAT	X	X		X		
ACT	X	X	X			X
LSAT			X		X	X
CBEST			X		X	
PPST	X		X		X	
PRAXIS II	X		X			
CLAST	X		X		X	
CLEP	X	X	X		X	

Locate your test in the table and find the corresponding sections recommended for study.

* Students who will be writing essays for exams and applications are strongly urged to review the Grammar and Usage section.

† The Verbal Ability chapter includes practice for the tests in antonyms, analogies, and sentence correction. Additionally, this chapter includes a vocabulary list and synonym drills to enhance your skills.

The **Critical Reading** section is included in both the SAT I and the PSAT. In this section you will be asked to analyze various reading passages, not only for straight content, but for the possible implications and inferences which can be drawn from them. You will be utilizing your critical and logical reasoning skills to make judgments and educated guesses based on the information presented. This chapter can help you enhance your reading and reasoning abilities, which is essential in doing well on almost all standardized exams.

The final chapter is on **Essay Writing**. This chapter is divided into two parts: timed essay writing for exams—which is applicable to the CLEP, LSAT, CLAST, MCAT, CBEST, and PPST—and essay writing for school applications, a skill that examinees will find helpful for the GRE, GMAT, LSAT, SAT I, ACT, and MCAT. This chapter will help you to focus on a topic and write under time restraints. It also offers many suggestions to improve your essay.

Finally, before you get started, here are a few guidelines:

➤ Study full chapters. If you think after a few minutes that the chapter appears easy, continue studying. Many chapters (like the tests themselves) become more difficult as they continue.

➤ Review the vocabulary. Having a solid "test vocabulary" will improve every verbal section of your standardized test, even if it is not being tested directly.

➤ Use this guide as a supplement to the review materials provided by the test administrators.

➤ Take the Grammar Diagnostic Test. Even if you don't have a grammar section on your exam, you will find that improving your grammar will help your Verbal Ability in general, and improve your essay writing significantly.

USING REA'S VERBAL BUILDER SOFTWARE GAMES TO BUILD YOUR VOCABULARY & READING SKILLS

See page 308 for CD-ROM Installation Instructions

Dictionary with Easy-Editor allows you to customize your own vocabulary word list or add words and definitions from the Verbal Builder master dictionary. The master dictionary comprises vocabulary words that are most often tested on standardized tests for college and graduate admission. The words are accompanied by definitions and examples of usage in full sentences.

Crossword Puzzles are created from the words and definitions in the master dictionary or from your own custom vocabulary list. The computer can create an "infinite" number of challenging puzzles from either word list.

Match & Link games are the perfect tool for building a stronger vocabulary. The object of the matching game is to link a word or phrase to its corresponding definition or synonym.

Reading Builder/Speed-Reader will help improve your reading speed and comprehension with several challenging activities. You can control the exercises to make them progressively harder as you increase your rate of perception. At the end of every passage are questions to test your reading comprehension.

Help Menu provides information and guidance for using the Verbal Builder software.

CHAPTER 2

Grammar and Usage

- ➤ Diagnostic Test
- ➤ Grammar and Usage Review
- ➤ Drills
- ➤ Grammar and Usage Practice Test

GRAMMAR AND USAGE
DIAGNOSTIC TEST

1. (A) (B) (C) (D) (E)	26. (A) (B) (C) (D) (E)
2. (A) (B) (C) (D) (E)	27. (A) (B) (C) (D) (E)
3. (A) (B) (C) (D) (E)	28. (A) (B) (C) (D) (E)
4. (A) (B) (C) (D) (E)	29. (A) (B) (C) (D) (E)
5. (A) (B) (C) (D) (E)	30. (A) (B) (C) (D) (E)
6. (A) (B) (C) (D) (E)	31. (A) (B) (C) (D) (E)
7. (A) (B) (C) (D) (E)	32. (A) (B) (C) (D) (E)
8. (A) (B) (C) (D) (E)	33. (A) (B) (C) (D) (E)
9. (A) (B) (C) (D) (E)	34. (A) (B) (C) (D) (E)
10. (A) (B) (C) (D) (E)	35. (A) (B) (C) (D) (E)
11. (A) (B) (C) (D) (E)	36. (A) (B) (C) (D) (E)
12. (A) (B) (C) (D) (E)	37. (A) (B) (C) (D) (E)
13. (A) (B) (C) (D) (E)	38. (A) (B) (C) (D) (E)
14. (A) (B) (C) (D) (E)	39. (A) (B) (C) (D) (E)
15. (A) (B) (C) (D) (E)	40. (A) (B) (C) (D) (E)
16. (A) (B) (C) (D) (E)	41. (A) (B) (C) (D) (E)
17. (A) (B) (C) (D) (E)	42. (A) (B) (C) (D) (E)
18. (A) (B) (C) (D) (E)	43. (A) (B) (C) (D) (E)
19. (A) (B) (C) (D) (E)	44. (A) (B) (C) (D) (E)
20. (A) (B) (C) (D) (E)	45. (A) (B) (C) (D) (E)
21. (A) (B) (C) (D) (E)	46. (A) (B) (C) (D) (E)
22. (A) (B) (C) (D) (E)	47. (A) (B) (C) (D) (E)
23. (A) (B) (C) (D) (E)	48. (A) (B) (C) (D) (E)
24. (A) (B) (C) (D) (E)	49. (A) (B) (C) (D) (E)
25. (A) (B) (C) (D) (E)	50. (A) (B) (C) (D) (E)

GRAMMAR AND USAGE
DIAGNOSTIC TEST

This diagnostic test is designed to help you determine your strengths and your weaknesses in grammar and usage. Follow the directions for each part and check your answers.

These types of questions are found in the following tests: PRAXIS II, ACT, CLAST, CLEP, and PPST.

You will also find these questions useful to sharpen your grammatical skills for these tests: GMAT, MCAT, GRE, LSAT, CBEST, PSAT and SAT I

---

50 Questions

DIRECTIONS: For each sentence in which you find an error, select the one underlined part that must be changed to make the sentence correct and blacken the corresponding space on your answer sheet.

If there is no error, blacken answer space (E).

EXAMPLE:

The player was so tired that thoughts of going to sleep was all that
           A   **B**   **C**

went through her mind. No error.   Ⓐ Ⓑ ● Ⓓ Ⓔ
    D   **E**

---

1. *Huckleberry Finn,* by general consensus agreement Mark Twain's greatest
                    A   **B**

  work, is supremely the American Classic; it is also one of the great books
           C   **D**

  of the world. No error.
        E

2. The U.S. Constitution supposes what the history of all governments
            A   **B**

demonstrate, that the executive is the branch <u>most</u> interested in war and
     C   D

most prone to it. <u>No error.</u>
                    E

3. Mama, the <u>narrator</u> of Alice Walker's short story "Everyday Use," <u>speaks</u>
           A   B

fondly of her daughter upon her return home after a long absence <u>like</u>
                                                                              C

Mama is <u>proud</u> of her. <u>No error.</u>
             D   E

4. <u>Nearly</u> one <u>hundred</u> years after the impoverished Vincent Van Gogh died,
   A   B

his paintings <u>had sold</u> for more than a <u>million dollars.</u> <u>No error.</u>
               C   D   E

5. Many athletes <u>recruited</u> for football by college coaches <u>expect</u> that they
              A   B

will, <u>in fact,</u> receive an education when they <u>accept</u> a scholarship.
        C   D

<u>No error.</u>
  E

6. <u>Hopefully,</u> by the end of the <u>Twentieth Century,</u> computer scientists will
   A   B

invent machines with <u>enough</u> intelligence to work without breaking down
                      C

<u>continually.</u> <u>No error.</u>
     D   E

7. Studies <u>showing</u> that the earth includes a <u>vast series</u> of sedimentary rocks,
        A   B

some with <u>embedded</u> fossils <u>that</u> prove the existence of ancient organisms.
          C   D

<u>No error.</u>
  E

8. When Martin Luther King, Jr., wrote his famous letter from the Birming-
   A

   ham jail, he advocated neither evading or defying the law; but he accepted
   B   C

   the idea that a penalty results from breaking a law, even an unjust one.
   D

   No error.
   E

9. The Eighteenth Century philosopher Adam Smith asserted that a nation
   A   B

   achieves the best economic results when individuals work both for their
   C

   own interests and to gain more goods. No error.
   D   E

10. According to Niccolo Machiavelli, wise rulers cannot and should not keep
    A   B

    their word when such integrity would be to their disadvantage and when the
    C

    reasons for the promise no longer exist. No error.
    D   E

11. The Milky Way galaxy, which comprises millions of stars, has both thin
    A   B

    and congested spots, but shines their brightest in the constellation
    C   D

    Sagittarius. No error.
    E

12. To learn an ancient language like Latin or Greek is one way to discover
    A   B

    the roots of Western Culture; studying Judaeo-Christian religious beliefs
    C

    is another. No error.
    D   E

13. Many political conservatives <u>contribute</u> the problems of modern American
             A

    society to the twin evils of the New Deal and <u>secular humanism</u>, both
                      B

    <u>of which are</u> presumed to <u>stem</u> from Marxism. <u>No error.</u>
     C   **D**   **E**

14. <u>Having minimal exposure</u> to poetry when they <u>attended</u> school, most
        A   **B**

    Americans <u>chose</u> to watch television or <u>to read</u> popular magazines for
        C   **D**

    entertainment. <u>No error.</u>
        E

15. What makes <u>we</u> humans <u>different from</u> other animals <u>can be defined</u> at
        A   **B**   **C**

    least <u>partly</u> by our powerful and efficient intelligence. <u>No error.</u>
      D   **E**

16. When one contrasts the ideas of the Romantic William Wordsworth <u>with</u>
                      A

    <u>those</u> of Neoclassicist John Dryden, <u>one finds</u> that neither of the poets
     B   **C**

    <u>differ</u> as much as one would expect. <u>No error.</u>
     D   **E**

17. Carl Jung's hypothesis of the collective unconscious <u>suggests</u> that we
                  A

    inherit <u>cultural-experimental</u> memory in the form of mythological arche-
        B

    type, <u>which arise</u> from repeated <u>patterns</u> of human behavior. <u>No error.</u>
      C   **D**   **E**

18. Bertrand Russell believed that a free <u>person's</u> liberation is <u>effected</u> by a
                                              A   **B**

    contemplation of <u>Fate</u>; one achieves emancipation through passionate
                  C

    pursuit of eternal things, <u>not through</u> the pursuit of private happiness.
                                         D

    <u>No error.</u>
      E

19. <u>Latin American</u> literature <u>includes</u> the works of Gabriel Garcia Marquez,
         A   **B**

    Pablo Neruda, and Jorge Luis Borges; each of these <u>acclaimed</u> artists has
                                                 C

    won <u>their</u> shares of prizes. <u>No error.</u>
         D   **E**

20. The reason a <u>large percentage</u> of American college students <u>located</u> Mos-
                A   **B**

    cow in California is <u>because</u> they <u>were not required</u> to learn the facts of
                     C   **D**

    geography. <u>No error.</u>
          E

21. <u>Viewing</u> the original "Las Meninas" painting by Velázquez at the Prado is
       A

    real interesting <u>compared</u> to viewing <u>it</u> in an art book. <u>No error.</u>
     B   **C**   **D**   **E**

22. Susan Sontag, who argued <u>against interpreting</u> artistic works, <u>urged</u> critics
                           A   **B**

    to <u>discontinue</u> their emphasis on content and to restore their attention
         C

    to form. <u>No error.</u>
      D   **E**

23. The movie <u>Amadeus</u> made <u>not only</u> Mozart's life intriguing, <u>but also</u>
             A   **B**   **C**

    <u>Antonio Salieri's works became popular.</u> <u>No error.</u>
                     D   **E**

24. In astronomy, a syzygy <u>is when</u> the earth, <u>the sun,</u> and the moon <u>converge;</u>
                        A   **B**   **C**

    that is, they <u>lie</u> in a straight line. <u>No error.</u>
              D   **E**

25. When the preamble to the <u>Declaration of Independence</u> <u>was read</u> to
                                    A   **B**

    a sample of the American people, <u>many</u> of them believe that it represents
                                  C

    <u>Communist beliefs.</u> <u>No error.</u>
             D   **E**

DIRECTIONS: In each of the following sentences, some part or all of the sentence is underlined. Below each sentence, you will find five ways of phrasing the underlined part. Select the answer that produces the most effective sentence, one that is clear and exact, without awkwardness or ambiguity, and blacken the corresponding space on your answer sheet. In choosing answers, follow the requirements of standard written English. Choose the answer that best expresses the meaning of the original sentence.

Answer (A) is always the same as the underlined part. Choose answer (A) if you think the original sentence needs no revision.

EXAMPLE:

The children swam in the lake all day <u>and that is because it was so hot.</u>

(A)   and that is because it was so hot.

(B)   when it was so hot.

(C)   since it was so hot.

(D)   which is why it was so hot.

(E)   at the time when it was so hot.

---

26.   Two-thirds of American seventeen-year-olds do not know that the Civil War <u>takes place</u> between 1850-1900.

  (A)   takes place   (D)   have taken place

  (B)   took place   (E)   is taking place

  (C)   had taken place

27.   Both professional and amateur ornithologists, <u>people that study birds,</u> recognize the Latin or scientific names of bird species.

  (A)   people that study birds

  (B)   people which study birds

  (C)   the study of birds

  (D)   people who study birds

  (E)   in which people study birds

28. Many of the oil-producing states spent their huge surplus tax revenues during the oil boom of the 1970s and early 1980s <u>in spite of the fact that</u> oil production from new wells began to flood the world market as early as 1985.

    (A) in spite of the fact that

    (B) even in view of the fact that

    (C) however clearly it was known that

    (D) even though

    (E) when it was clear that

29. The president of the community college reported <u>as to the expectability of the tuition increase as well as the actual amount.</u>

    (A) as to the expectability of the tuition increase as well as the actual amount

    (B) that the tuition will likely increase by a specific amount

    (C) as to the expectability that tuition will increase by a specific amount

    (D) about the expected tuition increase of five percent

    (E) regarding the expectation of a tuition increase expected to be five percent

30. Although Carmen developed an interest in classical music, <u>she did not read notes and had never played an instrument.</u>

    (A) she did not read notes and had never played an instrument

    (B) she does not read notes and has never played an instrument

    (C) it is without being able to read notes or having played an instrument

    (D) she did not read notes nor had she ever played them

    (E) it is without reading notes nor having played an instrument

31. Political candidates must campaign on issues and ideas that strike a chord within their constituency but <u>with their goal to sway</u> undecided voters to support their candidacy.

    (A) with their goal to sway

    (B) need also to sway

(C) aiming at the same time to sway

(D) also trying to sway

(E) its goal should also be in swaying

32. The major reasons students give for failing courses in college is that they have demanding professors and work at full- or part-time jobs.

(A) is that they have demanding professors and work at

(B) are demanding professors and they work at

(C) is having demanding professors and having

(D) are demanding professors, in addition to working at

(E) are that they have demanding professors and that they have

33. Having command of color, symbolism, as well as technique, Georgia O'Keeffe is considered to be a great American painter.

(A) Having command of color, symbolism, as well as technique

(B) Having command of color, symbolism, and her technical ability

(C) Because of her command of color, symbolism, and technique

(D) With her command of color and symbolism and being technical

(E) By being in command of both color and symbolism and also technique

34. Whether the ancient ancestors of American Indians actually migrated or did not cross a land bridge now covered by the Bering Strait remains uncertain, but that they could have has not been refuted by other theories.

(A) Whether the ancient ancestors of American Indians actually migrated or did not

(B) That the ancient ancestors of American Indians actually did migrate

(C) The actuality of whether the ancient ancestors of American Indians migrated

(D) Whether in actuality the ancient ancestors of American Indians migrated or did not

(E) That the ancient ancestors of American Indians may actually have migrated

35. Caution in scientific experimentation can sometimes be related more to integrity than to lack of knowledge.

   (A) sometimes be related more to integrity than to lack of knowledge

   (B) sometimes be related more to integrity as well as lack of knowledge

   (C) often be related to integrity as to lack of knowledge

   (D) be related more to integrity rather than lack of knowledge

   (E) be related often to integrity, not only to lack of knowledge

36. In freshman English classes, students sometimes believe that professors contrive all assignments for a purpose that is as often torture as it is for intellectual development.

   (A) as often torture as it is for intellectual development

   (B) as often torture as for intellectual development

   (C) as often for torture as for developing intellect

   (D) often for torture as for intellectual development

   (E) as often to torture as to develop intellect

37. Personal computers often feature tens of thousands of memory bytes, whose computing and storage ability far outstrips their need for most home and business users.

   (A) whose computing and storage ability far outstrips their

   (B) the computing and storage ability of them far outstrips

   (C) that computing and storage ability far outstrips their

   (D) whose computing and storage ability far outstrips its

   (E) whose computing and storage ability more outstrip their

38. Though heavily dependent on English tradition for direction in the early years of the republic, Ralph Waldo Emerson challenged American scholarship with a goal, but it established an identity separate from both.

   (A) republic, Ralph Waldo Emerson challenged American scholarship with a goal, but it established an identity

   (B) republic and challenged with a goal by Ralph Waldo Emerson, American scholarship established an identity

(C) republic, Ralph Waldo Emerson challenged American scholarship with a goal, while it established an identity

(D) republic and challenged with a goal by Ralph Waldo Emerson, the identity remains American scholarship

(E) republic while Ralph Waldo Emerson challenged American scholarship with a goal, as an identity it remains

39. Having heard all the evidence and having ruled that the football player plagiarized his research paper, that the academic vice president overturned the honor court's sentence disillusioned the student juror.

(A) that the academic vice president overturned the honor court's sentence disillusioned the student juror

(B) the student jurors were disillusioned about the academic vice president's overturning the honor court's sentence

(C) the students jurors found the academic vice president's decision to overturn the honor court's sentence disillusioning

(D) the student juror's disillusionment at the academic vice president's overturning of the honor court's sentence was disappointing

(E) the academic vice president's overturning the honor court's sentence was an extreme disillusionment to the student jurors

40. The United Nations is filled with representatives, who, although while there, have a stated common goal of maintaining peace in the world, their goals for their own nations range from working for accommodation to outright belligerence.

(A) their goals for their own nations range from working for accommodation to outright belligerence.

(B) work for their own nations toward goals that range from accommodations to outright belligerence.

(C) they are working toward goals for their own nations that ranging from accommodation to outright belligerence

(D) the goals range from accommodation to outright belligerence for their own nations

(E) work toward goals for their own nations that range from accommodation to outright belligerence

---

DIRECTIONS: For each sentence in which you find an error, select the one underlined part that must be changed to make the sentence correct and blacken the corresponding space on your answer sheet.

If there is no error, blacken answer space (E).

41. Astronomers and physicists <u>tell</u> us that the universe is <u>constant</u> expanding
                                      A   **B**

     <u>and that</u> it <u>comprises</u> numerous galaxies like ours. <u>No error.</u>
        C   **D**   **E**

42. <u>Less</u> students chose liberal arts and <u>sciences</u> majors in the 1990s than in the
     A   **B**

     1960s <u>because of</u> the contemporary view that a college education <u>is</u> a ticket
           C   **D**

     to enter the job market. <u>No error.</u>
                         E

43. Span of control is the term <u>that</u> refers to the <u>limits</u> of a leader's
                                   A   **B**

     <u>ability for managing</u> those employees <u>under</u> his/her supervision. <u>No error.</u>
              C   **D**   **E**

44. <u>Because some</u> people believe <u>strongly</u> that channelling, the <u>process by</u>
        A   **B**   **C**

     <u>which</u> an individual goes into a trance-like state and communicates the

     thoughts of an ancient warrior or guru to an audience, helps them cope with

     modern problems, but others condemn the whole idea <u>as</u> mere superstition.
                                                                  D

     <u>No error.</u>
      E

45. The reed on a woodwind instrument is <u>essential</u> <u>being that</u> it
                                            A   **B**

     <u>controls the quality</u> of <u>tone and sound.</u> <u>No error.</u>
            C   **D**   **E**

46. As far as taking an SAT preparation course, educators encourage it
     —————
       A   **B**

     because the course may alleviate test anxiety. No error.
     ———————   ————————   ————————
       C   **D**   **E**

47. In the South, they like to eat cured or smoked pork products such as ham,
            ———— ————   ————   ——————————
             A   **B**   **C**   **D**

     bacon, and barbecue. No error.
                          ————————
                            E

48. Both Japan and the United States want to remain a net exporter of goods
     ———————————————————————— ————   ——————————
                   A   **B**   **C**

     to avoid unfavorable trade imbalances. No error.
              ——————————————————————   ————————
                        D   **E**

49. As an avid cyclist, Jon rode more miles a day than his friend's bicycle
           ——————————   ————   ————   ———————
              A   **B**   **C**   **D**

     No error.
     ————————
       E

50. After the end of the Mesozoic Era, dinosaurs, once the dominant
                          —————————————   —————————————————
                              A   **B**

     species are extinct. No error.
     ——————— ———   ————————
       C   **D**   **E**

GRAMMAR AND USAGE DIAGNOSTIC TEST

ANSWER KEY

1.	(A)	14.	(C)	27.	(D)	40.	(B)
2.	(C)	15.	(A)	28.	(D)	41.	(B)
3.	(C)	16.	(D)	29.	(B)	42.	(A)
4.	(C)	17.	(E)	30.	(A)	43.	(C)
5.	(B)	18.	(E)	31.	(B)	44.	(A)
6.	(A)	19.	(D)	32.	(E)	45.	(B)
7.	(A)	20.	(C)	33.	(C)	46.	(A)
8.	(B)	21.	(B)	34.	(B)	47.	(B)
9.	(D)	22.	(E)	35.	(A)	48.	(C)
10.	(E)	23.	(D)	36.	(E)	49.	(D)
11.	(C)	24.	(A)	37.	(A)	50.	(C)
12.	(A)	25.	(B)	38.	(B)		
13.	(A)	26.	(B)	39.	(B)		

DETAILED EXPLANATIONS
OF ANSWERS

1.   **(A)**   Choice (A) is obviously wordy, "consensus" meaning the same as "general agreement," so it is the best choice. None of the others has a usage error. Choice (B) is acceptable in that it implies a well-known fact that Twain wrote many other works. Choice (C) underscores the claim made in the whole sentence by establishing the book as the "best" American work. Finally, choice (D) is acceptable because of commas in other parts of the sentence. Choice (E) clearly does not apply.

2.   **(C)**   This question has several potential errors. Choice (A) requires that you know to capitalize important historical documents, so it is correct. Choice (B) calls to question the attribution of human rationality to an inanimate object, but since the Constitution actually does have logical premises, we can correctly say that the document can posit the premise stated. Choice (D) is acceptable because the superlative is referenced within the sentence; one should know that the U.S. government has three branches. That leaves choices (C) and (E). Choice (C) is the verb in the clause beginning with the word "what"; it is plural, and therefore, incorrect because it does not agree with its subject "history," a singular noun. Do not be fooled by the intervening plural word "governments." Since choice (C) is the error, choice (E) would no longer be considered.

3.   **(C)**   Even though people use "like" as a conjunction in conversation and public speaking, it is a preposition, and formal written English requires "as," "as if," or "as though" when what follows is a clause. No other choice is even suspect.

4.   **(C)**   One could question the use of "nearly" (A), but it is correct. One might argue also that "million dollars" (D) should be written "$1 million," but the obvious choice (C) is so clearly an incorrect use of the past perfect tense that the other possibilities, remote at best, pale by comparison. The simple past tense ("sold"), the present progressive tense ("are selling"), or the present perfect progressive tense ("have been selling"), could each be used correctly depending on the meaning intended.

5.   **(B)**   This choice is not so obvious, and may be arguable, but authorities agree that the use of "expect" to mean "suppose" or "believe" (the usage here) is either informal or colloquial, but again not formal written English. The next most likely choice (E) would suggest that informal or colloquial usage is appropriate.

The third most likely trouble area (D) brings to mind the distinction between "accept" and "except," a word pair often confused. However, "accept" is correct here.

6. **(A)** Regardless of the popular usage by such pop grammarians as James Kilpatrick and William Safire, "hopefully" is an adverb trying to be a clause ("it is hoped" or "I hope"). However, instances still exist that require a distinction between the two uses. To be clear, use "hopefully" when you mean "in a hopeful manner." ("He wished hopefully that she would accept his proposal of marriage.") Choice (D) appears suspicious. "Continually" means recurrence at intervals over a period of time, so it is correctly used to imply that machines do break down often. Capitalizing "Twentieth Century" is also appropriate as it is here used as the specific historical period (like the "Middle Ages"). We would not capitalize the phrase if it were used simply to count, as in "The twentieth century from now will surely find enormous changes in the world." It is incorrect to hyphenate a number-noun phrase like this one when it stands alone as a noun phrase. Choice (C) is correct as used.

7. **(A)** The two most suspicious choices are (A) and (D) because the item is a sentence fragment. No reasonable substitute for (D) would solve both the logic problem (incomplete thought) and the punctuation problem (comma splice if you omit "that"). Changing "showing" to "show" would, however, make the clause into a complete sentence with correct punctuation. Neither of the choices (B) or (C) provokes suspicion.

8. **(B)** Again, the two most questionable choices, (B) and (C), compete for our attention. The use of "but" makes sense because it shows contrast to the previous idea. ("Don't evade or defy the law, but if caught breaking a law, accept the penalty.") The use of "or," however, is clearly not parallel to the immediately preceding use of "neither." The proper phrase is "neither....nor" for negative alternate choices. Neither choice (A) nor choice (D) demands a second look.

9. **(D)** This choice involves parallel construction, or the lack of it. The word "both" introduces a pair of phrases, one a prepositional phrase ("for their own interests"), the other an infinitive phrase ("to gain more goods"). Aside from being inelegant, "to gain more goods" is also not the same structure and should be changed to "their own gain" to make the two phrases perfectly parallel. Choices (B) and (C) are not problematic. Choice (A) is another candidate because of the capitalization and the lack of a hyphen between "Eighteenth" and "Century." The capitalization is correct (see explanation for answer 6), and no hyphen is needed when the phrase becomes an adjective that has meaning as a single phrase, which the capitalization suggests, or if the first word forms a familiar pair with the following word and if there is no danger of confusion. (The sentence clearly does not mean that Smith is the eighteenth (small "e") philosopher, but *the* Eighteenth Century philosopher.)

10. **(E)** The other choices all fail to exhibit inappropriate usage. Choice (A), "cannot," is spelled as one word; choice (B), "should not," is parallel to "cannot" and adds meaning necessary to the thought. Choice (C) is a correct plural possessive pronoun, the antecedent of which is "rulers." Finally, choice (D) is a third-person plural verb agreeing with its subject, "reasons."

11. **(C)** For the same reason "their" was correct in answer 10, it is incorrect here. "Milky Way galaxy" is the singular antecedent, for which the pronoun referent should be "its" (inanimate object). Do not be confused by the intervening words ("stars" and "spots"); it is the galaxy which shines in this sentence, not the stars or the spots. Choice (A) is the correct usage of "comprises." Choice (B) is an appropriate pair of adjectives with no apparent problem. Choice (D) is appropriate because the sentence has an internally supplied superlative sense; it does not need a "brightest of" phrase.

12. **(A)** Again, non-parallel structure is the key of this and many other test items. Because of the overwhelming importance of understanding balance and euphony in sentence structure, tests like this one emphasize parallel sentence structures. "To learn" clashes with "studying" in the parallel clause. You can't choose "studying." "Learning" substituted for "To learn" would make the clauses parallel. Choice (B) is a correct use of "like" as a preposition (objects: "Latin," "Greek"). Choice (D) is correctly singular as the verb of the noun phrase "studying ... beliefs." Nothing is incorrect about choice (C).

13. **(A)** This is a colloquial, nonstandard substitution for the correct word, "attribute." It is so obviously incorrect, there's hardly any point in proceeding once you read it. Choice (B) is correctly lower case, not capitalized. Choice (C) is a correct, if a bit stiff, phrase. Choice (D) is a correct plural verb the subject of which is "both," also plural.

14. **(C)** This is an incorrect simple past verb tense. You have to spot the context clue "most Americans" "attended" school (choice (B)) in the past, which suggests they no longer do so now. They must then "choose" their entertainment. You might believe that choice (A) is questionable, but the present participial phrase suggests coincidence with the time "most Americans" "attended school." It is, therefore, correct. Choice (D) is correctly an infinitive that is parallel to "to watch."

15. **(A)** The two most questionable choices to many students will be (A) and (B). Choice (A) is incorrectly a subjective case pronoun when it should be objective (object of verb "makes," subject "What"). If you know the difference between "different from" (correctly used in this sentence) and "difference than" (correctly used only to introduce a clause), then choice (B) is no longer viable.

Besides being passive construction, choice (C) has no objectionable qualities; it is grammatically correct. So is choice (D) correctly an adverb that has meaning in context.

16. **(D)** This is a case of subject-verb disagreement related to the definition of the word "neither" (subject) as singular. Its verb must also be singular, and "differ" is plural. Choice (A) correctly uses English idiom ("compare to" – "contrast with"). Choice (B) refers clearly to "ideas," its antecedent, and agrees with it (both plural). Choice (C) is a singular verb agreeing with its subject, "one."

17. **(E)** Everything in the sentence is acceptable or correct usage, even though some of it may be a bit stuffy and pedantic, i.e., choice (B). You might question choice (A) in that instead of suggesting, perhaps asserting or stating would be more appropriate. Even though these terms clearly differ, there is nothing wrong with using "suggests" (correct subject-verb agreement, with "hypothesis") because a hypothesis can suggest as well as theorize, assert, etc. Choice (C) correctly agrees with its subject "which" (plural, antecedent "archetypes"). Choice (D) might be considered redundant ("repeated" and "pattern"), but that is not apparent from the context.

18. **(E)** You are likely to have chosen either (B) or (C) here. The affect/effect word pair often confuses students, and this instance is one in which "effected" is correctly used as a verb meaning "brought about" or "caused to happen." The question of choice (C) is whether or not to capitalize the word "Fate." When it refers to the collective term for the Greek concept of destiny (actually gods, the Fates), as it does here, it is appropriately capitalized. Choices (A) and (D) do not seem questionable.

19. **(D)** Again, the problem here is pronoun-antecedent agreement. "Their" does not refer to the three writers collectively; its antecedent is "each," which is always singular, not plural ("each one"). There is nothing wrong with choices (A), (B), and (C).

20. **(C)** The error here is known as faulty predication ("reason … is because"). The usage rule is that "because" is redundant for "reason." Choice (A) is appropriate, if a bit general (not 30 or 70 percent, for example). The verb in choice (B) is correct in the past tense, as is the verb phrase in choice (D).

21. **(B)** "Real" is an adjective and should not be used as an adverb to modify, in this case, another adjective, "interesting." Choice (A) correctly uses a gerund (verbal noun) to introduce a phrase serving as the subject of the verb "is." Remember, we "compare to," so choice (C) is correct. Choice (D) is a singular pronoun referring properly to the inanimate object of the painting.

22. **(E)** Nothing in this sentence appears to be even questionable excepting perhaps choice (C). It is, however, a parallel construction to its coordinate phrase ("to restore their attention to form"). Choice (D) also is a parallel prepositional phrase matching "on content." Choices (A) and (B) are both appropriate uses in the context.

23. **(D)** This is a parallel structure problem. Choice (D) is part of a "not only ... but also" construction; it should read "works popular" to parallel "life intriguing," which was not a choice. Choice (C) correctly uses the possessive form, which, by the way, is parallel to "Mozart's."

24. **(A)** This is a faulty predication problem. To be correct, the verb "occurs" should be substituted for "is." "Is where" is also a faulty predication. The various forms of the verb "to be" are linking verbs and must link either nouns or pronouns or adjectives to the subject. (When, where, and because are adverbs). Choice (D) might draw your attention, but it is the correctly used form of "lie" (not "lay") because the various bodies are not placed there by humans. Choice (B) uses the comma correctly in the series. Choice (C) is also a correct use of the verb.

25. **(B)** The context clue is in the verb "believe," not a choice and presumed to be correct. In that case, the past tense passive verb "was read" must be changed to the appropriate present tense "is read." Choice (A) correctly capitalizes an important document. "Communist" is correctly capitalized as a proper adjective derived from the noun.

26. **(B)** This question of appropriate verb tense requires the simple past tense verb "took" because the Civil War happened in a finite time period in the past. The other choices all fail that test. The original and choice (E) are present tense, and do not logically fit the facts. Choice (D) is the present perfect tense, which suggests a continuous action from the past to the present. Choice (C) is the past perfect tense, which suggests a continuing action from one time in the past to another in the more recent past.

27. **(D)** We can eliminate fairly quickly choices (C) and (E) as either inappropriate or awkward appositives to "ornithology," instead of "ornithologists." Neither is (A) the best choice even though some may consider it acceptable. Likewise, choice (B) tends to be limited to nonrestrictive clauses, unlike this one. Choice (D) then correctly uses a "personal" relative pronoun.

28. **(D)** Choices (A), (D), and (E) are the best candidates because they are more concise than the other two choices. Each does express the same idea, but (E) does not as strongly indicate the contrast between the two clauses in the

sentence as do choices (A) and (D). Choice (D) clearly makes its point in fewer words and is the better choice.

29. **(B)** The phrase "as to" often is overblown and unclear, so it is best to eliminate it when there are other choices. Likewise, "expectability" does not exactly roll off your tongue. That leaves choices (B) and (D). Choice (D) adds a definite figure, unwarranted by the original sentence. It also is duller than (B), which does change the wording for the better and also indicates that the "actual amount" is to be announced, rather than that it is already known.

30. **(A)** Choices (C) and (D) introduce unnecessary absolute phrases beginning with "it," which make the sentences wordy. They can be eliminated immediately. Choice (D) has an illogical comparison suggesting notes = instrument, so it, too, is not the best choice. Between (A) and (B) the difference boils down to the present tense vs. the past tense. Choice (A) uses past tenses, which seem better in sequence to follow the past tense verb "developed."

31. **(B)** Choices (A), (C), and (D) can be disqualified quickly because they are not parallel to the structure of the main clause. Choice (E) is ungainly and introduces a vague pronoun "it" (unclear antecedent). Choice (B) reads well and has the virtue of brevity.

32. **(E)** The choices are easy to discern in this sentence. The original verb does not agree with its subject, nor is the structure parallel. The former reason also eliminates choice (C). Choice (B) does not have parallel structure (phrase and clause). Choice (D) does not logically agree with the subject ("reasons") since it names one ("demanding professors") but relegates the other reason to an afterthought. Choice (D) has both parallel structure and subject-verb agreement; it also names two reasons.

33. **(C)** The original suffers from inadequate causal relationship and nonparallel structure. Choices (D) and (E) are both unnecessarily wordy; (D) is still not parallel; and (E) is internally illogical ("both" with three things). Choice (B) switches its structure at the end. Although it is technically parallel, it is still awkward because of the addition of the possessive pronoun "her." Choice (C) solves both problems by clearly showing cause and by being parallel (three nouns in series).

34. **(B)** This sentence presents an incomplete comparison and a redundancy ("Whether"/"or did not"/"remains uncertain"), as well as syntactical mayhem. Choice (C) tries to undo the damage, but it remains inelegant in syntax and leaves partial redundancy ("Whether"/"remains uncertain"). Choice (D) is worse in both respects. Choice (E) clears up the syntax but leaves some redundancy

("may actually have"/"remains uncertain"). Choice (B) eliminates both problems cleanly.

35. **(A)** The sentence reads well as is; it is perfectly balanced. Choice (B) introduces an incomplete comparison ("more" but no "than"). Choice (C) awkwardly uses "as to." Choices (D) and (E) make a scrambled mess by introducing illogical structures.

36. **(E)** This is also a parallel structure case. However, here, we have to choose the solution that changes both the original phrases so that they are consistent with each other. (E) is the only answer to do that. Each of the other choices has a non-parallel pair compared.

37. **(A)** Not the best sentence, the only reasonable choice here is (A). (B) is incorrect because it introduces a clause which requires a semicolon to separate it from the rest of the sentence. (C) and (E) really do not make sense. (D) has an agreement problem ("its" and "computers").

38. **(B)** Even this answer may not be the best of all possible solutions, but it is the best one in this set. It properly makes the two ideas coordinate by putting them in a similar structure ("dependent" and "challenged"). The word "but" seems out of place in (A). (C) rambles along without making strict sense and using "while" inappropriately. (D) and (E) both make no sense at all.

39. **(B)** (B) uses the solution of a passive voice construction, again not necessarily the best way to rewrite the sentence, but better than the other choices. (A) has no noun to be modified by the phrase beginning with "Having." The same is true of (D) and (E), and they are also awkward. (C) unnecessarily suspends the disappointment until the end.

40. **(B)** Only two of the choices fulfill the "who" clause begun in the first part of the sentence: (B) and (E). The difference between them is the location of the phrase "for their own nations." In (E) the phrase separates "goals" from the relative clause describing the goals and induces confusion.

41. **(B)** (A) is a verb correctly in agreement with its compound subject. (C) is an appropriate parallel structure requiring no punctuation. (D) correctly uses the word "comprises" and makes it agree with its subject. Only (B) seems incorrect. The structure requires the adverb form "constantly," since it describes an adjective, "expanding."

42. **(A)** This is the classic confusion of "less" for the correct "fewer." "Few(er)" refers to countable things or persons; "little (less)" refers to things that

can be measured or estimated but not itemized. The only other choice to examine is (D), but it is the appropriate tense referring to the "contemporary" (now) view.

43. **(C)**   (A) is a correct use of the relative pronoun. Nothing is unusual about (B). (C) is the culprit here; it should be the infinitive form to adhere to the idiom, "ability to (verb)." (D) is an appropriate reference to hierarchy and responsibility.

44. **(A)**   The sentence is illogical as it stands. Removing "Because" will make it sensible. (B) is an appropriate adverb modifying "believe;" (C) is a clear and effective subordination of an explanation of a term. (D) uses "as" properly as a preposition.

45. **(B)**   "Being that" is colloquial for "because," which is better for at least the reason that it is shorter, but also that it is more formal. No other choices seem out of bounds.

46. **(A)**   "As far as" is an incomplete comparison that should always include "is" (or variant form of "to be") "concerned." "As for" can be substituted for "as far as ... is (are) concerned." The others are acceptable.

47. **(B)**   This is the classic vague pronoun reference. Out of context, there is no antecedent for "they." Every pronoun must have an identifiable antecedent. (A) is acceptable, by the way; geographical region is capitalized. No problems show up in the other choices.

48. **(C)**   This is a problem often called agreement of nominative forms. The compound subject ("Japan and the United States") is plural, and the form to match is "net exporters" in this case. (B) is a verb correctly agreeing with its plural subject. "Imbalances" is correct in (D) because all nations, particularly the two mentioned, want an imbalance of trade in their favor.

49. **(D)**   This problem demonstrates a faulty comparison: "Jon" and "his friend's bicycle" are not equivalents and should not be compared. "His friend" would have been correct. (B) is acceptable because it indicates the rides are in the past, which does not conflict with any other part of the sentence.

50. **(C)**   The problem here is appropriate verb tense. Both "After" and "once the dominant species" signal requirement of the past tense. Changing "are" to "became" would solve the problem. (A) is correctly capitalized as a geologic period. Nothing is amiss with either (B) or (D).

GRAMMAR AND USAGE REVIEW

After you have taken the Diagnostic Test, and have become familiar with the question types, you are ready to review grammar and usage. Use this review to brush up skills, as well as to learn new ones.

1. Subject-Verb Agreement

NO: The arrival of many friends promise good times.

Always remember to make the verb agree with the subject of the sentence. Be wary of the words that come between the subject and the verb. They may distract you.

YES: The <u>arrival</u> of many friends <u>promises</u> good times.

———————

NO: Into the darkness stares her black cats.

Don't be fooled by sentences where the subject follows the verb. Be especially careful to determine the subject and make it agree with the verb.

YES: Into the darkness <u>stares</u> her black <u>cat</u>.

———————

NO: Either the principal or the football coach usually attend the dance.

When singular subjects are joined by *either ... or, neither ... nor, or* or *nor,* the verb is also singular.

YES: Either the principal or the football <u>coach</u> usually <u>attends</u> the dance.

———————

NO: Neither the cat nor the dogs is eating today.

If one of the subjects is plural and one is singular, make the verb agree with the subject nearest it.

YES: Neither the <u>cat</u> nor the <u>dogs</u> are eating today,

2. Comparison of Adjectives

    NO: That was the most bravest thing he ever did.

Do not combine two superlatives.

    YES: That was the <u>bravest</u> thing he ever did.

    NO: Mary was more friendlier than Susan.

Do not combine two comparatives.

    YES: Mary was friendlier than Susan.

    NO: I can buy either the shirt or the scarf. The shirt is most expensive.

The comparative should be used when only two things are being compared.

    YES: I can buy either the shirt or the scarf. The shirt is <u>more</u> expensive.

3. Possessive Nouns

A common error to avoid is to write *it's* (the contraction for *it is*) for *its* (the possessive form) or vice versa.

Form the possessive singular of nouns by adding 's.

Mary's book

the Jones's family car

the sun's rays

my mother-in-law's suitcase

4. Prepositions

NO: She just couldn't start in to do her homework.

Do not overuse prepositions.

YES: She just couldn't start to do her homework.

5. Conjunctions

NO: She loved him dearly but not his dog.

When using a conjunction, be sure that the sentence parts you are joining are in agreement.

YES: She loved him dearly but she did not love his dog.

NO: They complimented them both for their bravery and they thanked them for their kindness.

When using conjunctions, a common mistake that is made is to forget that each member of the pair must be followed by the same kind of construction.

YES: They both complimented them for their bravery and thanked them for their kindness.

NO: While I'm usually interested in Fellini movies, I'd rather not go tonight.

While refers to time and should not be used as a substitute for *although, and* or *but*.

YES: Although I'm usually interested in Fellini movies, I'd rather not go tonight.

NO: We read in the paper where they are making great strides in DNA research.

Where refers to a place or location. Be careful not to use it when it does not have this meaning.

YES: We read in the paper that they are making great strides in DNA research.

6. Misplaced Modifiers

NO: Harold watched the painter gaping in astonishment.

The dangling participle is an error that results in an unclear sentence. The participle should appear immediately before or after the subject of the sentence.

YES: Gaping in astonishment, Harold watched the painter.

NO: On correcting the test, his errors became apparent.

Many modifiers cause confusion when they are out of place.

YES: His errors became apparent when the test was corrected.

NO: Jane almost polished the plate until it shined.

Words such as *almost, only, just, even, nearly, hardly, not,* and *merely* must appear immediately before the word they modify or they will cause confusion.

YES: Jane polished the plate until it almost shined.

7. Parallel Structure

NO: The janitor stopped, listened a moment, then he locked the door.

When ideas are similar, they should be expressed in similar forms. When elements of a sentence are similar, they too should appear in similar form.

YES: The janitor stopped, listened a moment, then locked the door.

8.   Run-On Sentences/Sentence Fragments

Run-On Sentences

> NO: It was a pleasant drive the sun was shining.

A run-on sentence is a sentence with too much in it. It usually contains two complete sentences separated by a comma, or two complete sentences merged together.

> YES: It was a pleasant drive because the sun was shining.

> NO: Talk softly, someone is listening.

Sometimes a writer will try to correct a run-on sentence by inserting a comma between the clauses, but this creates another error, a *comma splice*. The following examples illustrate various ways to correct the comma splice.

> YES: Talk softly; someone is listening.
>
> or
>
> Talk softly, because someone is listening.

Sentence Fragments

> NO: A tree as old as your father.

This is just the opposite of a run-on sentence. A sentence fragment does not have enough in it to make it a complete thought. It is usually missing a subject or a verb.

> YES: The tree is as old as your father.

9.   Tense of Verbs

Tense means time. Verbs have the ability to tell us not only what action is occurring, but also when it is occurring. The form of the verb changes to indicate when an action takes place.

> NO: I swum two miles last week.

Do not confuse the past participle for the past tense.

> YES: I <u>swam</u> two miles last week.

DRILL 1

Subject-Verb Agreement

DIRECTIONS: The following group of sentences may contain errors in subject-verb agreement. Make any necessary corrections.

1. Either her mother or her father usually drive her to school on rainy days.

2. There is, if I calculated right, two hundred dollars left in my bank account.

3. Mary and the rest of her friends were late for the test.

4. Economics are a major taught in many colleges.

5. The first years of high school is the most difficult.

6. Aristotle's *Poetics* have always been read widely.

7. The noise from all those fans were distracting.

8. Neither the chorus nor the actors knows their parts.

9. Each of us are going away for the weekend.

10. Neither the grass nor the flowers was growing well.

DETAILED EXPLANATIONS OF ANSWERS

Drill 1

Subject-Verb Agreement

NOTE: Subject(s) and verb(s) in a sentence must agree in number. Singular subjects must take singular verbs. Plural subjects must take plural verbs.

1. Either her mother or her father usually drives her to school on rainy days.

    If two or more subjects are joined by *either-or* (or *neither-nor*), the verb must agree with the subject which is nearer. In this case the subjects are *mother* and *father*, both of which are singular. Since *father* is nearer to the verb, however, and since it is singular, a singular verb is needed. The singular verb *drives* (not *drive*) is needed with the singular subject *father*.

2. There are, if I calculated right, two hundred dollars left in my bank account.

    The expletive *there* is not the subject of the sentence even when it is the first word in the sentence. Rather the expletive indicates that the subject is going to follow the verb. In this case, the plural subject (*dollars*) follows the verb. The plural verb (*are*) is needed for agreement between the subject and the verb.

3. Mary and the rest of her friends were late for the test.

    The subject of the sentence is plural: *Mary and the rest*. A plural verb is needed. Since *were* is plural, the sentence is correct as given and should not be changed.

4. Economics is a major taught in many colleges.

    Economics is the name of the subject; it is a singular noun and the singular subject of the sentence. A singular subject requires a singular verb. Since the verb *are*, which is given, is plural, the verb must be changed to *is* for subject-verb agreement.

5. The first years of high school are the most difficult.

    The subject of the sentence is *years*. It is a plural noun requiring a plural verb. The verb *is* is singular and must be changed to *are*. It is possible that some persons may think that *school* is the subject of the sentence; since *school* is singular, these persons may think the verb *is* is correct. Actually, however, *school* is the object of the preposition *of*, not the subject of the sentence. By changing the verb to *are* the sentence may be corrected.

6.   Aristotle's *Poetics* has always been read widely.

    Poetics is a singular title. Since it is singular (even though it ends in *s*), *Poetics* requires a singular verb. The verb *have* must be changed to *has*.

7.   The noise from all those fans was distracting.

    The subject of the sentence is *noise*, which is singular. The plural nouns *all* and *fans* are objects of the prepositions *from* and *of* (which is understood though not given). A singular verb is required; *were* must be changed to *was*.

8.   Neither the chorus nor the actors know their parts.

    When subjects are joined by *neither-nor* (or *either-or*), the verb must agree with the subject to which it is closer. In this case the subject *actors* is plural and is closer to the verb. The singular verb *knows* must be changed to the plural verb *know*.

9.   Each of us is going away for the weekend.

    Each (the subject of the sentence) is singular and requires a singular verb. The plural verb *are* must be changed to the singular verb *is*. The plural pronoun *us* is not the subject of the sentence but rather the object of the preposition *of*. The verb does not have to agree with the object of the preposition. Some persons may mistakenly leave the verb *are* in the sentence to make it agree with *us*.

10.   Neither the grass nor the flowers were growing well.

    When subjects are joined by *neither-nor* (or *either-or*), the verb must agree with the subject to which it is closer. In this case the subject *flowers* is closer to the verb form *was*. Since *was* is singular, *was* must be changed to *were* for subject-verb agreement.

DRILL 2

Comparison of Adjectives

DIRECTIONS: In the following sentences, make the changes indicated in the parentheses. Also, indicate if the comparative or superlative form is an adverb or an adjective.

1. He was sad to leave. (superlative)

2. She ran as fast as the others on the team. (comparative)

3. Throughout school, they were good in math. (superlative)

4. This class is as interesting as the European history class. (comparative)

5. He arrived as soon as I did. (comparative)

6. The test was as hard as we expected. (superlative)

7. He responded to the interviewer as candidly as Tom. (comparative)

8. The beggar had less possessions than she. (superlative)

9. That answer is perfectly correct. (superlative)

10. She read the part best. (comparative)

DETAILED EXPLANATIONS
OF ANSWERS

Drill 2

Comparison of Adjectives

NOTE: Positive, comparative, and superlative forms of both adjectives and adverbs show degrees of comparison. The positive form shows no comparison at all; examples are *pretty* and *rapidly*. The comparative form shows a greater degree or is used to make a comparison; examples are *prettier* and *more rapidly*. The superlative form shows the greatest degree or quality; examples are *prettiest* and *most rapidly*.

1.   He was *saddest* to leave. (adjective)

      The comparisons of *sad* are *sad, sadder, saddest*. The superlative form is *saddest* and is the word to be used in this sentence. *Saddest* is an adjective (specifically, a predicate adjective) modifying the subject pronoun *he*.

2.   She ran *faster* than the others on the team. (adverb)

      The comparisons of *fast* are *fast, faster*, and *fastest*. Since the comparative degree is sought, *faster* is the correct answer. *Faster* is an adverb modifying the verb *ran*; *faster* tells how she ran.

3.   Throughout school, they were *the best* in math. (adjective)

      The comparisons of *good* are *good, better*, and *best*. Since *best* is the superlative, it is the correct predicate adjective to use to describe the word *they*.

4.   This class is *more interesting* than European history class. (adjective)

      Interesting is an adjective. The comparisons are *interesting, more interesting*, and *most interesting*. Since the comparative degree is sought, *more interesting* is the correct choice.

5.   He arrived *sooner* than I did. (adverb)

      Soon, sooner, and *soonest* are the comparisons of *soon*. Since *sooner* is the comparative degree, it is the correct adverb to select.

6. The test was the *hardest* we expected. (adjective)

     There are three comparisons of *hard*: *hard*, *harder*, and *hardest*. *Hardest* is the correct adjective in the superlative degree to select for this answer.

7. He responded to the interviewer *more candidly* than Tom. (adverb)

     Candidly is an adverb. The comparisons of *candidly* are *candidly*, *more candidly*, and *most candidly*. Since the instructions ask for the comparative degree, *more candidly* should be selected.

8. This sentence (referring to "she") *cannot* be put in the superlative form.

     An adjective to modify *possessions* is sought in this sentence. In comparing the amount of possessions of two people (the beggar and she), the superlative degree — asked for in the sentence — should not be used; instead, one should use the comparative degree (lesser). The three comparisons of l*ess* are *less*, *lesser*, and *least*.

9. The answer is *most perfectly* correct. (adverb)

     The directions ask for the superlative degree of the adverb *perfectly*. The degrees are *perfectly*, *more perfectly*, and *most perfectly*. The superlative degree is *most perfectly*. (One might argue, however, if there can be comparisons of an answer which is already *perfectly correct*.

10. She read the part *better*. (adjective)

     The examinee is asked to give the comparative degree of the adverb *best*. The comparisons are w*ell*, *better*, and *best*. Since the comparative degree is sought, *better* is the correct choice.

DRILL 3

Possessive Nouns

> **DIRECTIONS:** The following group of sentences may contain errors in possession. Make any necessary corrections.

1. His suit, like James, was grey.

2. The president's adviser's past was investigated.

3. The pitcher's job is more difficult than the fielders.

4. The woman's cat's kittens were given away.

5. The majority leader of the House of Representatives' speech was well received.

6. The final plans of the Boy Scouts of America's meeting were made.

7. It was Susan, Ann, Joan and my idea.

8. The amateurs' life differs from the professionals.

9. That is Dr. White and her new house.

10. The play's ending satisfied the audience.

DETAILED EXPLANATIONS OF ANSWERS

Drill 3

Possessive Nouns

NOTE: To form the possession of nouns, a writer should use the following seven general rules:

---

1.   An inanimate object is usually made to show possession through the use of an *of* phrase.

2.   If two nouns show joint possession, the possessive form is taken by the last noun only; if two nouns show individual possession, the possessive form is taken by both nouns.

3.   If two possessive nouns follow each other in a sentence, the writer may use an *of* phrase.

4.   If a noun is compound (mother-in-law, someone else), the last word takes the possessive.

5.   If a noun (singular or plural) does not end in *s*, the apostrophe and *s* are added.

6.   If a noun is singular and ends in *s*, an apostrophe and *s* are added — unless the apostrophe and *s* make pronunciation difficult. For example, *Moses's* is difficult to say; one should use *Moses'*.

7.   If a plural noun ends in *s*, only the apostrophe is needed.

---

1.   His suit, like James's, was grey.

     An apostrophe and *s* must be added to *James* to make this proper noun show possession.

2.   The past of the president's adviser was investigated.

     The awkward construction of this sentence with two possessive nouns following each other can be improved by using an *of* statement. "The past of the president's adviser was investigated" is much better.

3.   The pitcher's job is more difficult than the fielder's.

     Since the pitcher's job is being compared to the fielder's job, an apostrophe *s* is needed on the word *fielder*. The word *job* is understood in the sentence. The corrected sentence should read, "The pitcher's job is more difficult than the fielder's."

4.   The kittens of the woman's cat were given away.

    To eliminate two possessive nouns in succession, the writer may use an *of* phrase. A way to do this with sentence four would be to write, "The kittens of the woman's cat were given away."

5.   The speech of the majority leader of the House of Representatives was well received.

    To eliminate the possession of an inanimate noun, the writer may use an *of* phrase. A way to improve the sentence would be to write, "The speech of the majority leader of the House of Representatives was well received."

6.   The final plans of the meeting of the Boy Scouts of America were made.

    The writer who wishes to eliminate the possession of the inanimate noun (Boy Scouts of America) can do so by rearranging the sentence and making use of an *of* phrase. "The final plans of the meeting of the Boy Scouts of America were made" would be a better way to arrange the sentence.

7.   It was Susan, Ann, Joan, and my idea.

    This sentence shows joint ownership. When several nouns/pronouns have joint ownership, only the last one in the sentence has to show possession. The sentence is correct as written.

8.   The amateur's life differs from the professional's.

    The entire sentence could read, "The amateurs' life differs from the professionals' life." Because life is singular and is understood by the reader, it is easy for the reader to see that the word *professionals* should be a possessive noun with the use of an apostrophe and *s*. The correct sentence should read as follows, "The amateur's life differs from the professional's."

9.   That is her and Dr. White's new house.

    Joint ownership is indicated by the sentence. Moving the noun *Dr. White* closer to the noun owned makes the sentence read more smoothly. An apostrophe and *s* is placed after *Dr.* White (a noun in the sentence) to show possession. *Her* already shows this possession; this sentence is correct when written, "That is her and Dr. White's new house."

10.   The ending of the play satisfied the audience.

    In sentence number 10 an inanimate noun shows possession. To avoid this, an *of* phrase can be used. The correct sentence should read as follows: "The ending of the play satisfied the audience."

DRILL 4

Prepositions

> **DIRECTIONS:** The following group of sentences may contain prepositional errors. Make any necessary corrections.

1. Let's finish up the assignment.

2. He was interested and fascinated with physics.

3. She had learned of his life and his times through reading.

4. They were both repelled and driven toward the space creature.

5. Tell me on what he left it.

6. Let's go over to James's house tomorrow.

7. She always had an interest and an aptitude for science.

8. It took a long time to get at the problem.

9. She looked like her sister and her mother.

10. Her belief and dedication to the cause were total.

DETAILED EXPLANATIONS
OF ANSWERS

Drill 4

Prepositions

1. Let's finish the assignment.

    The verb *finish* is complete in itself. The word *up* does not have to be included. The sentence should read, "Let's finish the assignment."

2. He was interested and fascinated by physics.

    After the verb *interested* the preposition *in* or *by* is needed. After the verb *fascinated*, the preposition *with* or *by* is needed. The way the sentence is constructed, only one preposition is used. The preposition used is *with*, which does not fit the verb *interested*. To correct the sentence, the preposition *by* should be inserted.

3. She had learned of his life and of his times through reading.

    An omission of a preposition is evident in sentence 3. To correct this sentence, the preposition *of* must be inserted. The sentence should read as follows, "She had learned of his life and of his times through reading."

4. They were both repelled by and driven toward the space creature.

    A preposition has been omitted here. Although *driven toward* does make sense, the preposition *toward* does not fit well with *repelled*. Another preposition is needed to follow *repelled*. One might use *repelled by*. The addition of the word *by* is needed.

5. Tell me what he left it on.

    No longer is it improper to end a sentence in a preposition. This sentence certainly is clearer to place the word *on* at the end of the sentence. The new sentence now reads, "Tell me what he left it on."

6. Let's go to James's house tomorrow.

    One should not insert or add extra prepositions when they are not needed. The sentence makes perfect sense to omit the *to* and read the sentence, "Let's go over to James's house tomorrow."

7. She always had an interest in and an aptitude for science.

Again, a preposition has been omitted. One does not have an *interest for*; a preposition is needed after the word *interest*; *in* is a perfect choice. The new sentence is, "She always had an interest in and an aptitude for science."

8. It took a long time to get through the problem.

The expression *to get at* is awkward. One might substitute *to get through*, *to work through*, or *to solve*. Any of these expressions is clearer to the reader. The new sentence might read, "It took a long time to get through the problem."

9. She looked like her sister and like her mother.

A good writer should be sure that needed prepositions are not omitted. Another *like* is needed before *her mother*. The new sentence now reads, "She looked like her sister and like her mother."

10. Her belief in and dedication to the cause were total.

Another preposition is needed in this sentence. It logically follows that one could have *dedication to* a cause, but another preposition is needed after the word *belief*. Since *in* could logically follow *belief*, that preposition might be inserted. The new sentence would read, "Her belief in and dedication to the cause were total."

DRILL 5

Conjunctions

> **DIRECTIONS:** The following group of sentences may contain errors in the use of conjunctions. Make any necessary corrections.

1. John's best assets are his personality and his swimming ability.

2. I heard on the radio where the play is closing this week.

3. I was reading the paper and the phone rang.

4. Susan ate vegetables often but not fruits.

5. Please send me an answer to the question or opinions on the project.

6. While I'm tired from the trip, I'll attend the concert tonight.

7. Mary's goal is to study hard and to pass the test.

8. He produced the play while she directed it.

9. A good essay is where the ideas are clearly articulated.

10. The class wanted neither to read the book nor do the assignment.

DETAILED EXPLANATIONS
OF ANSWERS

Drill 5

Conjunctions

1. John's best assets are his personality and his swimming ability.

    Sentence 1 (John's best assets are his personality and his swimming ability) is correct as written.

2. I heard on the radio that the play is closing this week.

    The correct answer for sentence 2 is, "I heard on the radio *that* the play is closing this week." If one places the conjunction close to the verb ("I heard where..."), it becomes obvious that the conjunction *that* is preferable.

3. I was reading the paper when the phone rang.

    The two clauses ("I was reading the paper" and "the phone rang") are not independent clauses and equal in rank. One of the clauses should be made a dependent clause telling *when*. One way of correcting the sentence is, "I was reading the paper when the phone rang." (One might also correct the sentence by writing, "While I was reading the paper, the phone rang."

4. Susan often ate vegetables but not fruits.

    It is better to connect two nouns with a conjunction without adding adverbs between them. Sentence 4 might be improved by writing, "Susan often ate vegetables but not fruits." This sentence now has the nouns connected without additional words between to confuse the reader.

5. Please send me either an answer to the question or opinions on the project.

    The conjunctions *either-or* are correlative conjunctions and are used together. The correlatives are needed in sentence 5. The sentence might be improved by inserting the word *either*. The correct sentence is, "Please send me either an answer to the question or opinions on the project."

6. Although I'm tired from the trip, I'll attend the concert tonight.

    The use of the adverbial clause "While I'm tired from the trip," does not really convey the sense of the sentence. Using the conjunction *although* will greatly improve the sentence by conveying the intent of the writer. Consider the following revised sentence: "Although I'm tired from the trip, I'll attend the concert tonight."

7. Mary's goal is not only to study hard but also to pass the test.

   Parallel structure in a sentence is indicated through the use of correlative conjunctions. In this sentence *not only-but also* would indicate this parallel structure. To connect the two infinitive phrases used as predicate nominatives, one might add these two correlatives successfully. The corrected sentence reads, "Mary's goal is not only to study hard but also to pass the test.

8. He produced the play and she directed it.

   The two independent clauses in sentence 8 are equal in importance. By using the word *while*, the writer has given less importance to the fact that the woman directed the play. A better way of writing the sentence would be to use the conjunction *and* which places equal weight to both clauses. The correct sentence might read, "He produced the play and she directed it."

9. A good essay is one in which the ideas are clearly articulated.

   Where (which introduces an adverbial clause) is not a proper conjunction to use with a predicate nominative. To improve the sentence, one might use the following: "A good essay is one in which the ideas are clearly articulated."

10. The class wanted neither to read the book nor to do the assignment.

   Neither-nor are correlative conjunctions which indicate parallel structure. In sentence 10 the correlative conjunctions are connecting the two infinitive phrases beginning "to read" and "to do." In the sentence as written, however, the second *to* has been omitted. To correct the sentence the *to* must be inserted. The sentence should read, "The class wanted neither to read the book nor to do the assignment."

DRILL 6

Misplaced Modifiers

DIRECTIONS: The following group of sentences may contain misplaced modifiers. Make any necessary corrections.

---

1.   I saw a stray dog riding the bus this afternoon.

2.   The clothing was given to the poor in large packages.

3.   I found five dollars eating lunch in the park.

4.   We saw two girls riding bicycles from our car.

5.   Reading my book quietly, I jumped up when the car crashed.

6.   He ran the mile with a sprained ankle.

7.   The history majors only were affected by the new requirements.

8.   Running quickly to catch the bus, Susan's packages fell out of her arms onto the ground.

9.   He just asked the man for directions to make sure.

10.   He discovered a new route driving home.

DETAILED EXPLANATIONS
OF ANSWERS

Drill 6

Misplaced Modifiers

1.   I saw a stray dog while I was riding on the bus this afternoon.

The modifier *riding the bus this afternoon* is placed closer to the noun *dog*; the reader is given the impression that the dog was riding the bus. To correct this misconception, *riding the bus this afternoon* should be moved closer to the word *I* which it modifies. The new sentence should read, "I saw a stray dog while I was riding on the bus this afternoon."

2.   The clothing was given in large packages to the poor.

The prepositional phrase *in large packages* is placed near *poor*, rather than near the word *clothing* which it modifies. To correct the impression that *the poor* (and not *the clothing*) were in large packages, the writer should change the arrangement slightly. The corrected sentence should read, "The clothing was given in large packages to the poor." or "The clothing in large packages was given to the poor."

3.   While I was eating lunch in the park, I found five dollars.

The adjective phrase *eating lunch in the park* does not modify the word *dollars*. The writer should place the phrase near the word *I* which the phrase modifies. The sentence should read, "While I was eating lunch in the park, I found five dollars." or "Eating lunch in the park, I found five dollars."

4.   While we were in our car, we saw two girls riding bicycles.

The way the sentence is written, it sounds as if the riding of bicycles occurred *from the car*. To correct the sentence, the writer can rearrange the words. "While riding in our car, we saw two girls riding bicycles."

5.   When the car crashed, I jumped up from quietly reading my book.

The sentence is not clear to the reader. The person did not continue *to read the book* and *to jump up* at the time *the car crashed*. An adverbial phrase can help to clarify the sequence and the sense for the reader. The writer might try revising the sentence to read like the following: "When the car crashed, I jumped up from quietly reading my book."

6. He ran the mile although his ankle was sprained.

Sentence 6 could be misinterpreted. The misplaced modifier might suggest that the person ran the mile with a sprained angle for company; the sentence does not even specify that a person is attached to the ankle! The sentence might be reworded as follows: "He ran the mile although his ankle was sprained."

7. Only the history majors were affected by the new requirements.

The word o*nly* is misplaced in this sentence. Since it is placed near *were affected*, the reader may be led to believe that the majors *were affected* but not *penalized* or *charged* or some other verb. The sense of the sentence is actually that only one group of majors — the history majors — was affected. By changing the placement of the word *only*, the writer can better convey the sense of the sentence.

8. As Susan was running quickly to catch the bus, her packages fell out of her arms onto the ground.

The way the sentence is written the writer conveys the picture of packages which ran to catch the bus. The dangling participle or misplaced modifier must be changed. One way of doing this is the following: "As Susan was running quickly to catch the bus, her packages fell out of her arms onto the ground.

9. He asked the man for directions just to make sure.

In sentence 9 the word *just* is misplaced. The writer did not mean that the man only asked or *just asked*. It seems that the writer is stating that the man was asking directions only to make sure he understood them. The following sentence expresses this: "He asked the man for directions just to make sure."

10. While driving home, he discovered a new route.

The misplaced modifier leads the reader to believe the new route was driving home. A better solution is the following: "While driving home, he discovered a new route."

DRILL 7

Parallel Structure

> **DIRECTIONS:** The following group of sentences may contain errors in parallel structure. Make any necessary corrections.

1. In the summer I usually like swimming and to water-ski.

2. The professor explained the cause, effect, and the results.

3. Mary read the book, studied the examples, and takes the test.

4. Mark watched the way John started the car and how he left the curb.

5. The essay was marked for organization and its clarity.

6. The movie was interesting and had a lot of excitement.

7. Shakespeare both wrote beautiful sonnets and complex plays.

8. The painting is done either in watercolors or with oils.

9. The lecturer spoke with seriousness and in a concerned tone.

10. Either we forget those plans, or accept their proposal.

DETAILED EXPLANATIONS OF ANSWERS

Drill 7

Parallel Structure

1. In the summer I usually like to swim and water-ski.

    The lack of parallel structure is evident with the words *swimming* and *to water-ski*. The sentence can be made parallel by making both terms into infinitives. The sentence now reads: "In the summer I usually like to swim and to water-ski." or "In the summer I usually like to swim and water-ski."

2. The professor explained the cause, the effect, and the results.

    The use of the word *the* is not used consistently with the three direct objectives of the word *explained*. To correct this, the word *the* can be inserted before each of the objectives. The new sentence would read, "The professor explained the cause, the effect, and the results."

3. Mary read the book, studied the examples, and took the test.

    The three verbs (*read, studied,* and *takes*) are not in the same tense. To correct the sentence, the writer needs to correct the tense of the verbs. This has been done in the following sentence: "Mary read the book, studied the examples, and took the test."

4. Mark watched how John started the car and how he left the curb.

    The two elements of the sentence which are not parallel are *the way* and *how*. A way of correcting this nonparallel structure is to preface both elements with *how*. The corrected sentence could read, "Mark watched how John started the car and how he left the curb."

5. The essay was marked for organization and clarity.

    The two elements without parallel structure are *organization* and *its clarity*. To achieve parallel structure the sentence may be reworded as follows: "The essay was marked for organization and clarity."

6. The movie was both interesting and exciting.

    The two predicate nominatives following the verb *was* are not parallel in structure. The writer must make *interesting* and *had a lot of excitement* show parallel structure. To do this the new sentence might read, "The move was interesting and exciting."

7.   Shakespeare wrote both (optional) beautiful sonnets and complex plays.

The word which is misplaced and results in a lack of parallel structure is the word *both*. To correct this sentence, the word *both* can be placed before the two elements to be made parallel. The words are *sonnets* and *plays*. The corrected sentence reads, "Shakespeare wrote both beautiful sonnets and complex plays."

8.   The painting is done with either watercolors or oils.

The elements which are not parallel in structure are the prepositional phrases *in watercolors* and *with oils*. By substituting the preposition *with* for the word *in* or the word *in* for the word *with*, the writer can achieve parallel structure. The corrected sentence might read, "The painting is done with either watercolors or oils"; an alternative might be, "The painting is done either in watercolors or oils."

9.   The lecturer spoke in a serious, concerned tone.

The adverbial phrases telling how the lecturer spoke are the ones which are not parallel. Specifically, the prepositional phrases are *with seriousness* and *in a concerned tone*. The writer might correct the sentence as follows: "The lecturer spoke in a serious, concerned tone."

10.   Either we forget those plans, or we accept their proposal.

The word *either* should precede the parallel elements. To achieve this result, the writer might change the sentence to read, "Either we forgot those plans, or we accept their proposal." An alternative might be for the writer to say, "We either forget those plans or accept their proposal."

DRILL 8

Run-On Sentences/Sentence Fragments

DIRECTIONS: The following sentences may be either run-on sentences or sentence fragments. Make any necessary corrections.

1.   After the rain stopped.

2.   Mow the lawn, it is much too long.

3.   The settlement you reached it seems fair.

4.   When I read, especially at night. My eyes get tired.

5.   It was impossible to get through on the phone, the lines were down because of the storm.

6.   Is this the only problem? The leaky pipe?

7.   Everyone saw the crime, no one is willing to come forth.

8.   The weather was bad, she played in the rain.

9.   Ellen paced the floor. Worrying about her economics final.

10.   Their season was over, the team had lost the playoffs.

DETAILED EXPLANATIONS
OF ANSWERS

Drill 8

Run-On Sentences/Sentence Fragments

1.   Fragment: We went out after the rain stopped.

   The first sentence is a fragment. The dependent adverbial clause cannot stand alone. To correct the sentence, the writer must insert an independent clause. The inserted independent clause must contain a subject and verb. An example might be, "We went out after the rain stopped."

2.   Run-on: Mow the lawn. It is much too long.

   Sentence 2 is a run-on sentence. To correct the sentence, the writer should make the one sentence into two sentences. The new sentences read, "Mow the lawn. It is much too long."

3.   Run-on: The settlement you reached seems fair.

   Since sentence 3 is a run-on sentence, it should be corrected. It can be made into one sentence which incorporates the sense of both sentences. The new sentence reads, "The settlement you reached seems fair."

4.   Fragment: My eyes get tired when I read, especially at night.

   Two "sentences" are given in sentence 4. The first "sentence," however, is really a fragment; the second sentence is a complete sentence. The two can be combined into one sentence which conveys the message. The new sentence reads, "My eyes get tired when I read, especially at night."

5.   Run-on: It was impossible to get through on the phone, since the lines were down because of the storm.

   Sentence 5 is actually two sentences joined together with only a comma. This is known as a comma splice or a run-on sentence. To correct this particular situation, a single sentence can be formed. A suggested correction is, "It was impossible to get through on the phone, since the lines were down because of the storm."

6. Fragment: Is the leaky pipe the only problem?

    A fragment ("The leaky pipe?") and a sentence ("Is this the only problem?") are found in sentence 6. To correct the fragment, the writer may combine the sentence and fragment into one sentence. The results read, "Is the leaky pipe the only problem?"

7. Run-on: Everyone saw the crime, but no one is willing to come forth.

    Two sentences are joined by a comma in sentence 7. The comma splice (run-on sentence) must be corrected. The two sentences can be joined with the conjunction *but* since they are equal in importance. The new sentence reads, "Everyone saw the crime, but no one is willing to come forth."

8. Run-on: The weather was bad. She played in the rain.

    Two sentences are joined by a comma. This run-on sentence can be corrected by making two separate sentences. The corrected sentences read, "The weather was bad. She played in the rain."

9. Fragment: Ellen paced the floor and worried about her economics final.

    Sentence 9 consists of a complete sentence ("Ellen paced the floor.") and a sentence fragment ("Worrying about her economics final."). To correct the situation, the two may be connected as a single sentence. The two may be connected as a single sentence with a compound verb. In this case, the corrected sentence reads, "Ellen paced the floor and worried about her economics final."

    Another remedy is to use the adjective phrase as a part of the complete sentence. The writer must be careful to place the modifier near the word which it modifies. The corrected sentence reads, "Worrying about her economics final, Ellen paced the floor."

10. Run-on: The team had lost the playoffs; their season was over.

    The two complete sentences in run-on sentence number 10 may be joined together by a semicolon. The new sentence reads, "The team had lost the playoffs; their season was over."

DRILL 9

Tense of Verbs

> **DIRECTIONS:** The following sentences contain a missing verb. Fill in the correct verb using the given information about the verb and the verb tense.

1. I _____ fifty pages by tomorrow. *(to read, future)*

2. We _____ in the concert. *(to sing, past)*

3. He _____ class on Mondays and Wednesdays. *(to teach, present)*

4. You _____ the dress without permission. *(to take, past)*

5. It _____ once spring arrives. *(to grow, future)*

6. The bee _____ her while she was on vacation. *(to sting, past)*

7. He _____ many Broadway plays. *(to cast, past perfect)*

8. He _____ the plane tomorrow if the skies are clear. *(to fly, future progressive)*

9. They _____ furniture all afternoon. *(to choose, present perfect progressive)*

10. You _____ your ticket before the train arrived. *(to buy, past perfect progressive)*

DETAILED EXPLANATIONS
OF ANSWERS

Drill 9

Tense of Verbs

1.   shall read

The principal parts of the verb *to read* are *read* (present), *read* (past), and *will read* or *shall read* (future). With the pronoun *I*, the future tense is indicated by *shall read* — unless strong intent is indicated. Since this does not seem to be the case here, *shall read* is the best choice.

2.   sang

The principal parts of the verb *to sing* are *sing* (present), *sang* (past), and *will sing* or *shall sing*. Since the past is sought, *sang* is the correct choice.

3.   teaches

The principal parts of the verb *to teach* are *teach* (present), *taught* (past), and *will teach* or *shall teach* (future). Since the present tense is sought, *teach* is needed. Notice that the verb must also agree in number with the pronoun *he* (singular). Since the singular of *teach* is needed, the reader should select *teaches*.

4.   took

The principal parts of *to take* are *take* (present), *took* (past), and *will take* or *shall take* (future). Since the past tense is needed, *took* is the correct choice.

5.   will grow

The principal parts of *to grow* are *grow* (present), *grew* (past), and *will grow* or *shall grow* (future). Since the future tense is sought and since the pronoun is *it*, *will grow* is the correct choice.

6.   stung

The verb *to sting* is an irregular one. The principal parts are *sting* (present), *stung* (past), and *will sting* or *shall sting* (future). The past is needed so the verb *stung* should be selected.

7. had cast

    The past perfect tense is asked for in this sentence. The perfect tenses for *cast* are *am cast*, *is cast*, or *are cast* (present perfect), *had cast* or *have cast* (past perfect), and *will have cast* or *shall have cast* (future perfect tense). Since the pronoun *he* must agree in number with the past perfect tense, *has cast* is the past perfect tense which should be selected.

8. will be flying

    Progressive tenses of *to fly* are *is flying* or *are flying* (present progressive), *was flying* or *were flying* (past progressive), and *will be flying* or *shall be flying* (future progressive). Since the future progressive must be used with the pronoun *he*, *will be flying* should be selected.

9. have been choosing

    Present perfect progressive of *choose* is *has been choosing* or *have been choosing*. Past perfect progressive of *choose* is *had been choosing*. Future perfect progressive of *choose* is *will have been choosing* or *shall have been choosing*. Since the present perfect progressive is needed with the pronoun *they*, *have been choosing* is the correct choice.

10. had been buying

    Present perfect progressive of *buy* is *has been buying* or *have been buying*. Past perfect progressive of *buy* is *had been buying*. Future perfect progressive of *buy* is *will have been buying* or *shall have been buying*. Since the past perfect progressive is needed with the pronoun *you*, *had been buying* is the correct choice.

GRAMMAR AND USAGE PRACTICE TEST

1. (A) (B) (C) (D) (E)
2. (A) (B) (C) (D) (E)
3. (A) (B) (C) (D) (E)
4. (A) (B) (C) (D) (E)
5. (A) (B) (C) (D) (E)
6. (A) (B) (C) (D) (E)
7. (A) (B) (C) (D) (E)
8. (A) (B) (C) (D) (E)
9. (A) (B) (C) (D) (E)
10. (A) (B) (C) (D) (E)
11. (A) (B) (C) (D) (E)
12. (A) (B) (C) (D) (E)
13. (A) (B) (C) (D) (E)
14. (A) (B) (C) (D) (E)
15. (A) (B) (C) (D) (E)
16. (A) (B) (C) (D) (E)
17. (A) (B) (C) (D) (E)
18. (A) (B) (C) (D) (E)
19. (A) (B) (C) (D) (E)
20. (A) (B) (C) (D) (E)
21. (A) (B) (C) (D) (E)
22. (A) (B) (C) (D) (E)
23. (A) (B) (C) (D) (E)
24. (A) (B) (C) (D) (E)
25. (A) (B) (C) (D) (E)

26. (A) (B) (C) (D) (E)
27. (A) (B) (C) (D) (E)
28. (A) (B) (C) (D) (E)
29. (A) (B) (C) (D) (E)
30. (A) (B) (C) (D) (E)
31. (A) (B) (C) (D) (E)
32. (A) (B) (C) (D) (E)
33. (A) (B) (C) (D) (E)
34. (A) (B) (C) (D) (E)
35. (A) (B) (C) (D) (E)
36. (A) (B) (C) (D) (E)
37. (A) (B) (C) (D) (E)
38. (A) (B) (C) (D) (E)
39. (A) (B) (C) (D) (E)
40. (A) (B) (C) (D) (E)
41. (A) (B) (C) (D) (E)
42. (A) (B) (C) (D) (E)
43. (A) (B) (C) (D) (E)
44. (A) (B) (C) (D) (E)
45. (A) (B) (C) (D) (E)
46. (A) (B) (C) (D) (E)
47. (A) (B) (C) (D) (E)
48. (A) (B) (C) (D) (E)
49. (A) (B) (C) (D) (E)
50. (A) (B) (C) (D) (E)

GRAMMAR AND USAGE
PRACTICE TEST

Here is a practice test to apply what you have learned in the Grammar and Usage chapter. After you complete the test, score yourself, and read the explanations to understand the concepts further.

These types of questions are found in the following tests: PRAXIS II, ACT, CLAST, CLEP, and PPST.

You will also find these questions useful to sharpen your grammatical skills for these tests: GMAT, MCAT, GRE, LSAT, CBEST, PSAT and SAT I

---

50 Questions

DIRECTIONS: For each sentence in which you find an error, select the one underlined part that must be changed to make the sentence correct and blacken the corresponding space on your answer sheet.

If there is no error, blacken answer space (E).

EXAMPLE:

The player was <u>so tired that</u> thoughts of <u>going to sleep</u> <u>was</u> all that
           A   B   C

<u>went through</u> her mind. <u>No error.</u>   Ⓐ Ⓑ ● Ⓓ Ⓔ
     D   E

---

1.   In 1877 Chief Joseph of the Nez Percés, <u>together with</u> 250 warriors and
                                              A

500 women and children, <u>were praised</u> by newspaper reporters for
                            B

<u>bravery</u> during the 115-day fight <u>for</u> freedom. <u>No error.</u>
  C   D   E

2.   The ideals <u>upon which</u> American society <u>is based</u> <u>are</u> primarily those of
               A   B   C

Europe, and not ones <u>derived from</u> the native Indian culture. <u>No error.</u>
                                       D   **E**

3. <u>An astute and powerful</u> woman, Frances Nadel <u>was</u> a beauty contest
            A   **B**

   winner before she <u>became</u> president of the company <u>upon the death</u> of
                      C   **D**

   her husband. <u>No error.</u>
                E

4. Representative Wilson <u>pointed out</u>, however, that the legislature <u>had not</u>
                            A   **B**

   <u>finalized</u> the state budget and salary increases <u>had depended</u> on decisions
                                                   C

   <u>to be made</u> in a special session. <u>No error.</u>
             D   **E**

5. Now the <u>city</u> librarian, doing more than checking out books, must help
             A

   to <u>plan</u> puppet shows and movies for children, garage sales for <u>used</u>
     B   **C**

   books, and <u>arranging for</u> guest lecturers and exhibits for adults. <u>No error.</u>
                  D   **E**

6. In order <u>to completely understand</u> the psychological <u>effects</u> of the Bubonic
                         A   **B**

   plague, <u>one must</u> realize that one-fourth to one-third of the population in
             C

   an affected area died. <u>No error.</u>
             D   **E**

7. Rural roads, <u>known</u> in the United States as farm-to-market roads, have
                A

   always been a vital <u>link in</u> the economy of <u>more advanced</u> nations
                     B   **C**

because transportation of goods to markets <u>is</u> essential. <u>No error.</u>
                                                  D   **E**

8. <u>Many a</u> graduate <u>wishes</u> to return to college and <u>abide in</u> the protected
    A   **B**   **C**

environment of a university, particularly if <u>someone else</u> pays the bills.
                                              D

<u>No error.</u>
E

9. <u>Confronted with</u> a choice of either <u>cleaning up</u> his room or <u>cleaning out</u>
        A   **B**   **C**

the garage, the teenager became very <u>aggravated</u> with his parents.
                                      D

<u>No error.</u>
E

10. My brother and <u>I</u> dressed as <u>quickly</u> as we could, but we missed the
                   A   **B**

school bus, <u>which</u> made <u>us</u> late for class today. <u>No error.</u>
         C   **D**   **E**

11. <u>Among</u> the activities <u>offered</u> at the local high school <u>through</u> the commun-
   A   **B**   **C**

ity education program <u>are</u> singing in the couples' chorus, ballroom dancing,
                  D

and Chinese cooking. <u>No error.</u>
               E

12. If you are <u>disappointed by</u> an <u>inexpensive</u> bicycle, then an option you
                A   **B**

might consider is to work this summer and <u>save</u> your money for a
                                      C

<u>more expensive</u> model. <u>No error.</u>
    D   **E**

13. Also being presented to the city council this morning is the mayor's city
                                                              —
                                                              A

    budget for next year and plans to renovate the existing music theater, so
                                       ————————   ————————
                                           B   C

    the session will focus on financial matters. No error.
                ————————   ————————
                    D   E

14. Even a movement so delicate as a fly's walking triggers the Venus flytrap
                      ——————————   ————————————
                           A   B

    to grow extra cells on the outside of its hinge, immediately closing the
    ————————   ———
       C   D

    petals of the trap. No error.
                        ————————
                            E

15. Although outwardly Thomas Hardy seemed quite the picture of
             ————————   ——————————
                 A   B

    respectability and contentment, his works, especially the prose, deals with
    ——————————   ——————————
         C   D

    the theme of man's inevitable suffering. No error.
                                             ————————
                                                 E

16. Though unequal in social standing, the everyday lives of ancient Egypt-
           ——————————
               A

    ian kings and commoners alike is visible in the pictures of them found
                            ————   ————
                              B   C

    inside of tombs and temples. No error.
    ————————   ————————
        D   E

17. Sometimes considered unsafe for crops, land around river deltas can be
                        ——————————   —————— ——————
                             A   B   C

    excellent land for farming because periodic flooding deposits silt rich

    in nutrients. No error.
    ————————   ————————
        D   E

18. For years <u>people</u> concerned with the environment <u>have compiled</u> infor-
    A   **B**

mation which <u>show</u> many species are extinct and others <u>are either</u> en-
    C   **D**

dangered or bordering on becoming endangered. <u>No error.</u>
                E

19. Little is known about Shakespeare's boyhood or his early career as an

actor and playwright, but he <u>appears to have been</u> a financial success
           A

because <u>he bought</u> many properties, including <u>one of the finest</u> homes
  B   **C**

in Stratford, the town <u>in which he was born.</u> <u>No error.</u>
        D   **E**

20. *Scared Straight*, a program designed <u>to inhibit</u> criminal <u>behavior in</u> juve-
             A   **B**

nile offenders <u>who</u> seemed bound for prison as adults, had a significant
      C

<u>affect</u> on the youngsters. <u>No error.</u>
 D   **E**

21. We would like to know if you are <u>one of those</u> women <u>who is</u> actively
            A   **B**

involved in politics because we need someone <u>to campaign for</u> a law
                C

legalizing maternity leave for men <u>as well as</u> for women. <u>No error.</u>
           D   **E**

22. <u>Because</u> one of Margaret Thatcher's main goals <u>are</u> to rid Britain of
 A   **B**

socialism, <u>we</u> followers of the news were pleased to hear of <u>her election</u>
    C   **D**

to a third term as Prime Minister. <u>No error.</u>
          E

23. The judge <u>solemnly</u> instructed the jury to <u>abide to</u> the rules for a unani-
           A   **B**

    mous verdict, but the jury <u>were</u> unable <u>to agree.</u> <u>No error.</u>
                           C   **D**   **E**

24. I do not know what Mr. Jones and <u>he</u> advised, but if I <u>was going</u> on a long
                                 A   **B**

    trip, I <u>would hire</u> a student to stay in my home <u>in order</u> to protect it.
              C   **D**

    <u>No error.</u>
     E

25. <u>Exhausted</u> by the cold and temporarily defeated by the <u>growing</u> darkness,
       A   **B**

    the rock climbers <u>laid</u> on a narrow ledge and <u>slept through</u> the night.
                       C   **D**

    <u>No error.</u>
     E

DIRECTIONS: In each of the following sentences, some part or all of the sentence is underlined. Below each sentence you will find five ways of phrasing the underlined part. Select the answer that produces the most effective sentence, one that is clear and exact, without awkwardness or ambiguity, and blacken the corresponding space on your answer sheet. In choosing answers, follow the requirements of standard written English. Choose the answer that best expresses the meaning of the original sentence.

Answer (A) is always the same as the underlined part. Choose answer (A) if you think the original sentence needs no revision.

EXAMPLE:

The children swam in the lake all day and that is because it was so hot.

(A)   and that is because it was so hot

(B)   when it was so hot

(C)   since it was so hot

(D)   which is why it was so hot.

(E)   at the time when it was so hot

---

26.   Being that you bring home more money than I do, it is only fitting you should pay proportionately more rent.

(A)   Being that you bring home more money than I do

(B)   Bringing home the more money of the two of us

(C)   When more money is made by you than by me

(D)   Because you bring home more money than I do

(E)   If you're bringing home more money than me

27.   So tenacious is their grip on life, that sponge cells will regroup and form a new sponge even when they are squeezed through silk.

(A)   when they are squeezed

(B)   since they have been

(C)   as they will be

(D)   after they have been

(E)   because they should be

28. Seeing as how the plane is late, wouldn't you prefer to wait for a while on the observation deck?

    (A) Seeing as how the plane is late

    (B) When the plane comes in

    (C) Since the plane is late

    (D) Being as the plane is late

    (E) While the plane is landing

29. Only with careful environmental planning can we protect the world we live in.

    (A) world we live in

    (B) world in which we live in

    (C) living in this world

    (D) world's living

    (E) world in which we live

30. In the last three years, we have added more varieties of vegetables to our garden than those you suggested in the beginning.

    (A) than those you suggested in the beginning

    (B) than the ones we began with

    (C) beginning with your suggestion

    (D) than what you suggested to us

    (E) which you suggested in the beginning

31. As you know, I am not easily fooled by flattery, and while nice words please you, they don't get the job done.

    (A) nice words please you

    (B) nice words are pleasing

    (C) nice words please a person

    (D) flattering words please people

    (E) flattering words are pleasing to some

32. Some pieces of the puzzle, in spite of Jane's search, <u>are still missing and probably will never be found</u>.

    (A) are still missing and probably will never be found

    (B) is missing still but never found probably

    (C) probably will be missing and never found

    (D) are still probably missing and to never be found

    (E) probably are missing and will not be found

33. *Gone With The Wind* <u>is the kind of a movie</u> producers would like to release because it would bring them fame.

    (A) is the kind of a movie

    (B) is the sort of movie

    (C) is the kind of movie

    (D) is the type of a movie

    (E) is the category of movie

34. Eighteenth century architecture, with its columns and balanced lines, <u>was characteristic of those of previous times in Greece and Rome</u>.

    (A) was characteristic of those of previous times in Greece and Rome

    (B) is similar to characteristics of Greece and Rome

    (C) is similar to Greek and Roman building styles

    (D) is characteristic with earlier Greek and Roman architecture

    (E) was similar to architecture of Greece and Rome

35. Plato, one of the famous Greek philosophers, won many wrestling prizes when he was a young man, thus <u>exemplifying the Greek ideal of balance between the necessity for physical activity and using one's mind</u>.

    (A) exemplifying the Greek ideal of balance between the necessity for physical activity and using one's mind

    (B) serving as an example of the Greek ideal of balance between physical and mental activities

    (C) an example of balancing Greek mental and athletic games

    (D) this is an example of the Greek's balance between mental physical pursuits

    (E) shown to be exemplifying the balancing of two aspects of Greek life, the physical and the mental

36. <u>When the American Constitution was written</u>, some people argued it gave too much power to the federal government, while others thought it did not give enough.

    (A) When the American Constitution was written

    (B) Since the American Constitution was written

    (C) The American Constitution having been written

    (D) Because the American Constitution was written

    (E) In order to write the American Constitution

37. In 1215 at Runnymede, King John <u>forced to sign the Magna Carta, a document which</u> guaranteed Britons fundamental rights and privileges.

    (A) forced to sign the Magna Carta, a document which

    (B) was forced to sign the Magna Carta, a document which

    (C) forcing the signature of the Magna Carta, a document which

    (D) forced into signing the Magna Carta, a document which

    (E) was signing the Magna Carta by force, a document which

38. When a person has developed an acceptable level of <u>fitness for them, side benefits sometimes includes the blood pressure lowered.</u>

    (A) fitness for them, side benefits sometimes includes the blood pressure lowered

    (B) fitness for him, side benefits sometimes include lowered blood pressure

    (C) fitness of him, side benefits sometimes include lowered blood pressure

    (D) his fitness, side benefits sometimes includes the blood pressure lowered

    (E) one's fitness, side benefits sometimes include lowered blood pressure

39. Boys have greater muscular strength <u>than girls, but even though they have better small motor skills.</u>

    (A) than girls, but even though they have better small motor skills

    (B) than girls, but they still have better small motor skills

    (C) than girls having better small motor shills

    (D) , but girls have better small motor skills

    (E) , even though girls having the best small motor skills

40. Current statistics <u>show where environmental factors may not be as significant as diet and lifestyle</u> in determining a person's good health.

    (A) show where environmental factors may not be as significant as diet and lifestyle

    (B) show environmental factors may not be so significant as diet and lifestyle

    (C) show environmental factors may not be as significant as diet and lifestyle

    (D) show environmental factors may not be as significant, and diet and lifestyle

    (E) show environmental factors may not be so significant, and diet and lifestyle

DIRECTIONS: For each sentence in which you find an error, select the one underlined part that must be changed to make the sentence correct and blacken the corresponding space on your answer sheet.

If there is no error, blacken answer space (E).

41. The <u>average</u> American tourist feels <u>quite</u> at home in a Japanese stadium
          A   **B**

    filled <u>at capacity</u> with sports fans watching Japan's <u>most</u> popular sport,
           C   **D**

    baseball. <u>No error.</u>
             E

42. My brother is <u>engaged</u> to a woman <u>who</u> my parents <u>have</u> not met because
               A   **B**   **C**

    she has not yet <u>emigrated from</u> her native country of Ecuador. <u>No error.</u>
                    D   **E**

43. Colonel Jones <u>denies</u> that he <u>illegally</u> delivered funds to a foreign govern-
                  A   **B**

    ment agent or that <u>he</u> was involved in <u>any other</u> covert activity. <u>No error.</u>
                C   **D**   **E**

44. In the United States, <u>testing for</u> toxicity, determining the <u>proper</u> dose and
                       A   **B**

    timing between doses, and evaluating the vaccine for <u>effectiveness</u> <u>is</u> the
                                             C   **D**

    method used in researching new drugs. <u>No error.</u>
                                    E

45. George wants <u>to know if</u> <u>it is her</u> driving that expensive red sports car
                   A   **B**

    <u>at a rate of speed</u> obviously <u>exceeding</u> the posted speed limit. <u>No error.</u>
           C   **D**   **E**

46. Unless an athlete is physically fit, there is no sense in <u>him</u> sacrificing
    A

    <u>himself</u> for victory in <u>any one game</u> and, <u>therefore, facing</u> a lifetime injury.
    B   C   D

    <u>No error.</u>
    E

47. <u>Insensible of</u> the pain from his burn, Father was <u>more concerned</u> with
    A   B

    cooling off the overheated car and <u>assessing any</u> <u>damage to</u> the engine.
    C   D

    <u>No error.</u>
    E

48. <u>Parasitic</u> plants, attaching <u>themselves</u> to other plants and <u>drawing</u>
    A   B   C

    <u>nourishment</u> from them, thereby <u>sapping</u> the strength of the host plant,
    D

    usually killing it. <u>No error.</u>
    E

49. The Alaskan pipeline <u>stretched from</u> Prudhoe Bay <u>through</u> three mountain
    A   B

    ranges and <u>over</u> eight hundred rivers to Valdez, the northernmost ice-free
    C

    <u>port</u> in the United States. <u>No error.</u>
    D   E

50. Current statistics show that <u>environmental</u> factors, once the most important
    A

    element <u>in determining</u> susceptibility to cancer, may not be <u>so</u> significant
    B   C

    <u>as diet and lifestyle</u> in maintaining a person's good health. <u>No error.</u>
    D   E

GRAMMAR AND USAGE
PRACTICE TEST

ANSWER KEY

1.	(B)	14.	(A)	27.	(D)	40.	(C)
2.	(E)	15.	(D)	28.	(C)	41.	(C)
3.	(B)	16.	(D)	29.	(E)	42.	(B)
4.	(C)	17.	(E)	30.	(A)	43.	(C)
5.	(D)	18.	(C)	31.	(B)	44.	(E)
6.	(A)	19.	(D)	32.	(A)	45.	(B)
7.	(C)	20.	(D)	33.	(C)	46.	(A)
8.	(E)	21.	(B)	34.	(E)	47.	(A)
9.	(D)	22.	(B)	35.	(B)	48.	(D)
10.	(C)	23.	(B)	36.	(A)	49.	(E)
11.	(E)	24.	(B)	37.	(B)	50.	(C)
12.	(A)	25.	(C)	38.	(B)		
13.	(A)	26.	(D)	39.	(D)		

DETAILED EXPLANATIONS
OF ANSWERS

1.   **(B)**   "Were praised" is a plural verb; since the subject is Chief Joseph, a singular proper noun, the verb should be "was praised." The intervening phrase of choice (A), "*together with* 250 warriors and 500 women and children," does not change the singular subject. Choice (C), "bravery," is the correct noun form, and choice (D), "for," is idiomatically correct in that phrase.

2.   **(E)**   Choice (A), "upon which," is a correct prepositional phrase. Choice (B), "is based," agrees with its subject, "society." In choice (C), "are," agrees with its subject, "Ideals." "Derived from" in choice (D) is correct idiomatic usage.

3.   **(B)**   Two past actions are mentioned. The earlier of two past actions should be indicated by past perfect tense, so the answer should read, "had been." Choice (A) contains two adjectives as part of an appositive phrase modifying the subject, and choice (D), "upon the death," is idiomatically correct.

4.   **(C)**   Choice (C) should be "depend," not "had depended" because that use of past perfect would indicate prior past action. There is a series of events in this sentence: first, the legislature "had not finalized," (B), the budget; then, Representative Wilson "pointed out," (A), this failure. Choice (C) needs to be present tense as this situation still exists, and (D) is future action.

5.   **(D)**   Choice (A) is a noun used as an adjective. "To plan" is an infinitive phrase followed by noun objects: "puppet shows and movies" and "garage sales." In order to complete the parallelism, choice (D) should be "arrangements." Choice (C), "used," is a participle modifying "books."

6.   **(A)**   An infinitive, "to understand," should never be split by an adverbial modifier, "completely." Choice (B), "effects," is the noun form, and choice (D), "affected," is the adjective form. "One must," choice (C), is used in standard English.

7.   **(C)**   "More" is used to compare two things. Since the number of nations is not specified, "more" cannot be used in this sentence. Choice (A), "known," modifies "roads"; choice (B) is idiomatically correct; choice (D), "is," agrees in number with its subject, "transportation."

8.   **(E)**   Choice (A), "many a," should always be followed by the singular verb, "wishes," of choice (B). Choice (C) is idiomatically correct. In "Someone

else," (D), "else" is needed to indicate a person other than the student would pay the bills.

9. **(D)** "To aggravate" means "to make worse"; "to irritate" means "to excite to impatience or anger." A situation is "aggravated" and becomes worse, but one does not become "aggravated" with people. Choice (D) should read, "became very irritated." Choices (A), (B), and (C) are correctly used idioms.

10. **(C)** The reference in choice (C) is vague because it sounds as if the bus made the two students late. Choice (A) is a correct subject pronoun; choice (B) is the correct adverb form to modify "dressed"; choice (D) is a correct object pronoun.

11. **(E)** Choice (A), "among," indicates choice involving more than two things. The prepositions in (B) and (C) are correct. "Are," (D), is a plural verb, agreeing in number with the compound subject "singing ... dancing ... cooking."

12. **(A)** One is "disappointed by" a person or action but "disappointed in" is not satisfactory. "Inexpensive," (B), is the adjective form. Parallel with "To work," choice (C), "save," has the word "to" omitted. Choice (D) compares the two models, one "inexpensive" and one "more expensive."

13. **(A)** The verb should be plural, "are," in order to agree with the compound subject, "budget ... plans." Choice (B) begins an infinitive phrase which included a participle, "existing," (C). Choice (D) is idiomatically correct.

14. **(A)** The expression should be phrased, "as delicate as." Choice (B) uses a possessive before a gerund; choice (C) is correctly used; and choice (D) is a possessive pronoun of neuter gender which is appropriate to use in referring to a plant.

15. **(D)** The verb "deal" must agree with the subject, "works," and not a word in the intervening phrase. "Outwardly," choice (A), is an adverb modifying "seemed." Choices (B) and (C), "the picture of respectability," describe the subject; (D) is idiomatically correct.

16. **(D)** The word "of" in "inside of" is redundant and should not be used. Choice (A) is idiomatically correct and signals two classes of people once considered unequal in merit, and choice (B), "alike," is appropriate when comparing the two. Choice (C), "them," is correct pronoun usage.

17. **(E)** Choice (A), "unsafe for," is idiomatically correct; choice (B), "deltas," is a plural noun. Choice (C), "can be," is grammatically correct. The proposition "in," choice (D), is correct.

18. **(C)**   The verb in this subordinate clause is incorrect; the clause begins with "which," and this word refers to "information." Therefore, the clause, in order to agree with antecedent, must read, "which shown." The verb "shows" should not be made to agree with "species" and "others." Choices (A), "people," and (B), "have compiled," agree in number. "Either" in choice (D) is correctly placed after the verb to show a choice of "endangered" or "becoming endangered."

19. **(E)**   No changes need be made in this passage. The verbs show proper time sequence in (A) and (B); choice (C) is correct pronoun usage and correct superlative degree of adjective.

20. **(D)**   The noun form, "effect," is the correct one to use. Choice (A), "to inhibit," is an infinitive; choice (B) is correctly worded; in choice (C), the nominative case "who" is the correct subject of "seemed."

21. **(B)**   Verbs in clauses following "one of those," choice (A), are always plural. Choice (C), "to campaign for," is correct; choice (D) is a correctly-worded conjunction.

22. **(B)**   Choice (A) introduces a subordinate clause in which the subject is "one," so the verb in choice (B) should be "is." "We" is a subject pronoun, and "her" is a possessive pronoun in (C) and (D).

23. **(B)**   People "abide by" not "to" the rules. The adverb "solemnly," choice (A), modifies "instructed"; choice (D) is a correctly used infinitive. In choice (C), "jury," a collective noun, can be singular or plural depending on its use; since individual members of the jury disagree with one another, "jury" requires a plural verb, thus you should use "were."

24. **(B)**   Subjunctive mood must be used in clauses indicating a condition contrary to face, "if I *were* going on a long trip" (but I am not). In choice (A), "he," is the correct nominative case pronoun used as the subject of the verb, "advised." Choice (C) is a conditional verb, and choice (D) is correctly worded.

25. **(C)**   The verb "laid" is a conjugation of "lay," meaning "to put" or "to place." The verb form that should be used is "lay" from the verb "lie," meaning "to be in a lying position." Choices (A) and (B) are two correctly used participles, and choice (D) is correct in common usage.

26. **(D)**   "Because" is the word to use in the cause and effect relationship in this sentence. Choice (A), "being that"; choice (E), "than me"; and choice (B), "the more," are not grammatically correct. Choice (C), "is made by you," is passive voice and not as direct as (D).

27. **(D)** "After they have been" completes the proper time sequence. Choice (A), "when"; choice (B), "have been"; and choice (C), "will be," are the wrong time sequences. Choice (E), "should be," is an idea not contained in the original sentence.

28. **(C)** "Since the plane is late" shows correct time sequence and good reasoning. Choice (A), "seeing as how," and choice (D), "being as," are poor wording. Choices (B), "when," and (E), "while," are the wrong time, logically, to be on the observation deck.

29. **(E)** Since a sentence should not end with a preposition, choices (A) and (B) are eliminated. Choices (C), "living in this world," and (D), "world's living," introduce new concepts.

30. **(A)** The construction, "than those," clarifies the fact that more vegetables have been added. Choice (C), "your suggestions"; choice (D), "than went"; and choice (E), "which," do not contain the idea of adding more varieties of vegetables. Choice (B) ends with a preposition.

31. **(B)** The voice must be consistent with "I", so (B) is the only possible correct answer. All other choices have a noun or pronoun that is not consistent with "I": choice (A), "you"; choice (C), "a person"; choice (D), "people"; and choice (E), "some."

32. **(A)** The correct answer has two concepts — pieces are missing and pieces will probably never be found. Choice (B) has a singular verb, "is." Choice (C) indicates the pieces "probably will be" missing, which is not the problem. Choice (D) and choice (E) both indicate the pieces are "probably" missing, which is illogical because the pieces either are or are not missing.

33. **(C)** Choice (A), "the kind of a," and choice (D), "the type of a," are incorrect grammatical structures. Choice (E) introduces the new concept of "category." Choice (B), "sort of," is poor wording.

34. **(E)** Choice (E) is clear and concise and has the comparison of architecture. The antecedent of "those" in choice (A) is not clear. Choice (B) is comparing "characteristics," not just architecture. Choice (C) is awkward, and choice (D) incorrectly uses an idiom, "characteristic with."

35. **(B)** Choice (B) is clear and direct. Choices (A) and (E) are too wordy. Choice (C) has the wrong concept, "balancing games." Choice (D) is poorly worded, "this is an example."

36. **(A)** The main emphasis is the time factor — debates occurring at the time the Constitution was written. Choice (B), choice (C), and choice (D) all sound as if the debates took place after the Constitution was written, and choice (E) places the debates before the writing.

37. **(B)** A complete sentence is formed with (B). Choices (A), (C), and (D) all produce fragments, and choice (E) changes the meaning of the sentence.

38. **(B)** Voice must be consistent; the appropriate pronoun to use with the singular "a person" is "he" or "him," not the plural pronoun "them" of choice (A). The pronoun "one" in choice (E) is also not appropriate to refer to "a person." In addition, "benefits" is a plural noun and requires the plural verb "include," so choice (D) is eliminated. In choice (C) the phrase "of him" is an incorrect preposition.

39. **(D)** The antecedent of "them" is unclear in choices (A) and (B). Choice (C) is awkward because it is not parallel with the first part of the sentence. Choice (E) is not parallel and creates an unclear, tangled fragment.

40. **(C)** The phrase for comparing two things is "as _____ as." Therefore, choice (C) is correct because it contains this correct construction. Choice (A) uses the grammatically incorrect "show where." Choice (B) uses the incorrect "so significant a." Choice (D) and choice (E) create incoherent sentences with "significant, and."

41. **(C)** The idiom should be "filled to capacity." The adjective in choice (A), "average," is correct, as is the adverb in choice (B). Choice (D), "most," is appropriate for the superlative degree.

42. **(B)** The subordinate clause, "who my parents have not met," has as its subject "parents," which agrees with choice (C), "have ... met." Therefore, the pronoun is a direct object of the verb and should be in the objective case, "whom." Both choice (A) and choice (D) are idiomatically correct.

43. **(C)** The pronoun reference is unclear. The meaning of the sentence indicated that Colonel Jones denies involvement in any other covert activity. The agent from a foreign country may or may not have been involved in other covert activities, but that is not the issue here. The verb tense of choice (A) is correct. Choice (B) is the correct adverb form, and "other" in choice (D) is necessary to the meaning of the sentence.

44. **(E)** Choice (A), "testing," is parallel to "determining" and "evaluating." "Proper" in choice (B) and "effectiveness" in choice (C) are correct. In choice

(D) "is" must be singular because all three steps mentioned comprise the one process.

45. **(B)**   Choice (A) is correct. Choice (B) should read, "it is she"; nominative case pronoun is required following a linking verb. Choice (C) is proper English, and correct form of the modifiers appears in choice (D).

46. **(A)**   "Sacrificing" is a gerund, and a possessive form is always used before a gerund. The phrase should read, "no sense in his sacrificing." Choice (B) is the reflexive form of the pronoun, and the pronoun in choice (C) is correct also. The punctuation in choice (D) is correct as "therefore" is an interrupter.

47. **(A)**   The correct idiom is "insensible to" pain. Choice (B), "more concerned," is the correct comparative degree; choices (C) and (D) are correct.

48. **(D)**   This is a fragment which can be corrected by changing "sapping" to "sap." Choice (A), "parasitic," is an adjective form; the pronoun "themselves," choice (B), refers to "plants." Choice (C), "drawing nourishment," is parallel to "attaching."

49. **(E)**   Every preposition in this sentence is used correctly.

50. **(C)**   The phrase should read, "as significant as," in order to complete the correctly written choice (B). Choice (A), "environmental," is an adjective form, and choice (B) is idiomatically correct.

CHAPTER 3

Verbal Builder

➤ Vocabulary Builder
➤ Knowing Your Word Parts
➤ Verbal Review
➤ Verbal Ability Test

VOCABULARY BUILDER

The verbal sections of the standardized test you will take measure your abilities in many areas. No area, however, will have a greater impact upon your degree of success on the verbal sections than your vocabulary knowledge. Without a strong, comprehensive vocabulary, it is virtually impossible to score well on the verbal sections. Therefore, in order to be successful on the test, you must build your vocabulary and sharpen your skills.

Although this may seem like a tough assignment, it's not as difficult as it sounds. Reading is a simple skill that is also the most effective way to build your vocabulary. Reading increases your familiarity with words and their uses in different contexts. By reading every day, you can increase your chances of recognizing a word and its meaning in a test question.

Remembering the words you read, however, is the tough part. Here is where REA's Comprehensive Vocabulary List is most helpful. After a solid education, you have naturally formed a fairly strong vocabulary. Therefore, rather than provide you with an extensive list of thousands of words, REA has focused the vocabulary list on the six hundred most frequently tested words, plus the four hundred more commonly tested words which will enable you to have the greatest advantage on your test. The Vocabulary List will give you a strong indication as to the appropriate level of vocabulary that may be found on your test. In conjunction with reading, REA's comprehensive vocabulary list can aid you in building your vocabulary and sharpening your skills.

The most effective way to utilize the Vocabulary List is to study one section at a time and to be sure to take the drill immediately following each section. Make a note of the words with which you are unfamiliar or that are defined in unusual ways. Any words that you are still unsure about should be studied as much as possible before the day of the test. These lists, along with your present vocabulary as a base and lots of reading, will prepare you to be successful on the verbal sections of your standardized test.

FREQUENTLY TESTED WORDS

GROUP 1

abase – *v.* – to degrade; humiliate; disgrace

aberration – *n.* – departure from what is right, true, correct

abeyance – *n.* – a state of temporary suspension

abhor – *v.* – to hate

abominate – *v.* – to loathe; to hate

absolve – *v.* – to forgive; to acquit

abstemious – *adj.* – sparingly used or used with temperance

abstinence – *n.* – the act or practice of voluntarily refraining from any action

abstruse – *adj.* – 1. hidden, concealed; 2. difficult to be comprehended

accolade – *n.* – approving or praising mention

accomplice – *n.* – co-conspirator; a partner; partner-in-crime

accretion – *n.* – growth in size by addition or accumulation

accrue – *v.* – collect; build up

acquiesce – *v.* – agree or consent to an opinion

acrid – *adj.* – sharp; bitter; foul smelling

adamant – *adj.* – not yielding; firm

adversary – *n.* – an enemy; foe

advocate – *v.* – 1. to plead in favor of; 2. *n.* – supporter; defender

aesthetic – *adj.* – showing good taste; artistic

aghast – *adj.* – 1. astonished; amazed; 2. horrified; terrified; appalled

alacrity – *v.* – 1. enthusiasm; fervor; 2. liveliness; sprightliness

alleviate – *v.* – to lessen or make easier

allocate – *v.* – set aside; designate; assign

allusion – *n.* – an indirect reference to something

aloof – *adj.* – distant in interest; reserved; cool

altercation – *n.* – controversy; dispute

altruistic – *adj.* – unselfish

amass –*v.* – to collect together; accumulate

ambiguous – *adj.* – not clear; uncertain; vague

ameliorate – *v.* – to make better; to improve

amiable – *adj.* – friendly

amorphous – *adj.* – having no determinate form

analogy – *n.* – similarity; correlation; parallelism; simile; metaphor

anarchist – *n.* – one who believes that a formal government is unnecessary

anomaly – *n.* – abnormality; irregularity; deviation from the regular arrangement

anonymous – *adj.* – nameless; unidentified

antagonism – *n.* – hostility; opposition

antipathy – *n.* – inherent aversion or antagonism of feeling

antiseptic – *adj.* – preventing infection or decay

apathy – *n.* – lack of emotion or interest

appease – *v.* – to make quiet; to calm

apprehensive – *adj.* – fearful; in expectation of evil

arbiter – *n.* – one who is authorized to judge or decide

arbitrary – *adj.* – based on one's preference or judgment

arduous – *adj.* – difficult; laborious

arid – *adj.* – 1. dry; parched; 2. barren; 3. uninteresting; dull

arrogant – *adj.* – acting superior to others; conceited

astute – *adj.* – cunning; sly; crafty

atrophy – *v.* – to waste away through lack of nutrition

audacious – *adj.* – fearless; bold

DRILL 1

> **DIRECTIONS:** Match each word in the left column with the word in the right column that is most **opposite** in meaning.

	Word		**Match**
1.	_____ audacious	A.	hostile
2.	_____ apathy	B.	fragrant
3.	_____ amiable	C.	selfish
4.	_____ altruistic	D.	reasoned
5.	_____ aberration	E.	ally
6.	_____ acrid	F.	disperse
7.	_____ acquiesce	G.	enthusiasm
8.	_____ arbitrary	H.	conformity
9.	_____ amass	I.	resist
10.	_____ adversary	J.	unadventurous

> **DIRECTIONS:** Match each word in the left column with the word in the right column that is most **similar** in meaning.

	Word		**Match**
11.	_____ adamant	A.	afraid
12.	_____ aesthetic	B.	disagreement
13.	_____ apprehensive	C.	tasteful
14.	_____ antagonism	D.	insistent
15.	_____ altercation	E.	hostility

Answers — Drill 1

11. (D)	12. (C)	13. (A)	14. (E)	15. (B)
6. (B)	7. (I)	8. (D)	9. (F)	10. (E)
1. (J)	2. (G)	3. (C)	4. (A)	5. (H)

GROUP 2

augment – *v.* – to increase or add to; to make larger

auspicious – *adj.* – 1. having omens of success; 2. prosperous; 3. favorable; kind

austere – *v.* – harsh; severe; strict

authentic – *adj.* – real; genuine; trustworthy

awry – *adv.* – 1. crooked(ly); uneven(ly); 2. *adj.* – wrong, askew

axiom – *n.* – an established principle or statement accepted as true

azure – *n.* – the clear blue color of the sky

baleful – *adj.* – sinister; threatening; evil; deadly

banal – *adj.* – common; trivial; trite

baroque – *adj.* – extravagant; ornate

bauble – *n.* – 1. that which is gay or showy; 2. a baby's toy

beget – *v.* – to produce, as an effect

behoove – *v.* – to be advantageous; to be necessary

benefactor – *n.* – one who helps others; a donor

beneficient – *adj.* – doing good

benevolent – *adj.* – kind; generous

benign – *adj.* – mild; harmless

berate – *v.* – scold; reprove; reproach; criticize

bereave – *v.* – to deprive

bereft – *adj.* – deprived, left sad because of someone's death

beseech – *v.* – 1. to ask or pray with urgency; 2. to beg eagerly for

biennial – *adj.* – 1. happening every two years; 2. *n.* – a plant which blooms
     every two years

blasphemous – *adj.* – irreligious, away from acceptable standards

blatant – *adj.* – 1. obvious; unmistakable; 2. crude; vulgar

blithe – *adj.* – happy; cheery; merry

bombastic – *adj.* – pompous; wordy; turgid

brevity – *n.* – briefness; shortness

brusque – *adj.* – abrupt, blunt, or short in manner or speech

bumptious – *adj.* – impertinent; conceited

burnish – *v.* – to make or become smooth, bright, and glossy

cabal – *v.* – to intrigue or plot; usually in a small group

cache – *n.* – 1. stockpile; store; heap; 2. hiding place for goods

cacophony – *n.* – a jarring or disagreeable sound of words

cajole – *v.* – to flatter; to coax

candid – *adj.* – honest; truthful; sincere

capricious – *adj.* – changeable; fickle

cascade – *n.* – 1. waterfall; 2. *v.* – pour; rush; fall

caustic – *adj.* – burning; sarcastic; harsh

censor – *v.* – to examine and delete objectionable material

censure – *v.* – to criticize or disapprove of

chagrin – *n.* – mortification or disappointment

charisma – *n.* – appeal; magnetism; presence

charlatan – *n.* – an imposter; fake

chastise – *v.* – punish; discipline; admonish; rebuke

chronology – *n.* – the arrangement of events, dates, etc. in a certain order of occurrence

circumlocution – *n.* – an indirect or lengthy way of expressing something

coalesce – *v.* – to combine into a single body or group

coda – *n.* – a musical passage which brings a composition to its definite close

cognizant – *adj.* – being informed or aware

cohesion – *n.* – the act of holding together

DRILL 2

DIRECTIONS: Match each word in the left column with the word in the right column that is most **opposite** in meaning.

	Word		*Match*
1. _____	augment	A.	permit
2. _____	bombastic	B.	heroine
3. _____	banal	C.	directness
4. _____	benevolent	D.	diminish
5. _____	censor	E.	dishonest
6. _____	authentic	F.	malicious
7. _____	candid	G.	modest
8. _____	circumlocution	H.	mournful
9. _____	charlatan	I.	unusual
10. _____	blithe	J.	bogus

DIRECTIONS: Match each word in the left column with the word in the right column that is most **similar** in meaning.

	Word		*Match*
11. _____	baleful	A.	harmless
12. _____	benign	B.	reprimand
13. _____	berate	C.	changeable
14. _____	censure	D.	ominous
15. _____	capricious	E.	criticize

Answers — Drill 2

11. (D)	12. (A)	13. (B)	14. (E)	15. (C)
6. (J)	7. (E)	8. (C)	9. (B)	10. (H)
1. (D)	2. (G)	3. (I)	4. (F)	5. (A)

GROUP 3

collaborate – *v.* – to work together; cooperate

colloquial – *adj.* – casual; common; conversational; idiomatic

compatible – *adj.* – in agreement with; harmonious

complacent – *adj.* – content; self-satisfied; smug

compliant – *adj.* – yielding; obedient

comprehensive – *adj.* – all–inclusive; complete; thorough

conciliatory – *adj.* – tending to make peace between persons at variance

concise – *adj.* – in few words; brief; condensed

condescend – *v.* – to deal with others in a patronizing manner

condone – *v.* – to overlook; to forgive

conglomeration – *n.* – mixture; collection

conjoin – *v.* – to unite; to combine

conjure – *v.* – 1. to call upon or appeal to; 2. to cause to be, appear, come

connoisseur – *n.* – expert; authority

consecrate – *v.* – to sanctify; make sacred; immortalize

consensus – *n.* – unanimity; agreement

consummation – *n.* – the completion; finish

contentious – *adj.* – argumentative; quarrelsome

contrite – *adj.* – regretful; sorrowful

contumacious – *adj.* – insubordinate; rebellious; disobedient

conundrum – *n.* – any question or thing of a perplexing nature

conventional – *adj.* – traditional; common; routine

correlate – *v.* – to bring one thing into mutual relation with another thing

corroborate – *v.* – 1. to strengthen; 2. to confirm; to make more certain

cower – *v.* – crouch down in fear; to shrink and tremble

craven – *adj.* – cowardly; fearful

culpable – *adj.* – blameworthy

cynic – *n.* – one who believes that others are motivated entirely by selfishness

dais – *n.* – a raised platform in a room where tables for honored guests are placed

dank – *adj.* – disagreeably damp or humid

dearth – *n.* – scarcity; shortage

debacle – *n.* – disaster; ruination

debauchery – *n.* – extreme indulgence of one's appetites, especially for sensual pleasure

debilitate – *v.* – deprive of strength

decorous – *adj.* – characterized by good taste

defamation – *n.* – the malicious uttering of falsehood respecting another

deference – *n.* – a yielding in opinion to another

deign – *v.* – condescend

deleterious – *adj.* – harmful to health, well-being

delineate – *v.* – to outline; to describe

demur – *v.* – to take exception; object

depict – *v.* – to portray in words; present a visual image

deplete – *v.* – to reduce; to empty

depravity – *n.* – moral corruption; badness

deride – *v.* – to ridicule; laugh at with scorn

derision – *n.* – ridicule; mockery

derogatory – *adj.* – belittling; uncomplimentary

desecrate – *v.* – to violate a holy place or sanctuary

desiccate – *v.* – to dry completely

destitute – *adj.* – poor; poverty-stricken

DRILL 3

DIRECTIONS: Match each word in the left column with the word in the right column that is most **opposite** in meaning.

	Word		*Match*
1. _____	deplete	A.	submissive
2. _____	colloquial	B.	disapprove
3. _____	concise	C.	innocent
4. _____	contumacious	D.	success
5. _____	depravity	E.	fill
6. _____	condone	F.	agree
7. _____	culpable	G.	beginning
8. _____	consummation	H.	sophisticated
9. _____	demur	I.	virtue
10. _____	debacle	J.	verbose

DIRECTIONS: Match each word in the left column with the word in the right column that is most **similar** in meaning.

	Word		*Match*
11. _____	compatible	A.	portray
12. _____	depict	B.	content
13. _____	conventional	C.	harmonious
14. _____	comprehensive	D.	thorough
15. _____	complacent	E.	common

Answers — Drill 3

1. (E) 2. (H) 3. (J) 4. (A) 5. (I)

6. (B) 7. (C) 8. (G) 9. (F) 10. (D)

11. (C) 12. (A) 13. (E) 14. (D) 15. (B)

GROUP 4

devoid – *adj.* – lacking; empty

dichotomy – *n.* – division of things by pairs

digress – *v.* – stray from the subject; wander from topic

disavow – *v.* – to deny; to refuse

discerning – *adj.* – distinguishing one thing from another

discomfit – *v.* – 1. to overthrow the plans or expectations of; 2. to confuse

discourse – *n.* – a communication of thoughts by words

disdain – *n.* – 1. intense dislike; 2. *v.* – look down upon; scorn

disheartened – *adj.* – discouraged; depressed

disinterested – *adj.* – impartial; unbiased

disparage – *v.* – to belittle; undervalue

disparity – *n.* – difference in form, character, or degree

disperse – *v.* – to scatter; separate

disseminate – *v.* – to circulate; scatter

dissonance – *n.* – discord

diverge – *v.* – separate; split

diverse – *adj.* – different; dissimilar

docile – *adj.* – manageable; obedient

doggerel – *adj.* – trivial; inartistic

dogmatic – *adj.* – stubborn; biased, opinionated

dowdy – *adj.* – drab; shabby

dubious – *adj.* – doubtful; uncertain; skeptical; suspicious

duress – *n.* – force; constraint

earthy – *adj.* – 1. not refined; coarse; 2. simple and natural

ebullient – *adj.* – showing excitement

eccentric – *adj.* – odd; peculiar; strange

eclectic – *adj.* – choosing or selecting from various sources

economical – *adj.* – not wasteful

educe – *v.* – draw forth

effeminate – *adj.* – having qualities generally attributed to a woman effervescence – *n.* – 1. liveliness; spirit; enthusiasm; 2. bubbliness

effigy – *n.* – the image or likeness of a person

effluvium – *n.* – an outflow in the form of a vapor

elusive – *adj.* – hard to catch; difficult to understand

eminence – *n.* – 1. high or lofty place; 2. superiority in position or rank

emulate – *v.* – to strive to equal or excel

engender – *v.* – to create; bring about

enhance – *v.* – to improve; complement; make more attractive

enigma – *n.* – mystery; secret; perplexity

ennui – *n.* – boredom; apathy

ephemeral – *adj.* – temporary; brief; short–lived

epitome – *n.* – model; typification; representation

equivocal – *adj.* – doubtful; uncertain

errant – *adj.* – wandering

erratic – *adj.* – unpredictable; strange

erudite – *adj.* – having extensive knowledge; learned

esoteric – *adj.* – incomprehensible; obscure

ethnic – *adj.* – native; racial; cultural

euphony – *n.* – pleasant sound

evanescent – *adj.* – vanishing; fleeting

DRILL 4

DIRECTIONS: Match each word in the left column with the word in the right column that is most **opposite** in meaning.

	Word		*Match*
1. _____	dowdy	A.	excitement
2. _____	erudite	B.	certain
3. _____	ennui	C.	acknowledge
4. _____	evanescent	D.	chic
5. _____	disheartened	E.	uninformed
6. _____	dubious	F.	wild
7. _____	disavow	G.	complement
8. _____	disdain	H.	sanctify
9. _____	docile	I.	appearing
10. _____	disparage	J.	uplifted

DIRECTIONS: Match each word in the left column with the word in the right column that is most **similar** in meaning.

	Word		*Match*
11. _____	effervescence	A.	native
12. _____	ethnic	B.	distribute
13. _____	disseminate	C.	confuse
14. _____	discomfit	D.	liveliness
15. _____	eccentric	E.	odd

Answers — Drill 4

11. (D)	12. (A)	13. (B)	14. (C)	15. (E)
6. (B)	7. (C)	8. (H)	9. (F)	10. (G)
1. (D)	2. (E)	3. (A)	4. (I)	5. (J)

GROUP 5

evoke – *v.* – call forth; provoke

exculpate – *v.* – to declare or prove guiltless

exemplary – *adj.* – serving as an example; outstanding

exigent – *n.* – an urgent occasion

exonerate – *v.* – to unload; to release from burden

exorbitant – *adj.* – going beyond what is reasonable; excessive

exotic – *adj.* – unusual; striking

expedient – *adj.* – helpful; practical; worthwhile

expedite – *v.* – speed up

exposition – *n.* – a setting forth of facts or ideas

extol – *v.* – praise; commend

exuberant – *adj.* – overflowing; lavish; superabundant

facade – *n.* – front view; false appearance

facetious – *adj.* – lightly joking

facilitate – *v.* – make easier; simplify

fallacious – *adj.* – misleading

fanatic – *n.* – enthusiast; extremist

fastidious – *adj.* – fussy; hard to please

feasible – *adj.* – reasonable; practical

fecund – *adj.* – fruitful in children; productive

ferret – *v.* – drive or hunt out of hiding

fervor – *n.* – passion; intensity

fickle – *adj.* – changeable; unpredictable

figment – *n.* – product; creation

finesse – *n.* – the ability to handle situations with skill and diplomacy

finite – *adj.* – measurable; limited; not everlasting

flag – *v.* – 1. to send a message by signaling; 2. to become limp

fledgling – *n.* – inexperienced person; beginner

flippant – *adj.* – 1. speaking with ease and rapidity; 2. impertinent

flout – *v.* – to mock; to sneer

fluency – *n.* – smoothness of speech

flux – *n.* – current; continuous change

forbearance – *n.* – patience; self-restraint

fortuitous – *adj.* – accidental; happening by chance; lucky

foster – *v.* – encourage; nurture; support

frenetic – *adj.* – frantic; frenzied

frugality – *n.* – thrift

fulsome – *adj.* – offensive, especially because of excess

furtive – *adj.* – secretive; sly

fustian – *n.* – an inflated style of talking or writing

gaffe – *n.* – a blunder

gainsay – *v.* – to deny or contradict

garbled – *adj.* – mixed up

garner – *v.* – to accumulate

garrulous – *adj.* – talking much about unimportant things

genial – *adj.* – 1. contributing to life and growth; 2. amiable; cordial

genre – *n.* – a kind, sort, or type

germane – *adj.* – pertinent; related; to the point

gerrymander – *v.* – to manipulate unfairly

DRILL 5

DIRECTIONS: Match each word in the left column with the word in the right column that is most **opposite** in meaning.

	Word		*Match*
1. _____	facetious	A.	combat
2. _____	extol	B.	delay
3. _____	foster	C.	considerate
4. _____	expedite	D.	rude
5. _____	fastidious	E.	quiet
6. _____	flippant	F.	denounce
7. _____	germane	G.	calm
8. _____	garrulous	H.	solemn
9. _____	genial	I.	immaterial
10. _____	frenetic	J.	neglectful

DIRECTIONS: Match each word in the left column with the word in the right column that is most **similar** in meaning.

	Word		*Match*
11. _____	furtive	A.	enable
12. _____	expedient	B.	stealthy
13. _____	facilitate	C.	unpredictable
14. _____	fallacious	D.	worthwhile
15. _____	fickle	E.	deceptive

Answers — Drill 5

1. (H)	2. (F)	3. (A)	4. (B)	5. (J)
6. (C)	7. (I)	8. (E)	9. (D)	10. (G)
11. (B)	12. (D)	13. (A)	14. (E)	15. (C)

GROUP 6

gibber – *v.* – speak foolishly

gloat – *v.* – brag; glory over

glutton – *n.* – overeater

goad – *v.* – to arouse or incite

grandiose – *adj.* – extravagant; flamboyant

guile – *n.* – slyness; deceit

gullible – *adj.* – easily fooled

hackneyed – *adj.* – commonplace; trite

haggard – *adj.* – tired-looking; fatigued

hamper – *v.* – interfere with; hinder

haphazard – *adj.* – disorganized; random

haughty – *adj.* – proud and disdainful

hedonistic – *adj.* – pleasure seeking

hierarchy – *n.* – body of people, things, or concepts divided into ranks

homeostasis – *n.* – the maintenance of stability or equilibrium

hone – *v.* – sharpen

humility – *n.* – lack of pride; modesty

hypocritical – *adj.* – two-faced; deceptive

hypothetical – *adj.* – assumed; uncertain

iconoclast – *n.* – a breaker or destroyer of images

ideology – *n.* – set of beliefs; principles

idyllic – *adj.* – pleasing and simple

ignoble – *adj.* – shameful; dishonorable

imbue – *v.* – inspire; arouse

immune – *adj.* – protected; unthreatened by

immutable – *adj.* – unchangeable; permanent

impale – *v.* – fix on a stake; stick; pierce

impede – *v.* – to stop in progress

imperious – *adj.* – authoritative

impervious – *adj.* – 1. incapable of being penetrated; 2. not affected or influenced by

impetuous – *adj.* – 1. rash; impulsive; 2. forcible; violent

implement – *v.* – to carry into effect

implication – *n.* – suggestion; inference

implicit – *adj.* – to be understood though not fully expressed

impromptu – *adj.* – without preparation

improvident – *adj.* – lacking foresight and thrift

impudent – *adj.* – shameless; immodest

impugn – *v.* – to contradict

inarticulate – *adj.* – speechless; unable to speak clearly

incessant – *adj.* – constant; continual

inchoate – *adj.* – existing in elementary or beginning form

incisive – *adj.* – cutting into

incognito – *adj.* – unidentified; disguised; concealed

incoherent – *adj.* – illogical; rambling

incompatible – *adj.* – disagreeing; disharmonious

incursion – *n.* – 1. a running in; 2. invasion; raid

indict – *v.* – charge with a crime

indignant – *adj.* – to consider as unworthy or improper

indolent – *adj.* – lazy; inactive

indulgent – *adj.* – lenient: patient

DRILL 6

DIRECTIONS: Match each word in the left column with the word in the right column that is most **opposite** in meaning.

	Word		**Match**
1.	_____ ignoble	A.	vigorous
2.	_____ haggard	B.	cynical
3.	_____ gloat	C.	simple
4.	_____ hedonist	D.	deter
5.	_____ grandiose	E.	belittle
6.	_____ gullible	F.	beneficial
7.	_____ goad	G.	admirable
8.	_____ furtive	H.	organized
9.	_____ futile	I.	candid
10.	_____ haphazard	J.	puritan

DIRECTIONS: Match each word in the left column with the word in the right column that is most **similar** in meaning.

	Word		**Match**
11.	_____ glutton	A.	hinder
12.	_____ impale	B.	principles
13.	_____ hamper	C.	trite
14.	_____ hackneyed	D.	overeater
15.	_____ ideology	E.	transfix

Answers — Drill 6

11. (D) 12. (E) 13. (A) 14. (C) 15. (B)

6. (B) 7. (D) 8. (I) 9. (F) 10. (H)

1. (G) 2. (A) 3. (E) 4. (J) 5. (C)

GROUP 7

ineluctable – *adj.* – not to be avoided or escaped

inept – *adj.* – incompetent; unskilled

inert – *adj.* – without power to move or to resist an opposite force

infamous – *adj.* – having a bad reputation; notorious

infer – *v.* – form an opinion; conclude

ingenuous – *adj.* – gifted with genius; innate or natural quality

inherent – *adj.* – innate; basic; inborn

innate – *adj.* – natural; inborn

innocuous – *adj.* – harmless; innocent

innovate – *v.* – introduce a change; depart from the old

innuendo – *n.* – an indirect remark, gesture or reference

insipid – *adj.* – uninteresting; bland

insolvent – *adj.* – bankrupt; not able to pay debts

intermittent – *adj.* – 1. stopping and starting again at intervals; 2. *n.* – a disease which entirely subsides or ceases at certain intervals

intransigent – *adj.* – refusing to compromise

invective – *n.* – a violent verbal attack

ironic – *adj.* – contradictory; inconsistent; sarcastic

jaded – *adj.* – 1. tired or worn-out; 2. dulled

jeopardy – *n.* – danger

judicious – *adj.* – possessing sound judgment

ken – *n.* – range of knowledge

kinship – *n.* – family relationship

kith – *n.* – acquaintances and relations

knavery – *n.* – dishonesty; trickery

labyrinth – *n.* – maze

laconic – *n.* – a brief, pithy expression

laggard – *n.* – a lazy person; one who lags behind

lament – *v.* – to mourn or grieve

languid – *adj.* – weak; fatigued

lascivious – *adj.* – indecent; immoral

latency – *n.* – the condition of being hidden or undeveloped

lax – *adj.* – careless; irresponsible

lecherous – *adj.* – impure in thought and act

lethal – *adj.* – deadly

lethargic – *adj.* – lazy; passive

levee – *n.* – the act or time of rising

levity – *n.* – silliness; lack of seriousness

liaison – *n.* – connection; link

ligneous – *adj.* – consisting of or resembling wood

litigate – *v.* – to contest in a lawsuit

livid – *adj.* – 1. black-and-blue; discolored; 2. enraged; irate

lucid – *adj.* – 1. shining; 2. easily understood

lucrative – *adj.* – profitable; gainful

luminous – *adj.* – giving off light; bright

lustrous – *adj.* – bright; radiant

macerate – *v.* – 1. to soften by soaking; 2. to cause to waste away; 3. to torment

magnanimous – *adj.* – forgiving; unselfish

malediction – *n.* – curse; evil spell

malicious – *adj.* – spiteful; vindictive

malleable – *adj.* – that which can be pounded without breaking; adaptable

DRILL 7

DIRECTIONS: Match each word in the left column with the word in the right column that is most **opposite** in meaning.

	Word		*Match*
1. _____	lamentable	A.	proper
2. _____	livid	B.	injurious
3. _____	lascivious	C.	responsible
4. _____	innocuous	D.	honor
5. _____	lecherous	E.	blissful
6. _____	levity	F.	encouraging
7. _____	lax	G.	compromising
8. _____	intransigent	H.	prudish
9. _____	invective	I.	gravity
10. _____	magnanimous	J.	resentful

DIRECTIONS: Match each word in the left column with the word in the right column that is most **similar** in meaning.

	Word		*Match*
11. _____	luminous	A.	bewail
12. _____	knave	B.	radiant
13. _____	liaison	C.	fatigued
14. _____	languid	D.	alliance
15. _____	lament	E.	rogue

Answers — Drill 7

11. (B)   12. (E)   13. (D)   14. (C)   15. (A)

6. (I)   7. (C)   8. (G)   9. (D)   10. (J)

1. (F)   2. (E)   3. (A)   4. (B)   5. (H)

GROUP 8

mandatory – *adj.* – authoritatively commanded or required

manifest – *adj.* – obvious; clear

maverick – *n.* – person who acts independent of a group

meander – *v.* – wind on a course; go aimlessly

mellifluous – *adj.* – flowing sweetly and smoothly

mentor – *n.* – teacher

mercenary – *n.* – working or done for payment only

metamorphosis – *n.* – change of form

meticulous – *adj.* – exacting; precise

mitigate – *v.* – alleviate; lessen; soothe

molten – *adj.* – melted

morose – *adj.* – moody; despondent

motif – *n.* – theme

motility – *n.* – the quality of exhibiting spontaneous motion

mundane – *adj.* – ordinary; commonplace

munificent – *adj.* – very generous in giving; lavish

myriad – *adj.* – innumerable; countless

nebulous – *adj.* – 1. cloudy; hazy; 2. unclear; vague

neophyte – *n.* – beginner; newcomer

nettle – *v.* – annoy; irritate

nostalgic – *adj.* – longing for the past; filled with bittersweet memories

notorious – *adj.* – infamous; renowned

nullify – *v.* – cancel; invalidate

oaf – *n.* – 1. a misshapen child; 2. a stupid, clumsy fellow

obdurate – *adj.* – stubborn; inflexible

obliterate – *v.* – destroy completely

obsequious – *adj.* – slavishly attentive; servile

obsolete – *adj.* – out of date; passé

occult – *adj.* – mystical; mysterious

ominous – *adj.* – threatening

omniscient – *adj.* – having universal knowledge

opaque – *adj.* – dull; cloudy; nontransparent

opulence – *n.* – wealth; fortune

ornate – *adj.* – elaborate; lavish; decorated

oscillate – *v.* – 1. to swing to and fro; 2. to be indecisive; to fluctuate

ossify – *v.* – to settle or fix rigidly in a practice, custom, attitude, etc.

ostensible – *adj.* – 1. proper to be shown; 2. apparent; declared

ostracize – *v.* – to cast out or banish

palliate – *v.* – 1. to alleviate or ease; 2. to make appear less serious

pallid – *adj.* – sallow; colorless

palpable – *adj.* – tangible; apparent

panegyric – *n.* – a formal speech written in praise of a distinguished person

paradox – *n.* – 1. a statement that seems contradictory but that may actually be true in fact; 2. something inconsistent with common experience

parallel – *adj.* – extending in the same direction and at the same distance apart at every point

paraphernalia – *n.* – equipment; accessories

partisan – *n.* – 1. supporter; follower; 2. *adj.* – biased; one-sided

passive – *adj.* – submissive; unassertive

pathology – *n.* – part of medicine dealing with the nature of diseases, their causes and symptoms, and the structural and functional changes

pedagogue – *n.* – a dogmatic teacher

penchant – *n.* – a strong liking or fondness

DRILL 8

DIRECTIONS: Match each word in the left column with the word in the right column that is most **opposite** in meaning.

	Word		Match
1.	ostensible	A.	aversion
2.	obsolete	B.	flexible
3.	nebulous	C.	unnoticeable
4.	penchant	D.	actual
5.	neophyte	E.	opponent
6.	partisan	F.	domineering
7.	obdurate	G.	distinct
8.	obsequious	H.	assertive
9.	palpable	I.	modern
10.	passive	J.	veteran

DIRECTIONS: Match each word in the left column with the word in the right column that is most **similar** in meaning.

	Word		Match
11.	nullify	A.	invalidate
12.	ominous	B.	irritate
13.	nettle	C.	dull
14.	palliate	D.	threatening
15.	opaque	E.	alleviate

Answers — Drill 8

1. (D) 2. (I) 3. (G) 4. (A) 5. (J)
6. (E) 7. (B) 8. (F) 9. (C) 10. (H)
11. (A) 12. (D) 13. (B) 14. (E) 15. (C)

GROUP 9

perceptive – *adj.* – full of insight; aware

pensive – *adj.* – reflective; contemplative

percussion – *n.* – the striking of one object against another

peripheral – *adj.* – marginal; outer

perjury – *n.* – the practice of lying

permeable – *adj.* – porous; allowing to pass through

pernicious – *adj.* – dangerous; harmful

perpetual – *adj.* – enduring for all time

pertinent – *adj.* – related to the matter at hand

pervade – *v.* – to occupy the whole of

pessimism – *n.* – seeing only the gloomy side; hopelessness

petulant – *adj.* – 1. forward; immodest; 2. impatient or irritable

philanthropy – *n.*– charity; unselfishness

phlegmatic – *adj.* – without emotion or interest

pinnacle – *n.* – 1. a small turret that rises above the roof of a building; 2. the highest point

pious – *adj.* – religious; devout; dedicated

piquant – *adj.* – 1. agreeably pungent or stimulating to the taste; 2. exciting interest or curiosity

pittance – *n.* – small allowance

placate – *v.* – pacify

placid – *adj.* – serene; tranquil

plethora – *n.* – condition of going beyond what is needed; excess; overabundance

plumb – *v.* – 1. to fall or sink straight down; 2. to hang vertically

polemic – *adj.* – controversial; argumentative

pragmatic – *adj.* – matter-of-fact; practical

preclude – *v.* – inhibit; make impossible

prattle – *v.* – to speak in a childish manner; babble

precipitate – *v.* – 1. to throw headlong; 2. to cause to happen

pristine – *adj.* – still pure or untouched

privy – *adj.* – private; confidential

probity – *n.* – true virtue or integrity; complete honesty

problematic – *adj.* – uncertain

prodigal – *adj.* – wasteful; lavish

prodigious – *adj.* – exceptional; tremendous

prodigy – *n.* – 1. an extraordinary happening; 2. something so extraordinary as to inspire wonder

profound – *adj.* – deep; knowledgeable; thorough

profusion – *n.* – great amount; abundance

progeny – *n.* – children; offspring

propinquity – *n.* – nearness in time or place, relationship, or nature

prosaic – *adj.* – tiresome; ordinary

proselytize – *v.* – to make a convert of

provocative – *adj.* – 1. tempting; 2. irritating

pundit – *n.* – a person of great learning

pungent – *adj.* – sharp; stinging

quandary – *n.* – dilemma

qualify – *v.* – 1. to render fit; 2. to furnish with legal power; 3. to modify

quiescent – *adj.* – inactive; at rest

quirk – *n.* – peculiar behavior; startling twist

rabid – *adj.* – furious; with extreme anger

rampart – *n.* – 1. anything that protects or defends; 2. an embankment of earth that surrounds a fort or castle

rancid – *adj.* – having a bad odor

rant – *v.* – to speak in a loud, pompous manner; rave

DRILL 9

DIRECTIONS: Match each word in the left column with the word in the right column that is most **opposite** in meaning.

	Word		*Match*
1. _____	pristine	A.	inexperienced
2. _____	phlegmatic	B.	anger
3. _____	profound	C.	central
4. _____	qualified	D.	cheerful
5. _____	placid	E.	shallow
6. _____	placate	F.	joyous
7. _____	pensive	G.	extraordinary
8. _____	peripheral	H.	contaminated
9. _____	petulant	I.	excited
10. _____	prosaic	J.	turbulent

DIRECTIONS: Match each word in the left column with the word in the right column that is most **similar** in meaning.

	Word		*Match*
11. _____	provocative	A.	nearness
12. _____	pungent	B.	tempting
13. _____	propinquity	C.	reverent
14. _____	pious	D.	flavorsome
15. _____	pragmatic	E.	practical

Answers — Drill 9

11. (B) 12. (D) 13. (A) 14. (C) 15. (E)

6. (B) 7. (F) 8. (C) 9. (D) 10. (G)

1. (H) 2. (I) 3. (E) 4. (A) 5. (J)

GROUP 10

rationalize – *v.* – to offer reasons for; account for

raucous – *adj.* – disagreeable to the sense of hearing; harsh

realm – *n.* – an area; sphere of activity

rebuff – *n.* – an abrupt, blunt refusal

recession – *n.* – withdrawal; depression

reciprocal – *adj.* – mutual; having the same relationship to each other

recluse – *n.* – solitary and shut off from society

recondite – *adj.* – beyond the grasp of ordinary understanding

redundant – *adj.* – repetitious; unnecessary

refute – *v.* – challenge; disprove

regal – *adj.* – royal; grand

reiterate – *v.* – repeat; to state again

relegate – *v.* – banish; put to a lower position

relevant – *adj.* – of concern; significant

relinquish – *v.* – to let go; abandon

renascence – *n.* – a new birth; revival

render – *v.* – deliver; provide; to give up a possession

replica – *n.* – copy; representation

reprehensible – *adj.* – wicked; disgraceful

reprobate – *adj.* – 1. vicious; unprincipled; 2. *v.* – to disapprove with detestation

repudiate – *v.* – reject; cancel

repugnant – *adj.* – inclined to disobey or oppose

rescind – *v.* – retract; discard

respite – *n.* – recess; rest period

reticent – *adj.* – silent; reserved; shy

retroaction – *n.* – an action elicited by a stimulus

reverie – *n.* – the condition of being unaware of one's surroundings; trance

rhetorical – *adj.* – having to do with verbal communication

ribald – *adj.* – characterized by coarse joking or mocking

rigor – *n.* – severity

rivet – *v.* – to fasten, fix, or hold firmly

rummage – *v.* – search thoroughly

saga – *n.* – a legend; story

sagacious – *adj.* – wise; cunning

salient – *adj.* – noticeable; prominent

salubrious – *adj.* – favorable to health

salvage – *v.* – rescue from loss

sanction – *n.* – 1. support; encouragement; 2. something which makes a rule binding

sanguine – *adj.* – 1. optimistic; cheerful; 2. red

sardonic – *adj.* – bitterly ironical

satiric – *adj.* – indulging in the use of ridicule or sarcasm to expose or attack vice, folly, etc.

saturate – *v.* – soak thoroughly; drench

saturnine – *adj.* – heavy; grave; gloomy

saunter – *v.* – walk at a leisurely pace; stroll

savor – *v.* – to receive pleasure from; enjoy

scrupulous – *adj.* – honorable; exact

seethe – *v.* – to be in a state of emotional turmoil; to become angry

serrated – *adj.* – having a sawtoothed edge

servile – *adj.* – slavish, groveling

shoddy – *adj.* – of inferior quality; cheap

DRILL 10

DIRECTIONS: Match each word in the left column with the word in the right column that is most **opposite** in meaning.

	Word		*Match*
1. _____	salient	A.	forward
2. _____	reticent	B.	promote
3. _____	raucous	C.	pleasant
4. _____	redundant	D.	minor
5. _____	relegate	E.	affirm
6. _____	repugnant	F.	unprincipled
7. _____	repudiate	G.	necessary
8. _____	rebuff	H.	pleasant
9. _____	scrupulous	I.	welcome
10. _____	sanguine	J.	pessimistic

DIRECTIONS: Match each word in the left column with the word in the right column that is most **similar** in meaning.

	Word		*Match*
11. _____	rescind	A.	deliver
12. _____	reprehensible	B.	blameworthy
13. _____	render	C.	retract
14. _____	sagacious	D.	drench
15. _____	saturate	E.	wise

Answers — Drill 10

1. (D)   2. (A)   3. (H)   4. (G)   5. (B)

6. (C)   7. (E)   8. (I)   9. (F)   10. (J)

11. (C)   12. (B)   13. (A)   14. (E)   15. (D)

GROUP 11

sinuous – *adj.* – winding; crooked

skulk – *v.* – to move secretly

sojourn – *n.* – temporary stay; visit

solicit – *v.* – ask; seek

soliloquy – *n.* – a talk one has with oneself (esp. on stage)

spendthrift – *n.* – one who spends money carelessly or wastefully

sporadic – *adj.* – rarely occurring or appearing; intermittent

spurious – *adj.* – false; counterfeit

squalid – *adj.* – foul; filthy

stagnant – *adj.* – motionless; uncirculating

stamina – *n.* – endurance

sterile – *adj.* – 1. incapable of producing others; 2. lacking in interest or vitality; 3. free from living microorganisms

stipend – *n.* – payment for work done

stupor – *n.* – a stunned or bewildered condition

suave – *adj.* – effortlessly gracious

subsidiary – *adj.* – subordinate

substantive – *adj.* – 1. existing independently; 2. having a real existence

subtlety – *n.* – 1. understatement; 2. propensity for understatement; 3. sophistication; 4. cunning

succinct – *adj.* – consisting of few words; concise

suffuse – *v.* – to overspread

sullen – *adj.* – 1. showing resentment; 2. gloomy; dismal

sunder – *v.* – break; split in two

superficial – *adj.* – on the surface; narrow–minded; lacking depth

superfluous – *adj.* – unnecessary; extra

surmise – *v.* – draw an inference; guess

surreptitious – *adj.* – done without proper authority

sycophant – *n* – a person who seeks favor by flattering people of wealth or influence

syllogism – *n.* – reasoning from the general to the particular synthesis – *n.* – 1. the putting together of two or more things; 2. a whole made up of parts put together

taciturn – *adj.* – reserved; quiet; secretive

tantalize – *v.* – to tempt; to torment

taut – *adj.* – 1. stretched tightly; 2. tense

temerity – *n.* – foolish boldness

temperament – *n.* – 1. a middle course reached by mutual concession; 2. frame of mind

tenacious – *adj.* – persistently holding to something

tepid – *adj.* – lacking warmth, interest, enthusiasm; lukewarm

terse – *adj.* – concise; abrupt

thwart – *v.* – prevent from accomplishing a purpose; frustrate

timbre – *n.* – the degree of resonance of a voiced sound

torpid – *adj.* – lacking alertness and activity; lethargic

toxic – *adj.* – poisonous

tractable – *adj.* – easily led or managed

transitory – *adj.* – of a passing nature; speedily vanishing

transpire – *v.* – to take place; come about

travesty – *n.* – a crude and ridiculous representation

trek – *v.* – to make a journey

trepidation – *n.* – apprehension; uneasiness

tribute – *n.* – expression of admiration

DRILL 11

> **DIRECTIONS:** Match each word in the left column with the word in the right column that is most **opposite** in meaning.

		Word		*Match*
1.	_____	scrutinize	A.	frivolity
2.	_____	skeptic	B.	enjoyable
3.	_____	solemnity	C.	prodigal
4.	_____	static	D.	chaos
5.	_____	tedious	E.	give
6.	_____	tentative	F.	skim
7.	_____	thrifty	G.	turbulent
8.	_____	tranquility	H.	active
9.	_____	solicit	I.	believer
10.	_____	stagnant	J.	confirmed

> **DIRECTIONS:** Match each word in the left column with the word in the right column that is most **similar** in meaning.

		Word		*Match*
11.	_____	symmetry	A.	understated
12.	_____	superfluous	B.	unnecessary
13.	_____	sycophant	C.	balance
14.	_____	subtle	D.	fear
15.	_____	trepidation	E.	flatterer

Answers — Drill 11

11. (C) 12. (B) 13. (E) 14. (A) 15. (D)

6. (J) 7. (C) 8. (D) 9. (E) 10. (G)

1. (F) 2. (I) 3. (A) 4. (H) 5. (B)

GROUP 12

trite – *adj.* – commonplace; overused

truculent – *adj.* – aggressive; eager to fight

tumid – *adj.* – swollen; inflated

tumult – *n.* – great commotion or agitation

turbulence – *n.* – condition of being physically agitated; disturbance

turpitude – *n.* – shameful wickedness

ubiquitous – *adj.* – ever present in all places; universal

ulterior – *adj.* – buried; concealed

uncanny – *adj.* – of a strange nature; weird

unequivocal – *adj.* – clear; definite

unique – *adj.* – without equal; incomparable

unruly – *adj.* – not submitting to discipline; disobedient

untoward – *adj.* – 1. hard to manage or deal with; 2. inconvenient

unwonted – *adj.* – not ordinary; unusual

urbane – *adj.* – cultured; suave

usury – *n.* – the act of lending money at illegal rates of interest

vacillation – *n.* – fluctuation

vacuous – *adj.* – containing nothing; empty

vantage – *n.* – position giving an advantage

vaunted – *v.* – boasted of

vehement – *adj.* – intense; excited; enthusiastic

veracious – *adj.* – conforming to fact; accurate

veracity – *n.* – 1. honesty; 2. accuracy of statement

verbose – *adj.* – wordy; talkative

versatile – *adj.* – having many uses; multifaceted

vertigo – *n.* – dizziness

vex – *v.* – to trouble the nerves; annoy

vilify – *v.* – slander

vindicate – *v.* – to free from charge; clear

virile – *adj.* – manly, masculine

virtuoso – *n*. – highly skilled artist

virulent – *adj*. – deadly; harmful; malicious

viscous – *adj*. – thick, syrupy, and sticky

visionary – *adj*. – 1. characterized by impractical ideas; 2. not real

vivacious – *adj*. – animated; gay

vogue – *n*. – modern fashion

volatile – *adj*. – changeable; undependable

voluble – *adj*. – fluent

vulnerable – *adj*. – open to attack; unprotected

waive – *v*. – to give up possession or right

wane – *v*. – grow gradually smaller

wanton – *adj*. – unruly; excessive

welter – *v*. – 1. to roll about or wallow; 2. to rise and fall

wheedle – *v*. – try to persuade; coax

whet – *v*. – sharpen

whimsical – *adj*.– fanciful; amusing

winsome – *adj*. – agreeable; charming; delightful

zealot– *n*. – believer, enthusiast; fan

zenith – *n*. – point directly overhead in the sky

zephyr – *n*. – a gentle wind; breeze

DRILL 12

	Word		Match
1.	uniform	A.	amateur
2.	virtuoso	B.	trivial
3.	vital	C.	visible
4.	wane	D.	placid
5.	unobtrusive	E.	unacceptable
6.	vigorous	F.	support
7.	volatile	G.	constancy
8.	vacillation	H.	lethargic
9.	undermine	I.	wax
10.	valid	J.	varied

	Word		Match
11.	wither	A.	intense
12.	whimsical	B.	deadly
13.	viable	C.	amusing
14.	vehement	D.	possible
15.	virulent	E.	shrivel

Answers — Drill 12

11. (E)   12. (C)   13. (D)   14. (A)   15. (B)

6. (H)   7. (D)   8. (G)   9. (F)   10. (E)

1. (J)   2. (A)   3. (B)   4. (I)   5. (C)

COMMONLY TESTED WORDS

abaft – *adv.* – on or toward the rear of a ship

abdicate – *v.* – to reject, denounce, or abandon

abjure – *v.* – to renounce upon oath

abnegation – *n.* – a denial

abscond – *v.* – to go away hastily or secretly; to hide

abstemious – *adj.* – 1. sparing in diet; 2. sparingly used

abysmal – *adj.* – bottomless; immeasurable

acerbity – *n.* – harshness or bitterness

acrimony – *n.* – sharpness

addle – *adj.* – barren; confused

adjure – *v.* – to entreat earnestly and solemnly

adulation – *n.* – praise in excess

adulterate – *v.* – to corrupt, debase, or make impure

agrarian – *adj.* – relating to land and the equal divisions of land

alchemy – *n.* – any imaginary power of transmitting one thing into another

allegory – *n.* – symbolic narration or description

anachronism – *n.* – representation of something existing at other than its proper
    time

annihilate – *v.* – to reduce to nothing

apocalyptic – *adj.* – pertaining to revelation or discovery

arrogate – *v.* – to claim or demand unduly

artifice – *n.* – skill; ingenuity; craft

askance – *adv.* – sideways; out of one corner of the eye

assay – *n.* – the determination of any quantity of a metal in an ore or alloy

attenuate – *v.* – 1. to make thin or slender; 2. to lessen or weaken

avarice – *n.* – inordinate desire of gaining and possessing wealth

batten – *v.* – to grow fat; to thrive

beholden – *adj.* – obliged; indebted

bellicose – *adj.* – warlike; disposed to quarrel or fight

besmirch – *v.* – to soil or discolor

bestial – *adj.* – having the qualities of a beast

betroth – *v.* – to promise or pledge in marriage

blighted – *adj.* – destroyed; frustrated

bode – *v.* – to foreshow something

boorish – *adj.* – rude; ill–mannered

brindled – *adj.* – streaked or spotted with a darker color

broach – *v.* – 1. to pierce; 2. to introduce into conversation

bucolic – *adj.* – pastoral

burlesque – *v.* – to imitate comically

cadaver – *n.* – a dead body

caliber – *n.* – 1. the diameter of a bullet or shell; 2. quality

callow – *adj.* – immature

calumny – *n.* – slander

canard – *n.* – a false statement or rumor

candid – *adj.* – open; frank; honest

captious – *adj.* – disposed to find fault

carnage – *n.* – slaughter

carte blanche – *n.* – unlimited power to decide

castigate – *v.* – to chastise

cataclysm – *n.* – 1. an overflowing of water; 2. an extraordinary change

catharsis – *n.* – purgation

cavil – *v.* – to find fault without good reason

celibate – *adj.* – unmarried, single; chaste

cessation – *n.* – a ceasing; a stop

chafe – *v.* – to rage; to fret

chaffing – *n.* – banter

chaste – *adj.* – virtuous; free from obscenity

choleric – *adj.* – easily irritated; angry

circumvent – *v.* – to go around

clandestine – *adj.* – secret; private; hidden

cogent – *adj.* – urgent; compelling; convincing

cohort – *n.* – a group; a band

collusion – *n.* – secret agreement for a fraudulent or illegal purpose

comport – *v.* – to agree; to accord

conclave – *n.* – any private meeting or close assembly

connivance – *n.* – passive cooperation

consort – *n.* – 1. a companion; 2. *v.* – to be in harmony or agreement

contravene – *v.* – to go against; to oppose

contusion – *n.* – a bruise; an injury where the skin is not broken

copious – *adj.* – abundant; in great quantities

covenant – *n.* – a binding and solemn agreement

coy – *adj.* – 1. modest; bashful; 2. pretending shyness to attract

crass – *adj.* – gross; thick; coarse

cursory – *adj.* – hasty; slight

dally – *v.* – to delay; to put off

dauntless – *adj.* – fearless; not discouraged

debonair – *adj.* – having an affable manner; courteous

decadence – *n.* – a decline in force or quality

deciduous – *adj.* – falling off at a particular season or stage of growth

decry – *v.* – to denounce or condemn openly

defunct – *adj.* – no longer living or existing

deliquesce – *v.* – to melt away

delusion – *n.* – a false statement or opinion

deposition – *n.* – 1. a removal from a position or power; 2. a testimony

depredation – *n.* – a plundering or laying waste

descant – *v.* – to talk at length

despoil – *v.* – to strip; to rob

despotism – *n.* – 1. tyranny; 2. absolute power or influence

desultory – *adj.* – without order or natural connection

dexterous – *adj.* – having or showing mental skill

diffidence – *n.* – 1. lack of self-confidence; 2. distrust

dilapidated – *n.* – falling to pieces or into disrepair

dilettante – *n.* – an admirer of the fine arts; a dabbler

dint – *n.* – a blow; a stroke

disarray – *n.* – 1. disorder; confusion; 2. incomplete or disorderly attire

divulge – *v.* – to become public; to become known

dormant – *adj.* – as if asleep

doting – *adj.* – excessively fond

doughty – *adj.* – brave; valiant

dregs – *n.* – waste or worthless manner

ecclesiastic – *adj.* – pertaining or relating to a church

edify – *v.* – 1. to build or establish; 2. to instruct and improve the mind

efface – *v.* – to erase; to remove from the mind

effrontery – *n.* – impudence; assurance

effusive – *adj.* – pouring out or forth; overflowing

egregious – *adj.* – eminent; remarkable

egress – *v.* – to depart; to go out

elegy – *n.* – a poem of lament and praise for the dead

elucidate – *v.* – to make clear or manifest; to explain

emanate – *v.* – to send forth; to emit

embellish – *v.* – to improve the appearance of

enamored – *adj.* – filled with love and desire

encroach – *v.* – to trespass or intrude

encumber – *v.* – to hold back; to hinder

endue – *v.* – to put on; to cover

enrapture – *v.* – to fill with pleasure

epilogue – *n.* – closing section of a play or novel providing further comment

epiphany – *n.* – an appearance of a supernatural being

epitaph – *n.* – an inscription on a monument, in honor or memory of a dead person

epitome – *n.* – a part that is typical of the whole

equinox – *n.* – precise time when the day and night everywhere is of equal length

equivocate – *v.* – to be purposely ambiguous

eschew – *v.* – to escape from; to avoid

estranged – *adj.* – kept at a distance; alienated

ethereal – *adj.* – 1. very light; airy; 2. heavenly; not earthly

euphemism – *n.* – the use of a word or phrase in place of one that is distasteful

euphoria – *n.* – a feeling of well-being

exhume – *v.* – to unearth; to reveal

expunge – *v.* – to blot out; to delete

exude – *v.* – to flow slowly or ooze in drops

faction – *n.* – a number of people in an organization having a common end view

fallible – *adj.* – liable to be mistaken or erroneous

fathom – *v.* – to reach or penetrate with the mind

fatuous – *adj.* – silly; inane; unreal

fealty – *n.* – fidelity; loyalty

feign – *v.* – to invent or imagine

ferment – *v.* – to excite or agitate

fervid – *adj.* – very hot; burning

fester – *v.* – to become more and more virulent and fixed

fetish – *n.* – anything to which one gives excessive devotion or blind adoration

fidelity – *n.* – faithfulness; honesty

fissure – *n.* – a dividing or breaking into parts

flaccid – *adj.* – 1. hanging in loose folds or wrinkles; 2. lacking force; weak

flamboyant – *adj.* – ornate; too showy

foible – *n.* – a slight frailty in character

foist – *v.* – to put in slyly or stealthily

foray – *v.* – to raid for spoils, plunder

forensic – *adj.* – pertaining to legal or public argument

fortitude – *n.* – firm courage; strength

fractious – *adj.* – rebellious; apt to quarrel

fraught – *adj.* – loaded; charged

froward – *adj.* – not willing to yield or comply with what is reasonable

fulminate – *v.* – to explode with sudden violence

galvanize – *v.* – to stimulate as if by electric shock; startle; excite

gamut – *n.* – 1. a complete range; 2. any complete musical scale

garish – *adj.* – gaudy; showy

gauche – *adj.* – awkward; lacking grace

gauntlet – *n.* – a long glove with a flaring cuff covering the lower part of the arm

germane – *adj.* – closely related; pertinent

glib – *adj.* – smooth and slippery; speaking or spoken in a smooth manner

gnarled – *adj.* – full of knots

gourmand – *n.* – a greedy or ravenous eater; glutton

gregarious – *adj.* – fond of the company of others

grisly – *adj.* – frightful; horrible

guffaw – *n.* – a loud, coarse burst of laughter

guise – *n.* – 1. customary behavior; 2. manner of dress; 3. false appearance

halcyon – *adj.* – calm; quiet; peaceful

hapless – *adj.* – unlucky; unfortunate

harangue – *v.* – to speak in an impassioned and forcible manner

heretic – *n.* – one who holds opinion contrary to that which is generally accepted

hiatus – *n.* – an opening or gap; slight pause

hoary – *adj.* – very aged; ancient

homily – *n.* – discourse or sermon read to an audience

hybrid – *n.* – anything of mixed origin

idiosyncrasy – *n.* – any personal peculiarity, mannerism, etc.

igneous – *adj.* – having the nature of fire

ignominious – *adj.* – 1. contemptible; 2. degrading

immaculate – *adj.* – 1. perfectly clean; perfectly correct; 2. pure

imminent – *adj.* – appearing as if about to happen

impasse – *n.* – a situation that has no solution or escape

impenitent – *adj.* – without regret, shame, or remorse

impiety – *n.* – 1. irreverence toward God; 2. lack of respect

impolitic – *adj.* – unwise; imprudent

imprecate – *v.* – to pray for evil; to invoke a curse

imputation – *n.* – attribution

incarcerate – *v.* – to imprison or confine

incommodious – *adj.* – uncomfortable; troublesome

incorporeal – *adj.* – not consisting of matter

incorrigible – *adj.* – not capable of correction or improvement

incubate – *v.* – to sit on and hatch (eggs)

inculcate – *v.* – to impress upon the mind by frequent repetition or urging

indemnify – *v.* – to protect against or keep free from loss

indigenous – *adj.* – innate; inherent; inborn

indomitable – *adj.* – not easily discouraged or defeated

indubitably – *adv.* – unquestionably; surely

inimical – *adj.* – unfriendly; adverse

iniquitous – *adj.* – unjust; wicked

inordinate – *adj.* – not regulated; excessive

intrepid – *adj.* – fearless; brave

inured – *adj.* – accustomed

irascible – *adj.* – easily provoked or inflamed to anger

irreparable – *adj.* – that which cannot be repaired or regained

jettison – *n.* – a throwing overboard of goods to lighten a vehicle in an emergency

jocund – *adj.* – merry; gay; cheerful

lacerate – *v.* – 1. to tear or mangle; 2. to wound or hurt

lambent – *adj.* – giving off a soft radiance

lassitude – *n.* – a state or feeling of being tired or weak

lewd – *adj.* – lustful; wicked

libertine – *n.* – one who indulges his desires without restraint

licentious – *adj.* – disregarding accepted rules and standards

lithe – *adj.* – easily bent; pliable

loquacious – *adj.* – talkative

lucent – *adj.* – shining; translucent

lugubrious – *adj.* – mournful; very sad

lurid – *adj.* – ghastly pale; gloomy

magnate – *n.* – a very influential person in any field of activity

malefactor – *n.* – one who commits a crime

malign – *v.* – to defame; speak evil of

marauder – *n.* – a rover in search of booty or plunder

maudlin – *adj.* – foolishly and tearfully sentimental

mendacious – *adj.* – addicted to deception

mercurial – *adj.* – quick, volatile; changeable

meretricious – *adj.* – alluring by false, showy charms; fleshy

mettle – *n.* – high quality of character

mien – *n.* – manner; external appearance

misanthropy – *n.* – hatred of mankind

mite – *n.* – 1. very small sum of money; 2. very small creature

modulate – *v.* – 1. to regulate or adjust; 2. to vary the pitch of the voice

mollify – *v.* – to soften; to make less intense

moot – *adj.* – subject to or open for discussion or debate

mordant – *adj.* – biting, cutting, or caustic

mutinous – *adj.* – inclined to revolt

nefarious – *adj.* – very wicked; abominable

nemesis – *n.* – just punishment; retribution

nexus – *n.* – a connection

nostrum – *n.* – a quack medicine

noxious – *adj.* – harmful to health or morals

nugatory – *adj.* – trifling; futile; insignificant

obeisance – *n.* – a gesture of respect or reverence

obfuscate – *v.* – to darken; to confuse

objurgate – *v.* – to chide vehemently

obloquy – *n.* – verbal abuse of a person or thing

obtrude – *v.* – to thrust forward; to eject

odious – *adj.* – hateful; disgusting

oligarchy – *n.* – form of government in which the supreme power is placed in the hands of a small exclusive group

opalescent – *adj.* – iridescent

opprobrious – *adj.* – reproachful or contemptuous

palatial – *adj.* – large and ornate, like a palace

palindrome – *n.* – a word, verse or sentence that is the same when read backward or forward

paltry – *adj.* – worthless; trifling

pandemonium – *n.* – a place of wild disorder, noise, or confusion

parapet – *n.* – a wall or railing to protect people from falling

pariah – *n.* – an outcast; someone despised by others

parity – *n.* – state of being the same in power, value, or rank

parley – *v.* – to speak with another; to discourse

parry – *v.* – to ward off; to avoid

parsimonious – *adj.* – miserly; stingy

paucity – *n.* – scarcity; small number

peculate – *v.* – to embezzle

pecuniary – *adj.* – relating to money

pellucid – *adj.* – transparent

penury – *n.* – lack of money or property

perdition – *n.* – complete and irreparable loss

peremptory – *adj.* – 1. barring future action; 2. that cannot be denied, changed, etc.

perfidious – *adj.* – violating good faith or vows

perquisite – *n.* – a fee, profit, etc. in addition to the stated income of one's employment

peruse – *v.* – to read carefully and thoroughly

pied – *adj.* – spotted

pinioned – *adj.* – 1. having wings; 2. having wings or arms bound or confined

platonic – *adj.* – 1. idealistic or impractical; 2. not amorous or sensual

plenary – *adj.* – full; entire; complete

plethora – *n.* – the state of being too full; excess

pommel – *n.* – the rounded, upward-projecting front of a saddle

portend – *v.* – to foreshadow

potable – *adj.* – drinkable

prate – *v.* – to talk much and foolishly

precept – *n.* – a rule or direction of moral conduct

precocious – *adj.* – developed or matured earlier than usual

prefatory – *adj.* – introductory

preponderate – *adj.* – to outweigh

prerogative – *n.* – a prior or exclusive right or privilege

prevaricate – *v.* – to evade the truth

prognosis – *n.* – a forecast, especially in medicine

prolific – *adj.* – fruitful

propagate – *v.* – to reproduce or multiply

propitiate – *v.* – to win the good will of

protocol – *n.* – an original draft or record of a document

provident – *adj.* – prudent; economical

proviso – *n.* – conditional stipulation to an agreement

pseudonym – *n.* – a borrowed or fictitious name

puerile – *adj.* – childish; immature

purloin – *v.* – to steal

purview – *n.* – the range of control, activity, or understanding

quaff – *v.* – to drink or swallow in large quantities

quagmire – *n.* – a difficult position, as if on shaky ground

qualm – *n.* – sudden feeling of uneasiness or doubt

quintessence – *n.* – 1. the ultimate substance; 2. the pure essence of anything

quixotic – *adj.* – extravagantly chivalrous

quizzical – *adj.* – odd; comical

ramification – *n.* – the arrangement of branches; consequence

rampant – *adj.* – violent and uncontrollable action

rancor – *n.* – a continuing and bitter hate or ill will

raze – *v.* – to scrape or shave off

recalcitrant – *adj.* – refusing to obey authority

recidivism – *n.* – habitual or chronic relapse

recumbent – *adj.* – leaning or reclining

recusant – *adj.* – disobedient of authority

redolent – *adj.* – sweet–smelling; fragrant

reminiscence – *n.* – a remembering

remonstrate – *v.* – to exhibit strong reasons against an act

rendition – *n.* – a performance or interpretation

repertoire – *n.* – stock of plays which can be readily performed by a company

reprehend – *v.* – to reprimand; to find fault with

reprieve – *v.* – to give temporary relief

resonant – *adj.* – resounding; re-echoing

resplendent – *adj.* – dazzling; splendid

resurgent – *adj.* – rising or tending to rise again

revile – *v.* – to be abusive in speech

risible – *adj.* – able or inclined to laugh

roseate – *adj.* – bright, cheerful, or optimistic

rote – *n.* – a fixed, mechanical way of doing something

rotundity – *n.* – condition of being rounded out or plump

rudimentary – *adj.* – elementary

ruminate – *v.* – to muse on

salutatory – *adj.* – of or containing greetings

sapid – *adj.* – having a pleasant taste

sardonic – *adj.* – bitterly ironical

savant – *n.* – a learned person

schism – *n.* – a division in an organized group

scourge – *v.* – to whip severely

scurrilous – *adj.* – using low and indecent language

sedentary – *adj.* – 1. characterized by sitting; 2. remaining in one locality

serendipity – *n.* – an apparent aptitude for making fortunate discoveries accidentally

shoal – *n.* – a great quantity

sloth – *n.* – disinclination to action or labor

slovenly – *adv.* – careless in habits, behavior, etc.; untidy

sordid – *adj.* – filthy; foul

specious – *adj.* – appearing just and fair without really being so

spelunker – *n.* – one who explores caves

splenetic – *adj.* – bad–tempered; irritable

staid – *adj.* – sober; sedate

stanch – *v.* – to stop or check the flow of blood

stigmatize – *v.* – to characterize or make as disgraceful

stoic – *adj.* – a person who is not easily excited

stolid – *adj.* – unexcitable; dull

striated – *adj.* – marked with fine parallel lines

strident – *adj.* – creaking; harsh; grating

stymie – *n.* – 1. to hinder or obstruct; 2. in golf, an opponent's ball lying in direct line between the player's ball and the hole

succor – *n.* – aid; assistance

sumptuous – *adj.* – involving great expense

sundry – *adj.* – 1. various; miscellaneous; 2. separate; distinct

supplant – *v.* – to take the place of

suppliant – *adj.* – asking earnestly and submissively

surfeit – *v.* – to feed or supply in excess

swathe – *v.* – to wrap around something; envelop

tawdry – *n.* – a gaudy ornament

teem – *v.* – 1. to be stocked to overflowing; 2. to pour out; to empty

tenet – *n.* – any principle, doctrine, etc. which a person, school, etc. believes or maintains

termagant – *n.* – a boisterous, scolding woman; a shrew

terrestrial – *adj.* – pertaining to the earth

tether – *n.* – the range or limit of one's abilities

thrall – *n.* – a slave

throe – *v.* – to put in agony

timorous – *adj.* – fearful

tortuous – *adj.* – pertaining to or involving excruciating pain

traduce – *v.* – 1. to exhibit; 2. to slander

transmute – *v.* – to transform

travail – *v.* – to harass; to torment

trenchant – *adj.* – 1. keen; penetrating; 2. clear-cut; distinct

tribunal – *n.* – the seat of judge

troth – *n.* – belief; faith; fidelity

turbid – *adj.* – 1. thick; dense; 2. confused; perplexed

tutelage – *n.* – the condition of being under a guardian or a tutor

umbrage – *n.* – shade; shadow

uncouth – *adj.* – uncultured; crude

unfeigned – *adj.* – genuine; real; sincere

untrowable – *adj.* – incredible

uxoricide – *n.* – the murder of a wife by her husband

vagary – *n.* – 1. an odd action or idea; 2. a wandering

vantage – *n.* – advantage; gain; profit

vaunt – *v.* – to brag or boast

venal – *adj.* – that can be readily bribed or corrupted

veneer – *n.* – 1. a thin surface layer; 2. any attractive but superficial appearance

verbiage – *n.* – wordiness

verity – *n.* – truthfulness

vertigo – *n.* – a sensation of dizziness

vestige – *n.* – a trace of something that no longer exists

vicarious – *adj.* – taking the place of another person or thing

vicissitude – *n.* – changes or variation occurring irregularly in the course of something

vigilance – *n.* – watchfulness

visage – *n.* – appearance

vitriolic – *adj.* – extremely biting or caustic

vociferous – *adj.* – making a loud outcry

volition – *n.* – the act of willing

voracious – *adj.* – greedy in eating

vouchsafe – *v.* – 1. to be gracious enough to grant; 2. to guarantee as safe

wan – *adj.* – pale; pallid

wily – *adj.* – cunning; sly

wizened – *adj.* – withered; shrunken

wreak – *v.* – to give vent or free play

wrest – *v.* – 1. to turn or twist; 2. usurp; 3. to distort or change the true meaning of

KNOWING YOUR WORD PARTS

Memorization and practice are not the only ways to learn the meanings of new words. While taking any standardized test, you are bound to come across some words you may not know. Although we have given you a list of frequently tested words, there will probably still be a few that do not seem familiar. Therefore, if you learn common prefixes, roots, and suffixes, you will be that much more prepared.

Learn the meanings of prefixes, roots, and suffixes in the same way that you learned the vocabulary words and their meanings. Be sure to use index cards for the items you don't know or find unusual. Look over the examples given and then try to think of your own. Testing yourself in this way will allow you to see if you really do know the meaning of each item. Knowledge of prefixes, roots, and suffixes is essential to a strong vocabulary.

Prefix

Prefix	Meaning	Example
ab –, a –, abs –	away, from	absent – away, not present
		abstain – keep from doing, refrain
ad –	to, toward	adjacent – next to
		address – to direct towards
ante –	before	antecedent – going before in time
		anterior – occurring before
anti –	against	antidote – remedy to act against an evil
		antibiotic – substance that fights against bacteria
be –	over, thoroughly	bemoan – to mourn over
		belabor – to exert much labor upon
bi –	two	bisect – to divide
		biennial – happening every two years
cata –, cat –, cath –	down	catacombs – underground passage-ways
		catalogue – descriptive list
circum –	around	circumscribe – to draw a circle around
		circumspect – watchful on all sides
com –	with	combine – join together
		communication – to have dealing with
contra –	against	contrary – opposed
		contrast – to stand in opposition
de –	down, from	decline – to bend downward
		decontrol – to release from government control

Prefix	Meaning	Example
di –	two	dichotomy – cutting in two diarchy – system of government with two authorities
dis –, di	apart, away	discern – to distinguish as separate dismiss – send away
epi –, ep –, eph –	upon, among	epidemic – happening among many people epicycle – circle whose center moves round in the circumference of a greater circle
ex –, e –	from, out	exceed – go beyond the limit emit – to send forth
extra –	outside, beyond	extraordinary – beyond or out of the common method extrasensory – beyond the senses
hyper –	beyond, over	hyperactive – over the normal activity level hypercritic – one who is critical beyond measure
hypo –	beneath, lower	hypodermic – parts beneath the skin hypocrisy – to be under a pretense of goodness
in –, il –, im –, ir –	not	inactive – not active irreversible – not reversible
in –, il –, im –, ir –	in, on, into	instill – to put in slowly impose – to lay on
inter –	among, between	intercom – to exchange conversations between people interlude – performance given between parts in a play

Prefix	Meaning	Example
intra –	within	intravenous – within a vein intramural – within a single college or its students
meta –	beyond, over, along with	metamorphosis – change over in form or nature metatarsus – part of foot beyond the flat of the foot
mis –	badly, wrongly	misconstrue – to interpret wrongly misappropriate – to use wrongly
mono –	one	monogamy – to be married to one person at a time monotone – a single, unvaried tone
multi –	many	multiple – of many parts multitude – a great number
non –	no, not	nonsense – lack of sense nonentity – not existing
ob –	against	obscene – offensive to modesty obstruct – to hinder the passage of
para –, *par* –	beside	parallel – continuously at equal distance apart parenthesis – sentence inserted within a passage
per –	through	persevere – to maintain an effort permeate – to pass through
poly –	many	polygon – a plane figure with many sides or angles polytheism – belief in existence of many gods

Prefix	Meaning	Example
post –	after	posterior – coming after postpone – to put off till a future time
pre –	before	premature – ready before the proper time premonition – a previous warning
pro –	in favor of, forward	prolific – bringing forth offspring project – throw or cast forward
re –	back, against	reimburse – pay back retract – to draw back
semi –	half	semicircle – half a circle semiannual – half-yearly
sub –	under	subdue – to bring under one's power submarine – travel under the surface of the sea
super –	above	supersonic – above the speed of sound superior – higher in place or position
tele –, *tel* –	across	telecast – transmit across a distance telepathy – communication between mind and mind at a distance
trans –	across	transpose – to change the position of two things transmit – to send from one person to another
ultra –	beyond	ultraviolet – beyond the limit of visibility ultramarine – beyond the sea
un –	not	undeclared – not declared unbelievable – not believable

Prefix	Meaning	Example
uni –	one	unity – state of oneness
		unison – sounding together
with –	away, against	withhold – to hold back
		withdraw – to take away

Root

Root	Meaning	Example
act, ag	do, act, drive	activate – to make active
		agile – having quick motion
alt	high	altitude – height
		alto – highest male singing voice
alter, altr	other, change	alternative – choice among two things
		altruism – living for the good of others
am, ami	love, friend	amiable – worthy of affection
		amity – friendship
anim	mind, spirit	animated – spirited
		animosity – violent hatred
annu, enni	year	annual – every year
		centennial – every hundred years
aqua	water	aquarium – tank for water animals and plants
		aquamarine – semiprecious stone of sea-green color
arch	first, ruler	archenemy – chief enemy
		archetype – original pattern from which things are copied

Root	Meaning	Example
aud, audit	hear	audible – capable of being heard audience – assembly of hearers
auto	self	automatic – self-acting autobiography – story about a person who also wrote it
bell	war	belligerent – a party taking part in a war bellicose – warlike
ben, bene	good	benign – kindly disposition beneficial – advantageous
bio	life	biotic – relating to life biology – the science of life
brev	short	abbreviate – make shorter brevity – shortness
cad, cas	fall	cadence – fall in voice casualty – loss caused by death
capit, cap	head	captain – the head or chief decapitate – to cut off the head
cede, ceed, cess	to go, to yield	recede – to move or fall back proceed – to move onward
cent	hundred	century – hundred years centipede – insect with a hundred legs
chron	time	chronology – science dealing with historical dates chronicle – register of events in order of time
cide, cis	to kill, to cut	homicide – one who kills incision – a cut

Root	Meaning	Example
clam, claim	to shout	acclaim – receive with applause proclamation – announce publicly
cogn	to know	recognize – to know again cognition – awareness
corp	body	incorporate – combine into one body corpse – dead body
cred	to trust, to believe	incredible – unbelievable credulous – too prone to believe
cur, curr, curs	to run	current – flowing body of air or water excursion – short trip
dem	people	democracy – government formed for the people epidemic – affecting all people
dic, dict	to say	dictate – to read aloud for another to transcribe verdict – decision of a jury
doc, doct	to teach	docile – easily instructed indoctrinate – to instruct
domin	to rule	dominate – to rule dominion – territory of rule
duc, duct	to lead	conduct – act of guiding induce – to overcome by persuasion
eu	well, good	eulogy – speech or writing in praise euphony – pleasantness or smoothness of sound
fac, fact, fect, fic	to do, to make	factory – location of production fiction – something invented or imagined

Root	Meaning	Example
fer	to bear, to carry	transfer – to move from one place to another
		refer – to direct to
fin	end, limit	infinity – unlimited
		finite – limited in quantity
flect, flex	to bend	flexible – easily bent
		reflect – to throw back
fort	luck	fortunate – lucky
		fortuitous – happening by chance
fort	strong	fortify – strengthen
		fortress – stronghold
frag, fract	break	fragile – easily broken
		fracture – break
fug	flee	fugitive – fleeing
		refugee – one who flees to a place of safety
gen	class, race	engender – to breed
		generic – of a general nature in regard to all members
grad, gress	to go, to step	regress – to go back
		graduate – to divide into regular steps
graph	writing	telegram – message sent by telegraph
		autograph – person's own handwriting or signature
ject	to throw	projectile – capable of being thrown
		reject – to throw away
leg	law	legitimate – lawful
		legal – defined by law

Root	Meaning	Example
leg, lig, lect	to choose, gather, read	illegible – incapable of being read election – the act of choosing
liber	free	liberal – favoring freedom of ideals liberty – freedom from restraint
log	study, speech	archaeology – study of human antiquities prologue – address spoken before a performance
luc, lum	light	translucent – slightly transparent illuminate – to light up
magn	large, great	magnify – to make larger magnificent – great
mal, male	bad, wrong	malfunction – to operate incorrectly malevolent – evil
mar	sea	marine – pertaining to the sea submarine – below the surface of the sea
mater, matr	mother	maternal – motherly matriarch – government exercised by a mother
mit, miss	to send	transmit – to send from one person or place to another mission – the act of sending
morph	shape	metamorphosis – a changing in shape anthropomorphic – having a human shape
mut	change	mutable – subject to change mutate – to change a vowel

Root	Meaning	Example
nat	born	innate – inborn native – a person born in a place
neg	deny	negative – expressing denial renege – to deny
nom	name	nominate – to put forward a name anonymous – no name given
nov	new	novel – new renovate – to make as good as new
omni	all	omnipotent – all powerful omnipresent – all present
oper	to work	operate – to work on something cooperate – to work with others
pass, path	to feel	pathetic – affecting the tender emotions passionate – moved by strong emotion
pater, patr	father	paternal – fatherly patriarch – government exercised by a father
ped, pod	foot	pedestrian – one who travels on foot podiatrist – foot doctor
pel, puls	to drive, to push	impel – to drive forward compulsion – irresistible force
phil	love	philharmonic – loving harmony or music philanthropist – one who loves and seeks to do good for others

Root	Meaning	Example
port	carry	export – to carry out of the country portable – able to be carried
psych	mind	psychology – study of the mind psychiatrist – specialist in mental disorders
quer, ques, quir, quis	to ask	inquiry – to ask about question – that which is asked
rid, ris	to laugh	ridiculous – laughable derision – to mock
rupt	to break	interrupt – to break in upon erupt – to break through
sci	to know	science – systematic knowledge of physical or natural phenomena conscious – having inward knowledge
scrib, script	to write	transcribe – to write over again script – text of words
sent, sens	to feel, to think	sentimental – feel great emotion sensitive – easily affected by changes
sequ, secut	to follow	sequence – connected series consecutive – following one another in unbroken order
solv, solu, solut	to loosen	dissolve – to break up absolute – without restraint
spect	to look at	spectator – one who watches inspect – to look at closely
spir	to breathe	inspire – to breathe in respiration – process of breathing

Root	Meaning	Example
string, strict	to bind	stringent – binding strongly restrict – to restrain within bounds
stru, struct	to build	misconstrue – to interpret wrongly construct – to build
tang, ting, tack, tig	to touch	tangent – touching, but not intersect- ing contact – touching
ten, tent, tain	to hold	tenure – holding of office contain – to hold
term	to end	terminate – to end terminal – having an end
terr	earth	terrain – tract of land terrestrial – existing on earth
therm	heat	thermal – pertaining to heat thermometer – instrument for measur- ing temperature
tort, tors	to twist	contortionist – one who twists violently torsion – act of turning or twisting
tract	to pull, to draw	attract – draw toward distract – to draw away
vac	empty	vacant – empty evacuate – to empty out
ven, vent	to come	prevent – to stop from coming intervene – to come between
ver	true	verify – to prove to be true veracious – truthful

Root	Meaning	Example
verb	word	verbose – use of excess words verbatim – word for word
vid, vis	to see	video – picture phase of television vision – act of seeing external objects
vinc, vict, vang	to conquer	invincible – unconquerable victory – defeat of enemy
viv, vit	life	vital – necessary to life vivacious – lively
voc	to call	provocative – serving to excite or stimulate to action vocal – uttered by voice
vol	to wish, to will	involuntary – outside the control of will volition – the act of willing or choosing

Suffix

Suffix	Meaning	Example
– *able*, – *ble*	capable of	believable – capable of being believed legible – capable of being read
– *acious*, – *icious*, – *ous*	full of	vivacious – full of life wondrous – full of wonder
– *ant*, – *ent*	full of	eloquent – full of eloquence expectant – full of expectation
– *ary*	connected with	honorary – for the sake of honor disciplinary – enforcing instruction

Suffix	Meaning	Example
– *ate*	to make	ventilate – to make public consecrate – to dedicate
– *fy*	to make	magnify – to make larger testify – to make witness
– *ile*	pertaining to, capable of	docile – capable of being managed easily civil – pertaining to a city or state
– *ism*	belief, ideal	conservationism – ideal of keeping safe pessimism – belief that there is more evil than good in the world.
– *ist*	doer	artist – one who creates art pianist – one who plays the piano
– *ose*	full of	verbose – full of words grandiose – striking, imposing
– *osis*	condition	neurosis – nervous condition psychosis – psychological condition
– *tude*	state	magnitude – state of greatness multitude – state of quantity

VERBAL ABILITY REVIEW

Study this section for tests:

GMAT, GRE, SAT I, PSAT, and ACT

Verbal Strategies

What do you do if you don't know the meaning of a word? How do you even begin to answer an analogy question? If you're not sure how to answer these questions, you're not alone. Many students feel uneasy with the verbal section of their standardized tests. This is mainly because students tend to think these sections are much more difficult than they really are.

To score well on the verbal section of your standardized test, you should not only know a large vocabulary, but also how to use that vocabulary in different contexts. That is why it is so important to study the verbal review. Specific strategies are presented to help you answer each type of question. These are solid hints as to the best way to answer a verbal question. Take advantage of the tips provided. The more familiar you are with these clues, the more successful and comfortable you will be in tackling the verbal part of your test.

I.   SYNONYM STRATEGIES

Synonyms are words which are the same or similar in definition to each other. There are no actual synonym questions on the standardized tests, however, you will be able to answer antonym, sentence completion, and analogy questions with confidence if you practice exercises in synonyms.

DIRECTIONS: Each of the following questions provides a given word in capitalized letters followed by five word choices. Choose the best word which is most similar in meaning to the given word.

Read the word carefully.

RESIGNATION

(A)   restriction   (B) submission   (C) interpretation

(D)   leaving   (E) remove

If you know the meaning of the word, this is your plan of attack:

➤ STRATEGY 1

Define the word in your own words.

RESIGNATION means to have given up.

➤ STRATEGY 2

Think of one word that might be similar to your definition.

A similar word would be surrender.

➤ STRATEGY 3

Find the answer choice that is closest in meaning to the word you came up with.

The only choice that means about the same as *surrender* is submission and is therefore the correct answer.

If you are familiar with a word, but are uncertain of its meaning, this is your plan of attack:

NEFARIOUS

(A) evil   (B) disgusting   (C) unloving

(D) cruel   (E) lying

➤ STRATEGY 1

Read over all the answer choices.

➤ STRATEGY 2

Define each of the answer choices in your own words.

(A) EVIL means *bad* or *wicked*.

(B) DISGUSTING means *offensive* or *sickening*.

(C) UNLOVING means *disliking* or *detesting*.

(D) CRUEL means *merciless* or *ruthless*.

(E) LYING means *falsifying* or *fibbing*.

➤ STRATEGY 3

Decide which of the similar words that you came up with best matches the meaning of the original word.

Assuming that you are slightly familiar with the capitalized word, by defining and finding a synonym for each answer choice, you may recognize the meaning of the original word. In this case, the correct choice would be (A) EVIL.

If you do not know the word at all, this is your plan of attack:

Use the clues outlined below to help you eliminate incorrect choices. Remember that hard questions (those that fall at the end of a set of questions) have hard answers and easy questions (those that fall in the very beginning of a set of questions) have easy answers.

IMPETUOUS

(A) thoughtful   (B) creative   (C) impish

(D) obnoxious   (E) impulsive

➤ STRATEGY 1

It is helpful to use knowledge of root words, prefixes, or suffixes if you are not sure of the meaning of a given word.

The prefix in IMPETUOUS is IMP which happens, in the case of the choices, to be the prefix of (E) *impulsive,* which is the correct answer.

II. ANTONYM STRATEGIES

Learn and understand the Directions so you don't waste valuable time reading them on the day of the exam.

DIRECTIONS: Each question below consists of a word in capital letters, followed by five lettered words or phrases. Choose the word or phrase that is most nearly **opposite** in meaning to the word in capital letters. Since some of the questions require you to distinguish fine shades of meaning, consider all the choices before deciding which is best.

Read the word carefully.

> TEMPORARY
>
> (A)   fortunate   (B)   permanent   (C)   flimsy
>
> (D)   gentle   (E)   repetitious

If you know the meaning of the word, this is your plan of attack:

➤ STRATEGY 1

Define the word using your own words.

TEMPORARY means only existing for a certain period of time.

➤ STRATEGY 2

Think of a word that means the opposite of your definition.

The opposite would be *lasting* or *endless.*

➤ STRATEGY 3

Find the answer choice that best matches the opposite that you came up with.

The only choice that means about the same as *lasting* or *endless* is *permanent* and is therefore the correct answer.

If you are familiar with the word, but are uncertain of its meaning, this is your plan of attack:

> REPUGNANT:
>
> (A)   sensible   (B)   delicate   (C)   clumsy
>
> (D)   attractive   (E)   athletic

➤ STRATEGY 1

Read over all the answer choices.

➤ STRATEGY 2

Define each of the answer choices in your own words.

(A) SENSIBLE means *logical* or *smart.*

(B) DELICATE means *easily broken* or *hurt.*

(C) CLUMSY means *awkward.*

(D) ATTRACTIVE means *appealing.*

(E) ATHLETIC means *active* or *sports-oriented.*

➤ STRATEGY 3

For each of the answer choices, think of a word that means the opposite of your definition.

(A) The opposite of logical is *illogical* or *irrational.*

(B) The opposite of easily broken is *sturdy* or *strong.*

(C) The opposite of awkward is *graceful.*

(D) The opposite of appealing is *repulsive.*

(E) The opposite of active is *sluggish.*

➤ STRATEGY 4

Decide which of the opposites that you came up with best matches the meaning of the original word.

Assuming you are slightly familiar with the capitalized word, by defining and finding the opposite of each answer choice, you may recognize the definition of the capitalized word. In this case, the correct choice would be (D) *ATTRAC-TIVE.*

If you do not know the word at all, this is your plan of attack:

Use the clues outlined below to help you eliminate incorrect choices. Remember that hard questions (those that fall at the end of a set of questions) have hard answers and easy questions (those that fall in the very beginning of a set of questions) have easy answers.

➤ ADDITIONAL STRATEGIES

➤ **Study your vocabulary. The key to solving antonym questions is to be able to define all the words involved.**

➤ **If you do not know a word, use its root, prefixes, and suffixes to determine its meaning.**

➤ **If you know whether a word's connotation is negative or positive, you can eliminate choices with similar connotations.**

HOSPITABLE

(A) private   (B) tasteful   (C) qualified

(D) unfriendly   (E) pathetic

HOSPITABLE has positive connotations. Therefore, its opposite must have negative connotations. Both TASTEFUL and QUALIFIED can be eliminated since they have positive connotations. The correct answer is (D) UNFRIENDLY.

➤ **Beware of words that seem simple, but have more than one meaning.**

The word GNAW is most commonly defined as *to eat away at* or *munch*. However, there is another meaning of GNAW, *to trouble* or *torment*, which would change the whole question.

➤ **Watch out for words that act as reminders of the capitalized word.**

SYMPATHETIC

(A) organized   (B) unfeeling   (C) frozen

(D) emphathetic   (E) symmetrical

In the above example, both (D) EMPATHETIC and (E) SYMMETRICAL are reminders of the capitalized word. In this case, neither are correct. Be aware of choices like these when choosing your answer.

➤ **Pay extra attention to answer choices that seem strange and out of place.**

GREGARIOUS

(A) compulsory   (B) aggressive   (C) despondent

(D) reclusive   (E) cold

The word GREGARIOUS could be considered a medium-hard vocabulary word. Among the answer choices, the word COLD seems too easy to be the correct answer to this question. Watch out for words like COLD that do not seem to belong among the other choices.

> ➤ **If you are unclear about the part of speech of the capitalized word, look at the first answer choice to determine the part of speech.**

> ➤ **If you cannot determine the correct answer after eliminating all answer choices possible, make an educated guess.**

III. SENTENCE COMPLETION STRATEGIES

Learn and understand the Directions so you don't waste valuable time reading them on the day of the exam.

DIRECTIONS: Each sentence below has one or two blanks, each blank indicating that something has been omitted. Beneath the sentence are five lettered words or sets of words. Choose the word or set of words that **best** fits the meaning of the sentence as a whole.

Read the sentence carefully.

Although the babysitter was actually quite _____ after the mysterious phone call, she portrayed complete _____ in front of the children.

(A) relaxed ... fear   (D) distressed ... confidence

(B) indifferent ... ignorance   (E) intrigued ... immaturity

(C) confused ... apathy

Look for clue words in the sentence. These are words that provide important tips as to the meaning and general flow of the sentence. Before looking at the answer choices, use the clue words to predict what the missing words may be.

Own words: disturbed ... confidence

If you are able to determine what words are left out of the sentence, this is your plan of attack:

➤ **STRATEGY 1**

Go through each answer choice to see if the words you have come up with appear among the answer choices.

➤ STRATEGY 2

If your words do not appear as choices, look for their synonyms among the answer choices.

The second word in answer choice (D) is the same as the second word that we came up with. Disturbed and distressed are synonyms. Therefore, the correct answer is (D). None of the other choices are appropriate.

If you are unable to fill in the blanks with your own words, this is your plan of attack:

Her determination to succeed no matter what the costs made her _____ to the _____ of other people.

(A) responsive … opinions   (D) attractive … aspirations

(B) helpful … needs   (E) communicative … lives

(C) insensitive … concerns

➤ STRATEGY 1

Plug in each answer choice in its corresponding blank, eliminating choices that do not make sense.

After plugging the answer choices into the sentence, we find that choice (D) and choice (E) can be eliminated since they do not make sense in the sentence.

➤ STRATEGY 2

Use the context of the sentence to determine if the missing word has a positive or negative connotation. Eliminate choices that do not agree.

By analyzing the context of the sentence, we see that the first blank needs a word with a negative connotation since this will be an adjective that is associated with someone who is determined to succeed no matter what the costs. Therefore, choices (A) and (B) can be eliminated. As a result, only choice (C) remains and is therefore the correct choice.

➤ STRATEGY 3

Remember the rules concerning the level of difficulty of the questions. Easy questions will have easy answers. Hard questions will have hard answers.

➤ **ADDITIONAL STRATEGIES**

➤ **Watch for key phrases that provide clues to the meaning of the sentence.**

> I do not _____ new challenges, but rather _____ them with great energy and anticipation.

In this sentence, the phrase, *but rather*, suggests that the word that follows is the opposite or a contradiction to the phrase that precedes it.

➤ **Use word parts — roots, prefixes, suffixes — to find the meanings of words you do not know.**

IV. ANALOGY STRATEGIES

Learn and understand the Directions so you don't waste valuable time reading them on the day of the exam.

> **DIRECTIONS**: Each question below consists of a related pair of words or phrases, followed by five lettered pairs of words or phrases. Select the lettered pair that best expresses a relationship similar to that expressed in the original pair.

Read both capitalized words carefully.

> SUCCESS : PROMOTION ::
>
> (A) emotion : tear   (D) happiness : laugh
>
> (B) marriage : ring   (E) occupation : prestige
>
> (C) intelligence : tie

If you know the meaning of both capitalized words, this is your plan of attack:

➤ **STRATEGY 1**

Using both words, form a sentence stating the simple and direct relationship between them. A relationship is simple and direct only if it logically stems from the meanings of the words and does not require a third word to relate the first to the second.

SUCCESS in business is marked by a *PROMOTION*.

➤ STRATEGY 2

Substitute the words in the answer choices for the capitalized words. Eliminate any choice which does not make sense in your sentence.

(A) EMOTION in business is marked by a TEAR. — NO

(B) MARRIAGE in business is marked by a RING. — NO

(C) INTELLIGENCE in business is marked by a TIE. — NO

(D) HAPPINESS in business is marked by a LAUGH. — NO

(E) OCCUPATION in business is marked by PRESTIGE. — NO

➤ STRATEGY 3

If none of the choices makes sense in your sentence, revise your sentence to make the relationship broader.

A *PROMOTION* can be a symbol representing SUCCESS.

(A) A TEAR can be a symbol representing EMOTION. — YES

(B) A RING can be a symbol representing MARRIAGE. — YES

(C) A TIE can be a symbol representing INTELLIGENCE. — NO

(D) A LAUGH can be a symbol representing HAPPINESS. — YES

(E) PRESTIGE can be a symbol representing OCCUPATION. — NO

If more than one choice remains, revise your sentence to make the relationship more specific and try again. Do this until only one answer choice remains.

SUCCESS is symbolized by a *PROMOTION*.

(A) EMOTION is symbolized by a TEAR. — NO

This is not a simple and direct relationship. Emotion can be symbolized in many different ways.

> (B) MARRIAGE is symbolized by a RING. — YES

> (D) HAPPINESS is symbolized by a LAUGH. — NO

This is not a simple and direct relationship. Happiness can be symbolized in many different ways.

If you don't know all the words in the answer choices, this is your plan of attack.

➤ STRATEGY 1

Using the sentence you have already formed, substitute the answer pairs whose meanings you do know and eliminate any which do not fit.

➤ STRATEGY 2

If you know one of the words in an answer pair, substitute that word for the corresponding word in the sentence and leave the other word out. Could another word possibly fill in the blank so that the sentence would make sense and the exact relationship would be preserved? If not, eliminate the answer choice. Do this with any remaining pairs where you know the meaning of one word.

Let's assume that you have the same analogy problem as above, but you do not know the meaning of *PRESTIGE*. Again, using the first sentence created, none of the choices would fit, so you would have to make the sentence broader. This time you would not eliminate choice (E) *OCCUPATION : PRESTIGE* since you do not know the meaning of the word *PRESTIGE*. However, by substituting *OCCUPATION* in the sentence, you could determine that there is no word that could make the sentence simple and direct.

> _____ can be a symbol representing OCCUPATION. — NO

➤ STRATEGY 3

If more than one answer pair remains, revise your sentence to make the relationship more specific and again plug in the remaining word choices, eliminating those which don't fit. Do this until only one word choice remains or until you can't narrow down the relationship any more.

If you don't know either of the choices in an answer pair, this is your plan of attack.

In a different analogy question, suppose you have eliminated any choices possible, but there is still one answer choice that contains two words you do not know. Use word parts to find the meanings of these words.

➤ STRATEGY 1

First eliminate any answer choices you can, using the previously described methods.

➤ STRATEGY 2

Look at the words you don't know. Can you determine their meanings from word parts (roots, prefixes, suffixes) or from ways in which you've heard them used? If so, use the same process you've been using all along to eliminate incorrect choices.

fortuitous : premeditated

The prefix *fort-* means *luck*. The suffix *-ous* means *full of*. Therefore, *fortuitous* means *full of luck* or *chance*.

The prefix *pre-* means *before* and *meditate* means to *think about*. Therefore, *premeditated* means to *think about before* or *to plan*. Using word parts, we see that these two words are opposites. If this is not the same relationship that exists for the capitalized words, then eliminate this answer choice.

➤ STRATEGY 3

If you've eliminated all the choices you can and you still don't have the answer, guess from among the remaining choices.

If you don't know one of the capitalized choices, this is your plan of attack.

Since you don't know one of the capitalized words, you can't possibly form a sentence expressing the simple and direct relationship. You need to work backwards from the answer choices to determine which choice is correct.

PLACID: TEMPESTUOUS ::

(A)   minimum : maximum   (D)   logical : compassionate

(B)   scared: terrified   (E)   calm : soothing

(C)   elegant: pure

➤ STRATEGY 1

Quickly form a sentence stating the simple and direct relationship between the two words in each answer choice. Eliminate those choices in which no direct relationship exists.

(A) MINIMUM is the opposite of MAXIMUM.

(B) TERRIFIED is a more intense degree of being SCARED.

(C) No simple and direct relationship exists. — ELIMINATE

(D) No simple and direct relationship exists. — ELIMINATE

(E) CALM is a synonym for SOOTHING.

➤ STRATEGY 2

Substitute the capitalized word that you do know for the corresponding word in the sentence you've created for each remaining answer choice. Leave the other space in the sentence blank. In each case, determine whether another word could possibly complete the sentence and preserve the exact relationship. If not, eliminate that answer choice.

➤ STRATEGY 3

If more than one answer choice remains, revise your sentences to make the relationships more specific and try again.

Assuming that *PLACID* is the word that is known, you can substitute it in any of the remaining three answer choices and it could make sense. Therefore, the best thing to do in this case is use word parts to determine the meaning of *TEMPESTUOUS*. A tempest is a violent storm. The suffix *-ous* means *full of*. Therefore, *TEMPESTUOUS* means *full of storm*. Since *PLACID* means *calm*, the relationship between the capitalized words is one of opposites. The same relationship exists between the words in choice (A) MINIMUM : MAXIMUM.

Whenever you aren't familiar with one of the words in an answer pair, try to figure it out from the word parts. Remember, even if you can't find the meanings of all the words, you can often eliminate some or all of the wrong choices using these techniques.

If you don't know either of the capitalized words, this is your plan of attack.

Again, quickly form a sentence expressing the simple and direct relationship between the words in the answer pairs. Eliminate any pair in which there is no simple and direct relationship. Then guess from among the remaining answers.

Using the same analogy as above, if you didn't know what either *PLACID* or *TEMPESTUOUS* meant, you could try to use word parts for both words. If that didn't work, you could guess among the choices that were determined as having simple and direct relationships.

➤ ADDITIONAL STRATEGIES

➤ **The analogy sections on the SAT start with easy questions and end with difficult ones. If a question is easy, the answer will probably be straightforward. If a question is difficult, you should look for trick answers and avoid them. The answers to difficult questions are more likely to include words you don't know than the answers to easy questions.**

➤ **Remember uncommon meanings of common words. SAT questions test not only your knowledge of uncommon meanings, but also your ability to recognize when an uncommon meaning fits the analogy better than a common one. Always be flexible enough to look for the most useful definition of a word.**

EYEBROWS : KNIT ::

The most common meaning of *KNIT* is *to form a fabric using yarn or thread by means of needles or a machine*. However, this is not the meaning that fits this analogy. The less common meaning of *KNIT* which is used in this analogy is *to contract*, as in *to contract the eyebrows*.

➤ **Parts of speech can alert you to uncommon meanings. The part of speech of a word in a SAT analogy is always the same as the part of speech of the corresponding words in the answer choices. If you think the first word in an analogy is a noun, but**

**all the first words in the answer choices are verbs, you should
look for another meaning for the word.**

The first answer choice of each question sets the part of speech for the words
in the question. So, if you are unsure of how a particular word is being used,
simply look at the first answer choice to determine the parts of speech.

DOCTOR : INJURY ::

(A)   sing : song   (D)   stare : eye

(B)   feed : baby   (E)   score : game

(C)   write : pencil

At first glance, the words in capital letters seem to be in the relationship
NOUN : NOUN. However, if you look at the first answer choice, SING : SONG,
you will see that the relationship between these two words is VERB : NOUN
and, therefore, DOCTOR is being used as a verb rather than a noun.

➤ **Watch out for look alikes. Especially in hard questions, words
which "just look right" are often there to fool you. You need to
find the answer pair that expresses the right relationship, not
the one with similar word structures to the stem, nor the one
with words that seem related to the words in the stem.**

BIOLOGY : LIFE ::

(A)   biography : lifetime   (D)   psychology : mind

(B)   archaeology : death   (E)   horticulture : growth

(C)   geology : planet

BIOLOGY is the *study of LIFE*, just as *PSYCHOLOGY* is the *study of the
MIND*. Don't be fooled by such words as LIFETIME, DEATH, GROWTH, and
PLANET, which are all associated with LIFE. If you look only at the relationships between the words, and not how they look or sound, you will be able to
determine the correct answer.

➤ **Beware of mirror relationships. The mirror is a common trap. In
a mirror analogy, one of the answers has the exact relationship
you're looking for, stated backwards. Mirror choices are always
wrong.**

DOWNPOUR : FLOODING ::

(A) movie : entertainment   (D) surgeon : scalpel

(B) sleeplessness : exhaustion (E) slice : pie

(C) sunburn : sunbathing

The relationship between the capitalized words is one of CAUSE : EFFECT. This same relationship exists for (B) sleeplessness : exhaustion. Choice (C), sunburn : sunbathing, is a mirror analogy. The relationship is EFFECT : CAUSE. You must be aware of these mirror relationships since they are incorrect.

FREQUENTLY USED SIMPLE AND DIRECT RELATIONSHIPS

The following are some of the word relationships frequently found on the Standardized Tests.

Type	Description	Examples
Synonyms	The words have similar meanings and the same part of speech.	happy : joyful intractable : immovable
Synonym Extensions	The words have similar meanings but different parts of speech.	despise : hatred ingenuous : naivety
Antonyms	The words have opposite meanings but the same part of speech.	love : hate dynamic : static
Antonym Extensions	The words have opposite meanings and different parts of speech.	passive : activity disinterested : enthusiasm
Agent and Action	One word represents the action necessarily taken by the other.	fish : swim architect : design
Set and Element	One word describes a category; the other, a thing that belongs to it.	fish : minnow gem : agate
Degree	Size; Intensity	sleepy : exhausted rain : torrent
Part to Whole	One word represents a piece of what the other represents	slice : pie torso : body
Cause and Effect	One word represents the outcome of the other.	downpour : flooding sunbathing : sunburn
Fashion	One word describes a way in which the action described by the other can be taken.	laugh : chuckle dance : waltz
Purpose	One word represents a reason for the existence of the thing represented by the other.	movie : entertain handcuffs : restrict
Person and Her Work		lawyer : litigation carpenter : building
Person and Her Place of Work		lawyer : courtroom surgeon : hospital
Person and the Tools He Uses		surgeon : scalpel chef : oven
Person and the Fruit of His Labor		chef : food musician : song

VERBAL ABILITY PRACTICE TEST

1. Ⓐ Ⓑ Ⓒ Ⓓ Ⓔ
2. Ⓐ Ⓑ Ⓒ Ⓓ Ⓔ
3. Ⓐ Ⓑ Ⓒ Ⓓ Ⓔ
4. Ⓐ Ⓑ Ⓒ Ⓓ Ⓔ
5. Ⓐ Ⓑ Ⓒ Ⓓ Ⓔ
6. Ⓐ Ⓑ Ⓒ Ⓓ Ⓔ
7. Ⓐ Ⓑ Ⓒ Ⓓ Ⓔ
8. Ⓐ Ⓑ Ⓒ Ⓓ Ⓔ
9. Ⓐ Ⓑ Ⓒ Ⓓ Ⓔ
10. Ⓐ Ⓑ Ⓒ Ⓓ Ⓔ
11. Ⓐ Ⓑ Ⓒ Ⓓ Ⓔ
12. Ⓐ Ⓑ Ⓒ Ⓓ Ⓔ
13. Ⓐ Ⓑ Ⓒ Ⓓ Ⓔ
14. Ⓐ Ⓑ Ⓒ Ⓓ Ⓔ
15. Ⓐ Ⓑ Ⓒ Ⓓ Ⓔ
16. Ⓐ Ⓑ Ⓒ Ⓓ Ⓔ
17. Ⓐ Ⓑ Ⓒ Ⓓ Ⓔ
18. Ⓐ Ⓑ Ⓒ Ⓓ Ⓔ
19. Ⓐ Ⓑ Ⓒ Ⓓ Ⓔ
20. Ⓐ Ⓑ Ⓒ Ⓓ Ⓔ
21. Ⓐ Ⓑ Ⓒ Ⓓ Ⓔ
22. Ⓐ Ⓑ Ⓒ Ⓓ Ⓔ
23. Ⓐ Ⓑ Ⓒ Ⓓ Ⓔ

24. Ⓐ Ⓑ Ⓒ Ⓓ Ⓔ
25. Ⓐ Ⓑ Ⓒ Ⓓ Ⓔ
26. Ⓐ Ⓑ Ⓒ Ⓓ Ⓔ
27. Ⓐ Ⓑ Ⓒ Ⓓ Ⓔ
28. Ⓐ Ⓑ Ⓒ Ⓓ Ⓔ
29. Ⓐ Ⓑ Ⓒ Ⓓ Ⓔ
30. Ⓐ Ⓑ Ⓒ Ⓓ Ⓔ
31. Ⓐ Ⓑ Ⓒ Ⓓ Ⓔ
32. Ⓐ Ⓑ Ⓒ Ⓓ Ⓔ
33. Ⓐ Ⓑ Ⓒ Ⓓ Ⓔ
34. Ⓐ Ⓑ Ⓒ Ⓓ Ⓔ
35. Ⓐ Ⓑ Ⓒ Ⓓ Ⓔ
36. Ⓐ Ⓑ Ⓒ Ⓓ Ⓔ
37. Ⓐ Ⓑ Ⓒ Ⓓ Ⓔ
38. Ⓐ Ⓑ Ⓒ Ⓓ Ⓔ
39. Ⓐ Ⓑ Ⓒ Ⓓ Ⓔ
40. Ⓐ Ⓑ Ⓒ Ⓓ Ⓔ
41. Ⓐ Ⓑ Ⓒ Ⓓ Ⓔ
42. Ⓐ Ⓑ Ⓒ Ⓓ Ⓔ
43. Ⓐ Ⓑ Ⓒ Ⓓ Ⓔ
44. Ⓐ Ⓑ Ⓒ Ⓓ Ⓔ
45. Ⓐ Ⓑ Ⓒ Ⓓ Ⓔ

VERBAL ABILITY
PRACTICE TEST

45 Questions

DIRECTIONS: Each question below consists of a word in capital letters, followed by five lettered words or phrases. Choose the word or phrase that is most nearly **OPPOSITE** in meaning to the word in capital letters. Since some of the questions require you to distinguish fine shades of meaning, consider all the choices before deciding which is best.

EXAMPLE:

EASY:

(A)   cold   (B)   hard   (C)   low

(D)   small   (E)   sweet   Ⓐ ● Ⓒ Ⓓ Ⓔ

---

1.   IMITATE:

   (A)   modify   (B)   initiate   (C)   act

   (D)   impair   (E)   sustain

2.   HEAR:

   (A)   deafen   (B)   attend   (C)   answer

   (D)   disregard   (E)   muffle

3.   BLEAK:

   (A)   blind   (B)   sheltered   (C)   binding

   (D)   absent   (E)   open

4.   YIELD:

   (A)   contact   (B)   ascend   (C)   frustrate

   (D)   advance   (E)   uphold

5. ZEAL:

    (A)   miracle   (B)   reluctance   (C)   zenith

    (D)   doom   (E)   bias

6. LIVID:

    (A)   lively   (B)   overdone   (C)   fantastic

    (D)   level   (E)   brilliant

7. AGILE:

    (A)   obstinate   (B)   lifeless   (C)   capable

    (D)   conscious   (E)   jovial

8. AUSTERE:

    (A)   awful   (B)   indulgent   (C)   contrite

    (D)   timid   (E)   tenuous

9. ESOTERIC:

    (A)   erroneous   (B)   mediocre   (C)   healthy

    (D)   accessible   (E)   essential

10. OPPRESS:

    (A)   impress   (B)   encourage   (C)   apprehend

    (D)   apportion   (E)   impugn

11. HEAVY:

    (A)   stoic   (B)   confining   (C)   trivial

    (D)   heaping   (E)   hearty

12. DISSEMBLE:

    (A)   transmit   (B)   dismantle   (C)   create

    (D)   aver   (E)   discover

13. PANACEA:

   (A) nostril   (B) rostrum   (C) virus

   (D) nostalgic   (E) tenure

14. PHILISTINE:

   (A) cosmopolitan   (B) philanthropist (C) criminal

   (D) defender   (E) malingerer

15. ICONOCLAST:

   (A) servant   (B) perfectionist   (C) counselor

   (D) conformist   (E) inventor

DIRECTIONS: Each sentence below has one or two blanks, each blank indicating that something has been omitted. Beneath the sentence are five lettered words or sets of words. Choose the word or set of words that **BEST** fits the meaning of the sentence as a whole.

EXAMPLE:

Although the critics found the book _____, many of the readers found it rather _____.

   (A) obnoxious ... perfect   (D) comical ... persuasive

   (B) spectacular ... interesting (E) popular ... rare

   (C) boring ... intriguing   Ⓐ Ⓑ ● Ⓓ Ⓔ

---

16. Frustrated by the many _____ , the scientist reluctantly _____ his experiment.

   (A) complications ... terminated

   (B) dangers ... extended

   (C) successes ... finished

   (D) situations ... submitted

   (E) liabilities ... studied

17. During the Middle Ages, the majority of the population were _____ since working the land was an _____ job.

   (A) nobles ... enjoyable

   (B) serfs ... endless

   (C) monks ... everlasting

   (D) merchants ... impersonal

   (E) knights ... inconsequential

18. The speaker's monotone delivery made his hour-long speech seem _____ and the audience became _____ waiting for the end.

   (A) exciting ... interested

   (B) interminable ... impatient

   (C) unbelievable ... skeptical

   (D) long ... doubtful

   (E) uninteresting ... grumpy

19. When he first began buying stock, the businessman felt _____ , but his successes now give him great _____ .

   (A) uncertain ... assurance

   (B) scared ... distrust

   (C) incompetent ... ability

   (D) timid ... concern

   (E) confident ... wealth

20. Because the actor's temperament was so _____, directors often rejected him for parts since no one could be sure how he would behave.

   (A) confident

   (B) mercurial

   (C) pessimistic

   (D) overpowering

   (E) inhibited

DIRECTIONS: Each passage below is followed by questions based on its content. Answer all questions following a passage on the basis of what is **STATED** or **IMPLIED** in that passage.

Schizophrenia is a term used to describe a complex, extremely puzzling condition–the most chronic and disabling of the major mental illnesses. Schizophrenia may be one disorder, or it may be many disorders, with different causes. Because of the disorder's complexity, few generalizations hold true for all people who are diagnosed as schizophrenic.

Just as "normal" individuals view the world from their own perspectives, schizophrenic people, too, have their own perceptions of reality. Their view of the world, however, is often strikingly different from the usual reality seen and shared by those around them.

Living in a world that can appear distorted, changeable, and lacking the reliable landmarks we all use to anchor ourselves to reality, a person with schizophrenia may feel anxious and confused. This person may seem distant, detached, or preoccupied, and may even sit as rigidly as a stone, not moving for hours and not uttering a sound. Or he or she may move about constantly, always occupied, wide awake, vigilant, and alert. A schizophrenic person may exhibit very different kinds of behavior at different times.

The world of a schizophrenic individual may be filled with hallucinations; a person actually may sense things that in reality do not exist, such as hearing voices telling the person to do certain things, seeing people or objects that are not really there, or feeling invisible fingers touching his or her body. These hallucinations may be quite frightening. Hearing voices that other people don't hear is the most common type of hallucination in schizophrenia. Such voices may describe the patient's activities, carry on a conversation, warn of impending dangers, or tell the person what to do.

Delusions are false personal beliefs that are not subject to reason or contradictory evidence and are not part of the person's culture. They are common symptoms of schizophrenia and can involve themes of persecution or grandeur, for example. Sometimes delusions in schizophrenia are quite bizarre–for instance, believing that a neighbor is controlling the schizophrenic individual's behavior with magnetic waves, or that people on television are directing special messages specifically at him or her, or are broadcasting the individual's thoughts aloud to other people. Delusions of persecution, which are common in paranoid schizophrenia, are false and irrational beliefs that a person is being cheated, harassed, poisoned, or conspired against. The patient may believe that he or she, or a member of the family or other group, is the focus of this imagined persecution.

21. The word "chronic" would more likely be defined as

   (A) fleeting.   (D) persistent.

   (B) temporary.   (E) occasional.

   (C) infrequent.

22. According to psychiatrists, a schizophrenic's perception of reality is

   (A) uncontrollable.   (D) distorted.

   (B) indifferent.   (E) apathetic.

   (C) inappropriate.

23. According to the passage, the behavior exhibited by the schizophrenic may not result from

    (A)   imagined persecution.
    (B)   hallucinations.
    (C)   delusions.
    (D)   feelings of grandeur.
    (E)   society's expectations.

24. According to the passage, inner voices that describe the schizophrenic's activities are known as

    (A)   delusions.
    (B)   paranoia.
    (C)   hallucinations.
    (D)   persecution.
    (E)   grandeur.

25. Paranoid schizophrenics commonly have irrational beliefs including all but one of the following.

    (A)   They are being cheated.

    (B)   They are being poisoned.

    (C)   They are being conspired against.

    (D)   They are being told what to do.

    (E)   They are not in touch with reality.

The ambivalence of women, characteristic of nearly all generations today, is perhaps most clearly seen among those who came to maturity during the uncertainty of the last two decades and who found themselves as young women just out of college supported by the society to seek an important job or significant post-graduate study. Many of them did so successfully and now in their mid or late 30s or even early 40s, having forthrightly pursued an elusive goal called "success" with its concomitants of money, prestige, and recognition, they discover that other elements of their lives need attention. For those who are married, there is the question of children. Their biological clock is running down. But what will children do to their lifestyle? The one answer to that question is that children will change their lifestyle, but in what ways? For those who are not married, there may also be the question of children, either of their own, or adopted or jointly reared with the child's natural parent. In any case, well-educated women are concerned about the matter. The higher the level of a woman's education, the fewer children she is likely to have and the later in life she is likely to have them.

What is obvious is that in the older generation of women, ones now in their 40s and 50s, the opportunities for combining successful career and parenthood were limited. Whether those limitations occurred because women and society in general discouraged such combinations or because women were not prepared to undertake such responsibilities is unclear. Undoubtedly both factors contribute to an explanation. Now it is reasonably clear that women are prepared to undertake such responsibilities and are educated through undergraduate and professional schools to do so. Whether society is yet ready for these women when they are middle-aged to have the same opportunities as middle age men is much less clear.

One may observe that, while ambivalence may be characteristic of many modern women, it is not socially sanctioned. Women may be ambivalent, but society does not expect them to be ambivalent the way they are expected to be active, attractive and ambitious. I would argue that indeed society at the present time does expect women to be ambivalent about the commitments to job and to personal life. This ambivalence is expected, I believe, because we are in a transitional period in which we as a society have not yet resolved what, ultimately, we believe should be the priorities of adult lives for persons of both sexes. In the face of this ambiguity, we prescribe ambivalence for women.

26. The author of the article implies that the role for women in the future should be

   (A)   pursuit of prestige and recognition.

   (B)   pursuit of a family.

   (C)   combination of career and parenthood.

   (D)   ambivalent.

   (E)   attractive and ambitious.

27. The article infers that women's ambivalence has occurred primarily

   (A)   during the last two decades.

   (B)   since the educational level of women has been raised.

   (C)   since the standard of living has risen.

   (D)   since women have experienced success in the workplace.

   (E)   during the last century.

28. The factor which has not contributed to the ambivalence of women is

   (A)   a successful career.   (D)   education.

   (B)   parenthood.   (E)   low wages.

   (C)   acceptance of responsibilities.

29. The passage infers that opportunities for combining successful careers and parenthood were not limited to

    (A)   women in their 20s and 30s.

    (B)   women in their 40s and 50s.

    (C)   women in their 50s and 60s.

    (D)   women in their 60s and 70s.

    (E)   women in their 40s and 60s.

30. The author implies that ambivalence is the result of

    (A)   the lack of role definition for both sexes.

    (B)   the desires of women.

    (C)   the current transitional period.

    (D)   commitments to jobs and personal life.

    (E)   equal opportunities.

DIRECTIONS: Select the word or set of words that best completes each of the following sentences.

---

31. Even though most of his published verses were _____ , the poet received great acclaim for his work.

    (A)   grand   (D)   inane

    (B)   impressive   (E)   unlikely

    (C)   musical

32. Finishing a marathon can be a _____ task when leg cramps _____ the runner.

    (A)   herculean ... debilitate   (D)   invigorating ... slow

    (B)   hard ... impel   (E)   thrilling ... sedate

    (C)   frustrating ... spur

33. Since the athlete thought he was _____ , he was willing to challenge the limits of his strength without fear of injury.

    (A)   capable

    (B)   judicious

    (C)   competent

    (D)   incurable

    (E)   invulnerable

34. The crushing _____ suffered by the soccer team left the fans feeling _____ with the bragging goalie.

    (A)   blow ... overwhelmed

    (B)   failure ... indecisive

    (C)   defense ... angry

    (D)   defeat ... disenchanted

    (E)   loss ... placid

35. The westward _____ from the Midwest to California in the 1930s created a large population of _____ workers on the Western produce farms.

    (A)   influx ... wandering

    (B)   movement ... incapable

    (C)   expansion ... lackadaisical

    (D)   highways ... hopeful

    (E)   exodus ... migrant

DIRECTIONS: Each question below consists of a related pair of words or phrases, followed by five lettered pairs of words or phrases. Select the lettered pair that best expresses a relationship similar to that expressed in the original pair.

EXAMPLE:

SMILE : MOUTH ::

(A)   wink : eye

(B)   teeth : face

(C)   voice : speech

(D)   tan : skin

(E)   food : gums

● ⒝ ⒞ ⒟ ⒠

---

36. WATER : CHLORINE ::

    (A)   dough : yeast

    (B)   city : mayor

    (C)   parents : children

    (D)   fire : water

    (E)   soda : ice

37. MINISTER : BIBLE ::

    (A) secretary : shoes   (D) carpenter : hammer

    (B) Shakespeare : play   (E) swimmer : dive

    (C) comb : cosmetologist

38. BRACKISH : MURKY ::

    (A) color : temperature   (D) purity : density

    (B) taste : appearance   (E) breadth : depth

    (C) density : weight

39. WALK : SAUNTER ::

    (A) desecrate : profane   (D) nullify : annul

    (B) rise : risen   (E) talk : whisper

    (C) banter : converse

40. PHILANTHROPIST : MONEY ::

    (A) bigot : prejudice   (D) mother : cookies

    (B) humanitarian : time   (E) attorney : law

    (C) doctor : medicine

41. MARRIAGE : DIVORCE ::

    (A) sermon : benediction   (D) opera : aria

    (B) employee : termination   (E) play : curtain call

    (C) life : death

42. THIEF : FURTIVE ::

    (A) teenager : young   (D) fame : illusory

    (B) glutton : obese   (E) men : irrational

    (C) delinquent : intractable

43. COLLABORATION : COLLUSION ::

   (A)   guile : illusion   (D)   fame : notoriety

   (B)   clarity : brightness   (E)   covert : overt

   (C)   hypocrite : deceiver

44. CONTRITE : PENITENT

   (A)   reticent : punctual   (D)   sanguine : pessimistic

   (B)   concise : succinct   (E)   facsimile : original

   (C)   dogmatic : levelheaded

45. ALTRUISTIC : SELFISH ::

   (A)   bright : dim   (D)   in : out

   (B)   sweet : sour   (E)   right : wrong

   (C)   industrious : lazy

VERBAL ABILITY
PRACTICE TEST

ANSWER KEY

1.	(A)	13.	(C)	25.	(E)	37.	(D)
2.	(D)	14.	(A)	26.	(D)	38.	(B)
3.	(B)	15.	(D)	27.	(A)	39.	(E)
4.	(C)	16.	(A)	28.	(E)	40.	(B)
5.	(B)	17.	(B)	29.	(A)	41.	(C)
6.	(E)	18.	(B)	30.	(A)	42.	(C)
7.	(B)	19.	(A)	31.	(D)	43.	(D)
8.	(B)	20.	(B)	32.	(A)	44.	(B)
9.	(D)	21.	(D)	33.	(E)	45.	(C)
10.	(B)	22.	(D)	34.	(D)		
11.	(C)	23.	(E)	35.	(E)		
12.	(D)	24.	(C)	36.	(A)		

DETAILED EXPLANATIONS
OF ANSWERS

1. **(A)** To IMITATE means to copy, to try to do the same thing as someone else. To MODIFY is to change the original in some way, to not copy exactly, and is the opposite.

2. **(D)** To HEAR may be thought of initially as to receive sound. However, it can also mean to pay attention to, to heed. While DEAFEN may seem a possible choice, this word implies action "done to" not "done by" as the original word implies. To DISREGARD is the opposite word because it implies not paying attention to or heeding.

3. **(B)** BLEAK means bare and unsheltered, worn out. SHELTERED implies a place of protection and security, making it the opposite of bleak.

4. **(C)** To YIELD is to give in or give up, or to cede. It can also mean to give someone easy access to or to open up a way for someone. To FRUSTRATE is to keep someone from attaining a goal or access to something.

5. **(B)** ZEAL means ardor, devotion, excitement, energy. To pursue a cause with zeal would mean to devote one's whole self to that cause. RELUCTANCE is the best choice because it implies a hesitancy to commit.

6. **(E)** LIVID means pale, ashy, bloodless. It has also come to mean extremely angry, "livid with rage." Because of this second meaning, livid is often thought to mean the same as being very RED in the face from anger, which is misleading. The first meaning needs to be kept in mind to know that BRILLIANT, meaning bright and colorful is the proper choice.

7. **(B)** AGILE means active, limber, perhaps even athletic-like. LIFELESS implies without energy, limp, without spirit.

8. **(B)** AUSTERE means stern, strict, and plain or severe. It can apply to a person, a way of life, or even decor. All these areas need to be kept in mind when looking for the opposite word. In this case, INDULGENT, which means flexible and easygoing, would be the proper choice.

9. **(D)** ESOTERIC means something that is known by only a few people. It could refer to specialized knowledge, or codes and passwords, something that is not generally available to all. ACCESSIBLE is the best choice here because it implies something that is open to all.

10. **(B)** OPPRESS means "to burden or weigh down." (B) ENCOURAGE is to reassure and help, and is the antonym of oppress. (A) IMPRESS and (C) APPREHEND are misleading because of their similarity to the word oppress.

11. **(C)** HEAVY can mean of great weight, but it can also mean something of great importance, or a great problem bearing down on one. Realizing this meaning, the antonym is TRIVIAL, something of little importance, or no weight.

12. **(D)** DISSEMBLE means "to lie." (D) AVER, "to certify or guarantee," is the opposite of not telling the truth. (B) DISMANTLE and (E) DISCOVER can be misleading because of the sound and look of each word.

13. **(C)** A PANACEA is a cure-all or a medication. Choices (A), (B), and (D) are completely unrelated. A VIRUS is something that causes disease and is the antonym.

14. **(A)** PHILISTINE in the modern sense means someone who is a total boor, unsophisticated, and artless. Choice (B) misleads because of sound and look. Choices (C), (D), and (E) describe different types of people. A COSMO-POLITAN is one who is at home and comfortable anywhere; who knows and appreciates all in the world.

15. **(D)** An ICONOCLAST is one who rejects the religious beliefs or philo-sophical and governmental ideals of others. Choice (A) SERVANT might not reject the beliefs of others, but is not the exact opposite of the original word. Choices (B), (C), and (E) designate various types of people. A CONFORMIST would comply with, rather than reject, the beliefs of others and is therefore the correct answer.

16. **(A)** The word FRUSTRATE should indicate some sort of problem faced by the scientist. RELUCTANTLY leads the reader to realize that the scientist had to do something that she didn't want to do because she was frustrated with the experiment. The second choice words in (B), (C), (D), and (E) are not actions that would be made reluctantly in this case. (A) is the best combination of words to properly complete the sentence.

17. **(B)** While some knowledge of history may be required in this sentence, most students are aware of the word SERF and the type of life that the word entails. The other first-choice words do not logically go with those types of society who worked the land. Therefore, SERF becomes the marker word to focus on the proper choice.

18. **(B)** The reader should look for two word clues at the beginning of this sentence: MONOTONE and HOUR-LONG SPEECH. Anyone who has been in a situation like this would know that an hour can seem like an eternity. The reader then needs to consider what the audience reaction might be.

19. **(A)** The thrust of the sentence is toward a change in attitude as expertise is developed in a certain area. Therefore, the word choice should be one that shows growth as well as change. (C) might be considered as a possible choice, but ABILITY does not adequately complete the sentence. (A) demonstrates the growth and change that is called for by the sentence.

20. **(B)** The last part of the sentence leads the reader to conclude that the actor has a temperament that changes. MERCURIAL is the only choice of the five that offers this sense of change and wide mood swings that would cause the problems for directors.

21. **(D)** (A), (B), (C), (E) are antonyms for the word "chronic." (D) is the correct choice since it is a synonym of "chronic."

22. **(D)** Answer (D) is correct since the article states that the schizophrenic's perception of reality is distorted. None of the other choices are stated in the passage.

23. **(E)** Answers (A), (B), (C), and (D) are stated. Answer (E) is the correct choice since it is not mentioned in the article.

24. **(C)** Answer (C) is correct as stated in the article, but hallucinations may be exhibited through delusions, paranoia, persecutions or feelings of grandeur.

25. **(E)** Answers (A), (B), (C), and (D) are stated in the passage. Answer (E) is correct since the last paragraph does not list this as an irrational belief.

26. **(D)** Answer (D) is the correct answer since it is stated in the article. (A), (B), (C), and (E) are incorrect choices as they describe the options of ambivalent women of today.

27. **(A)** Answer (A) is correct since the first paragraph states that it is "perhaps most clearly seen ... during the uncertainty of the last two decades." Answers (B), (C), and (D) are contributing factors to the ambivalence. Answer (E) is incorrect since there was no inference that this ambivalence extended over such a long period of time.

28. **(E)** Answers (A), (B), (C), and (D) are stated. Answer (E) is the correct choice since it is not mentioned in the article.

29. **(A)** The article states that women in their 40s and 50s did not have the opportunity to combine careers and parenthood, so therefore, one could infer that younger women did have that opportunity. This reasoning makes answer (A) correct and all other choices incorrect.

30. **(A)** Answer (A) is the correct answer since the author states that society has not "yet resolved what, ultimately, we believe should be the priorities of adult lives for persons of both sexes." This implies that there is no definitive role for both sexes. Answers (B), (C), (D), and (E) are contributing factors stated in the article.

31. **(D)** The reader needs to realize that a contradiction is being set up here because of the "Even though ..." opening. Therefore, the verses are not going to be described as those that would signal fame. INANE (D), meaning silly or absurd, best fulfills the contradiction. (E) UNLIKELY is a possibility, but (D) fits better. (A), (B), and (C) would not create a contradiction.

32. **(A)** Taking a clue from the word MARATHON should lead the reader to look for a first word that would connote a task requiring fortitude. LEG CRAMPS should make the reader look for a second word that would mean the runner has problems. Choice (A) is the only pair of words which conveys the necessary effort implied by the sentence.

33. **(E)** INVULNERABLE (E) implies one who feels he could not be injured or wounded, which is the case in this sentence. This is the correct answer. While (A) CAPABLE and (C) COMPETENT are possible choices, they do not totally lead to the conclusion of the sentence. Someone who is (B) JUDICIOUS would not challenge everything and everyone, nor would one who is (D) INCURABLE.

34. **(D)** The word CRUSHING should lead the reader to realize that something bad has happened. The word BRAGGING describing the goalie connotes that his boasts have not come true. Therefore, the reader needs to look for two words that show this in the sentence. Only (D) completes the sentence with the full sense of what is implied.

35. **(E)** The phrase "from the Midwest to California" should lead the reader to look for a first word that shows movement out from an area. This then excludes (A) and (D). (B) and (C) are possibilities, but neither INCAPABLE or LACKADAISICAL give the full thrust of the necessary outward movement. MIGRANT also shows workers on the move. Choice (E) fulfills the needs of the sentence.

36. **(A)** CHLORINE is a chemical that causes a change in WATER just as YEAST brings about a change in DOUGH. (B) in the other choices can also bring about changes in (A), but not as a chemical effects a change.

37. **(D)** A MINISTER uses a BIBLE in his work like a CARPENTER uses a HAMMER in his work. A COSMOTOLOGIST also uses a COMB in her work, but that is in the reverse order from the first pair. SHAKESPEARE did not use a PLAY; he wrote them.

38. **(B)** BRACKISH, meaning salty, deals with the sense of TASTE while MURKY, meaning unclear, deals with the sense of SIGHT. The other choices do not demonstrate qualities associated with the capitalized pair.

39. **(E)** SAUNTERING is an action that is a variation of WALKING as WHISPERING is a variation of TALKING. Choice (A) is synonymous meaning to violate and choice (D) is synonymous meaning to cancel. Choice (C) is also a variation of the same thing, but the pair is presented in the opposite order from the capitalized pair since CONVERSE means generally to talk while BANTER, meaning talking playfully, is more specific.

40. **(B)** A PHILANTHROPIST is known for being charitable with MONEY while a HUMANITARIAN is known for his generosity in giving of his TIME to help others. Choices (C) and (E) are also known for the second item in each pair, but those are occupations rather than charitable endeavors.

41. **(C)** A DIVORCE is the negative conclusion of a MARRIAGE as DEATH is the negative ending of LIFE. Choices (A) and (E) are also the endings of an activity, but do not imply the negative as the capitalized pair does. Choice (B) is the ending of an employee's job, not the employee.

42. **(C)** A THIEF is FURTIVE or sly and a DELINQUENT is INTRAC-TABLE or difficult to control. A TEENAGER is YOUNG, but that is a relative term so it's difficult to determine to say whether that is true. A GLUTTON is OBESE, but that is a physical trait rather than a personality trait. Some MEN are IRRATIONAL, but that is not a trait normally assigned them.

43. **(D)** COLLUSION is a negative synonym of COLLABORATION since both deal with working together, but collusion is for negative purposes. FAME and NOTORIETY are also synonyms, but notoriety is due to negative deeds. Choices (A), (B), and (C) are synonyms, and choice (E) antonyms.

44. **(B)** CONTRITE and PENITENT are synonyms meaning to be regretful for one's sins. CONCISE and SUCCINCT are also synonyms meaning brief. Choices (D) and (E) are antonyms. In choice (A) RETICENT (reluctant to speak) and PUNCTUAL have no clear relationship. In choice (C) DOGMATIC means stubborn, so there is no clear relationship there either.

45. **(C)** ALTRUISTIC and SELFISH are human characteristics that are an-tonyms. The other choices are also antonyms, but they are not normally used in describing people.

CHAPTER 4

Reading Comprehension

➤ Reading Comprehension Review
➤ Sample Passages

READING COMPREHENSION REVIEW

Study this chapter for the following tests:

GMAT, MCAT, GRE, ACT, LSAT, CBEST, CLAST, PPST, CLEP, and PRAXIS II

You will find reading comprehension on virtually all standardized tests. Reading comprehension tests your ability to understand, analyze, and apply information based on passages. These passages will range from short, one- to two-paragraph types with a moderate vocabulary, to longer, denser passages on technical subjects where there is a substantial vocabulary. You will not need to have any prior knowledge of the material presented, since the questions are based only on the given passages.

Since this book is used for a wide range of standardized tests, we need to clarify difficulty levels for each type of test. The shorter passages with an average vocabulary are commonly seen on tests such as the CLAST, CLEP, PRAXIS II and other State Teacher Certification Tests, such as the CBEST and the PPST. Passages of a more moderate length, with a challenging vocabulary and many inferential questions can be found in tests such as the GRE, GMAT, and ACT. The most challenging passages (which also tend to be the longest, have the most intensive vocabulary, and more analytical questions) can be found in the LSAT and the MCAT. We urge you, however, to study passages of all lengths and difficulty levels. You will then be sufficiently prepared and more confident when you take your test.

SUGGESTED STRATEGIES

➤ Skim some of the questions first before reading the passage. This will help you to look for answers in the passage.

➤ As you read, underline key words, phrases, and ideas. When you answer a question and need to refer to the passage, the important ideas will stand out.

➤ Try not to spend too much time deciphering the meaning of words and statements upon the initial reading of the passage. It will be helpful to go back over specific parts of the passage for in-depth understanding after reading each question.

➤ While reading the passage, look specifically for inferences, the mood or tone of the passage, and the main idea. These can indicate the questions that will be asked.

➤ Passages usually have their main idea or theme in the first and/ or last sentences.

There are three types of questions that you will encounter on the reading comprehension section of your exam. They are:

1. Memory/Recall,

2. Interpretation, and

3. Analytical Reasoning.

Memory/Recall questions simply ask you facts about the passage you have just read.

Interpretation questions ask you to make inferences and then to draw conclusions based on the given passage. Examples of these questions include asking the reader to choose a title for the passage, or to infer the meaning of a word within that passage.

Analytical Reasoning questions ask you to analyze an idea or concept and then to make a judgment based on that analysis. These questions often ask you to judge the author's mood throughout the passage, or to determine a cause and effect relationship within the passage.

The following example passage and questions illustrate the different types of questions.

SAMPLE PASSAGE

DIRECTIONS: The passage below is followed by questions based on the content. Answer all questions following the passage based on what is stated or implied in the passage. Determine whether the question type is memory/recall, interpretation, or analytical reasoning.

Helping your children enjoy reading is one of the most important things you can do as a parent and well worth the investment of your time and energy. Kids will learn reading skills in school, but often they come to associate reading with work, not pleasure. As a result, they lose their desire to read. And it is that desire — the curiosity and interest — that is the cornerstone to using reading and related skills successfully.

By far the most effective way to encourage your children to love books and reading is to read aloud to them, and the earlier you start, the better. Even a baby of a few months can see pictures, listen to your voice, and turn cardboard pages. Make this time together a special time when you hold your children and share the pleasure of a story without the distractions of TV or telephones. You may be surprised to find that a well-written children's book is often as big a delight to you as it is to the kids.

And don't stop taking the time to read aloud once your children have learned to read for themselves. At this stage, encourage them to read to you some of the time. This shared enjoyment will continue to strengthen your children's interest and appreciation.

Simply having books, magazines, and newspapers around your home will help children to view them as part of daily life. And your example of reading frequently and enjoying it will reinforce that view.

While your children are still very small, it's a good idea to start a home library for them, even if it's just a shelf or two. Be sure to keep some books for little children to handle freely. Consider specially made, extra-durable books for infants, and pick paperbacks and plastic covers for kids who are older but still not quite ready for expensive hardbacks. Allowing little children to touch, smell, and even taste books will help them to develop strong attachments.

How you handle books will eventually influence how your kids treat them. Children imitate, so if they see that you enjoy reading and treat books gently and with respect, it is likely that, in time, they will do the same.

When you read aloud together, choose books that you both like. If a book seems dull, put it down and find one that is appealing.

1. A baby of a few months can

    (A)   recognize the title of a favorite book.

    (B)   associate reading with play rather than work.

    (C)   talk, if read to all the time.

    (D)   hold a book.

    (E)   see pictures, listen to your voice, and turn cardboard pages.

2. A good title for this passage would be

    (A)   How to Get Children Interested in Reading.

    (B)   Teaching Children to Read at a Young Age.

    (C)   Reading Through Schoolwork.

    (D)   Choosing Good Books.

    (E)   Finding Time for Reading.

3. The attitude of the author toward children's reading is

    (A)   neutral, it doesn't really matter how or when children learn to read.

    (B)   boredom, there is little to say on the subject.

    (C)   positive, it is a pleasure to help children to appreciate reading.

    (D)   pessimistic, getting children to learn to like reading is hard work.

    (E)   hard to pin down, he or she doesn't express a clear attitude one way or the other.

DETAILED EXPLANATIONS
OF SAMPLE PASSAGE

1. **(E)** **Memory/Recall Question.** There is no validity to (A) since nowhere in the passage is there a statement that a baby of a few months can recognize the title of a favorite book. In answer (B), you would recognize the concept of associating reading with play rather than with work, but when you look back in the paragraph, you would see that it refers to "Kids" and not specifically to babies of a few months. (C) also has no validity — there is nothing in the passage that states or infers that babies will talk if read to all the time. (D) might seem correct at first, since the passage describes how to let children become familiar with books, but it is not stated that babies of a few months can do that. (E) is the only correct answer, then, because it is a statement actually found in the passage.

2. **(A)** **Interpretation Question.** (B) is incorrect because the passage reinforces the idea of helping children to enjoy reading; there is nothing in the passage that implies that a parent should teach his or her young child to read — only to enjoy it. (C) is almost opposite to the idea of the passage. It talks about reading through schoolwork, whereas the author wants parents to emphasize reading for pleasure. (D) is obviously wrong because there is nothing in the passage which suggests how to choose good books. (E) doesn't fit because the author doesn't suggest how to find time for reading, nor is there a reference to finding time to read. The correct choice is (A) because the passage talks specifically about how to motivate children's interest through early reading, encouraging children to read to you, keeping books, magazines, and newspapers at home, and creating a home library.

3. **(C)** **Analytical Reasoning Question.** (A) is obviously incorrect, because this passage is about getting children interested in reading, and the author says in the first paragraph that children who only read through school lose their desire to read. (B) is incorrect because the author remains upbeat and positive about children's reading and this feeling is not associated with forcing reading. (D) is incorrect because the passage is optimistic and encourages children to read. It does not treat reading like hard work. (E) suggests that the process of teaching children reading is not pleasurable, yet the tone is clearly one which suggests it is pleasurable to teach children the value of reading. (C) is correct because the author has a pleasant tone, many suggestions, and is encouraging. This means that he is viewing the subject positively, and this matches the key phrase "pleasure" in (C).

Now that you have seen how all three questions might appear on your exam, take the following Reading Comprehension exercises. There are four practice passages with questions followed by detailed explanations.

Each corresponds to specific tests, although it is a good idea to study all of the following passages.

Please note that the length of the essay does not always suggest its degree of difficulty.

PASSAGE I

> ## This sample passage may apply to these tests:
>
> ## PRAXIS II, CLAST, CBEST, CLEP, and PPST

DIRECTIONS: Each passage is followed by questions based on its content. After reading the passage, choose the best answer to each question. Answer all questions based on what is indicated or implied in that passage.

Questions 1-3 are based on the following passage.

The high school drop out rate remains high in many southern states. An average of 18% of the students who finish sixth grade in Texas, Mississippi, Louisiana, and Alabama do not stay in school long enough to graduate from high school. Maintaining a precise count of the number of dropouts is difficult. Some students may still be listed as enrolled when in fact they have stopped attending school and do not plan to return. A slightly larger percentage of male students drop out of school than females. More students tend to leave school during the eleventh grade. Other times most frequently cited reasons for dropping out include failing grades, suspensions and expulsions, conflict with the school, pregnancy, marriage and economic hardship. Generally, students who are incarcerated are not counted in the total number of dropouts. Some school districts have implemented special programs to encourage teens to stay in school. These retention programs usually include tutoring, counseling and opportunities for part-time employment at the school or in the neighborhood.

1. What is the main idea of the passage?

    (A) Everyone should graduate from high school.

    (B) More males drop out of school than females.

    (C) There are many reasons why students drop out of school.

    (D) Some southern states have large numbers of students who do not graduate from high school.

    (E) Many students would stay in school if they could work part time.

2. Which of the following is not stated in the passage?

    (A) Students in jail are not included in the total number of dropouts.

(B)   Some states have dropout rates of 18%.

(C)   Some students are labeled dropouts when they have moved out of the district.

(D)   Tutoring programs before and after school may be successful in encouraging some teens to stay in school.

(E)   Many students drop out in the eleventh grade.

3.   Which statement best summarizes the author's attitude?

(A)   The drop out problem is of little importance to the author.

(B)   The author believes that teachers should spend more time encouraging students to stay in school.

(C)   The author feels that the dropout problem is complex.

(D)   Dropout prevention programs are a simple solution.

(E)   The author has the attitude that anyone who drops out of school is stupid.

DETAILED EXPLANATIONS
OF PASSAGE I

1.   **(D)**   Although the author of the passage might agree with answer (A), this belief is not expressed in the paragraph. Answers (B) and (C) are both included in the paragraph but neither statement summarizes the content of the whole passage. Answer (E) refers to programs designed to keep students in school, but this is only a small portion of the entire passage, and therefore is not the main idea. The correct answer is (D) because it paraphrases the topic of the entire passage which is stated in the first and second sentences.

2.   **(C)**   Answer (A) is specifically stated in the eighth sentence of the passage. Answer (B) is stated in the second sentence. Answer (D) is stated in the last two sentences. Answer (E) is stated in the sixth sentence. Answer (C) is correct because the paragraph does not discuss students moving out of the district.

3.   **(C)**   This question requires you to determine the author's attitude, although it is not specifically stated in the passage. Answer (A) is not appropriate because the entire passage discusses the dropout problem, and the topic must be of concern to the author. Answer (B) is incorrect because there is no mention of teachers in the passage. Answer (D) is possible because the author does discuss dropout prevention programs; however, the author does not state or imply that such programs are simple solutions to the problem. Although the author might agree with answer (E), there is no evidence of this in the passage. Answer (C) is the best answer because it refers to the main idea, and it can be inferred from the discussion that the author feels the dropout problem is complex and has many contributing factors.

PASSAGE II

This sample passage may apply to these tests:

ACT

DIRECTIONS: Each passage below is followed by questions based on its content. Answer all questions following a passage on the basis of what is STATED or IMPLIED in that passage.

Dr. Robert H. Goddard, at one time a physics professor at Clark University, Worcester, Massachusetts, was largely responsible for the sudden interest in rockets back in the 1920s. When Dr. Goddard first started his experiments with rockets, no related technical information was available. He started a new science, industry, and field of engineering. Through his scientific experiments, he pointed the way to the development of rockets as we know them today. The Smithsonian Institute agreed to finance his experiments in 1920. From these experiments he wrote a paper titled "A Method of Reaching Extreme Altitudes," in which he outlined a space rocket of the step (multistage) principle, theoretically capable of reaching the moon.

Goddard discovered that with a properly shaped, smooth, tapered nozzle he could increase the ejection velocity eight times with the same weight of fuel. This would not only drive a rocket eight times faster, but 64 times farther, according to his theory. Early in his experiments he found that solid-fuel rockets would not give him the high power or the duration of power needed for a dependable supersonic motor capable of extreme altitudes. On March 16, 1926, after many trials, Dr. Goddard successfully fired, for the first time in history, a liquid-fuel rocket into the air. It attained an altitude of 184 feet and a speed of 60 mph. This seems small as compared to present-day speeds and heights of missile flights, but instead of trying to achieve speed or altitude at this time, Dr. Goddard was trying to develop a dependable rocket motor.

Dr. Goddard later was the first to fire a rocket that reached a speed faster than the speed of sound. He was first to develop a gyroscopic steering apparatus for rockets. He was the first to use vanes in the jet stream for rocket stabilization during the initial phase of a rocket flight. And he was first to patent the idea of step rockets. After proving on paper and in actual tests that a rocket can travel in a vacuum, he developed the mathematical theory of rocket propulsion and rocket flight, including basic designs for long-range rockets. All of this information was available to our military men before World War II, but evidently its immediate use did not seem applicable. Near the end of World War II we started intense work on rocket-powered guided missiles, using the experiments and developments of Dr. Goddard and the American Rocket Society.

1. The passage implies that Dr. Goddard, a physics professor,

    (A)   was the father of the science of rocketry.

    (B)   started a new science, industry, and field of engineering.

    (C)   pointed the way to the development of rockets.

    (D)   outlined the principle of multistage space rockets.

    (E)   was responsible for interest in rockets in the 1920s.

2. One can assume from the article that

    (A)   , all factors being equal, a proper shape of the rocket nozzle would increase the ejection velocity and travel distance.

    (B)   solid-fuel rockets would give higher power and duration.

    (C)   blunt nozzle would negatively affect speed and distance.

    (D)   supersonic motors are needed for extreme altitudes.

    (E)   the first successfully fired liquid fueled rocket was for developing a dependable rocket motor.

3. Among Dr. Goddard's many achievements, the most far-reaching was

    (A)   the development of a rocket stabilizing steering mechanism.

    (B)   the development of liquid rocket fuel.

    (C)   the development of use of vanes for rocket stabilizing.

    (D)   the development of the gyroscope.

    (E)   his thesis for multistage rocket design.

4. It can be inferred from the selection that Goddard's mathematical theory and design

    (A)   are applicable to other types of rocket-powered vehicles.

    (B)   included basic designs for long-range rockets.

    (C)   utilized vanes in jet streams for rocket stabilization.

    (D)   tested rocket travel in a vacuum.

    (E)   produced gyroscopic steering apparatus.

5.   Dr. Goddard made which of the following assumptions about rockets?

(A)   The amount of fuel had to be in direct proportion to the ejection velocity desired.

(B)   All other factors being equal, the shape of the rocket nozzle increases the ejection velocity and distance to the desired effect.

(C)   A medium of air was not a required component for rocket flight.

(D)   Dependability was more important than speed and distance.

(E)   Solid rocket fuel failed to deliver high power for an extended duration.

DETAILED EXPLANATIONS
OF PASSAGE II

1.   **(A)**   (B), (C), (D), and (E) are stated in paragraph one. (A) is the correct choice. It is inferred from sentence three, paragraph one, "He *started* a new science."

2.   **(C)**   (A) is stated in paragraph two, sentence one. (B) is a negative statement; paragraph two, sentence three states the opposite. (D) is an incorrect choice; paragraph two, sentence four states "a dependable supersonic motor." Paragraph two, the last sentence states (E). (C) is the correct choice. Paragraph two, sentence one states "smooth, tapered nozzle increases velocity by eight times and distance by 64 times," implying that a blunt nozzle negatively affects both speed and distance.

3.   **(E)**   (A), (B), (C), and (D) are stated and share a part-to-whole relationship with (E). Without the whole, the multistage principle contained within Goddard's thesis, the development of the parts would have been directionless; therefore, (E) is the correct answer.

4.   **(A)**   (B), (C), (D), and (E) are explicitly stated. (A) is the correct choice. It is inferred from the statement "proving on paper and in actual test that a rocket can travel in a vacuum ... basic designs...."

5.   **(C)**   (A) is a false statement. (B), (D), and (E) are stated in the passage. (C) is the correct choice. "A rocket could travel in a vacuum" suggests that a medium of air is not necessary for rocket flight.

PASSAGE III

This sample passage may apply to these tests:

GRE General and GMAT

DIRECTIONS: Each passage below is followed by questions based on its content. Answer all questions following a passage on the basis of what is STATED or IMPLIED in that passage.

Being born female and black were two handicaps Gwendolyn Brooks states that she faced from her birth, in 1917, in Kansas. Brooks was determined to succeed. Despite the lack of encouragement she received from her teachers and others, she was determined to write and found the first publisher for one of her poems when she was eleven.

In 1945 she marketed and sold her first book; national recognition ensued. She applied for and received grants and fellowships from such organizations as the American Academy of Arts and Letters and the Guggenheim Foundation. Later she received the Pulitzer Prize for Poetry; she was the first black woman to receive such an honor.

Brooks was an integrationist in the 1940s and an advocate of black consciousness in the 1960s. Her writing styles show that she is not bound by rules; her works are not devoid of the truth, even about sensitive subjects like the black experience, life in the ghetto, and city life.

Brooks' reaction to fame is atypical. She continues to work—and work hard. She writes, travels, and helps many who are interested in writing. Especially important to her is increasing her knowledge of her black heritage and encouraging other people to do the same. She encourages dedication to the art to would-be writers.

1. From the article one could say that Brooks could be best described as which of the following?

   (A) Humanistic

   (B) Circumspect

   (C) Obscure

   (D) Craven

   (E) Alienated

2. The passage implies that Brooks received less credit than she deserved primarily because of which of the following?

(A)   She tried to publish too early in her career.

(B)   She was aided by funds received through grants.

(C)   She was a frequent victim of both racial and gender discrimination.

(D)   Her work was too complex to be of widespread interest to others.

(E)   She had no interest in the accolades of her colleagues.

3.   If the next sentence in the passage were a statement from Brooks, which of the following might most likely be her words?

(A)   "Awards are not important; write what you want to say."

(B)   "Develop a style of your own and do not depart from this art form."

(C)   "*Art* is what the public calls *art*. Find out what this is and 'go for it'."

(D)   "If you sincerely dedicate yourself to your art form, there will be little room left for current events and loneliness."

(E)   "Study the classics before you begin; they are essential elements after which you must pattern your writing if you are to be dedicated to the arts."

DETAILED EXPLANATIONS
OF PASSAGE III

1.   **(A)**   Brooks can best be described, from the list of words given, as HU-MANISTIC. Her concern with integration, black consciousness, would-be writers, and her choice of writing topics illustrate why choice (A) is appropriate. (B) is incorrect. Brooks is not afraid to pursue a cause which causes criticism of her from some groups. For those who seek to criticize, she is not CIRCUMSPECT. (C) is false; Brooks is not OBSCURE. She is the most famous black poet writing in our country today. (D) is incorrect; Brooks is not cowardly or CRAVEN. She is not afraid to work for that which she believes is right—even if it might not give her popularity in all circles. (E) is a poor choice. Brooks is not withdrawn or ALIENATED from society. She continues to write and to travel about working with would-be writers.

2.   **(C)**   Brooks was a published writer by eleven; (A) is incorrect. Grants did not lessen, but heighten, her prestige; (B) is incorrect. (C) is the correct answer. After her first book was sold, she received nationwide recognition; (D) is wrong. Brooks takes an interest in others; (E) is incorrect.

3.   **(A)**   Brooks believes in writing what one has to say regardless of whether one is rewarded by others. (A) is a statement similar to what she tells would-be writers on her travels. Brooks does not use just one style of writing; she writes different poems using different styles. She is not bound by tradition. This does not sound like the advice she would give others. (B) is incorrect. (C) Brooks would not believe in writing just to please others. She would believe it more important to please one's self. Brooks would not tell others to write just to sell; (C) is not typical of Brooks. Brooks has always found room for causes and people in her busy life. She would not encourage others to withdraw from life but to experience life. It is from her life experiences that she draws most of her writing ideas; (D) is incorrect. Brooks does not pattern her writing after one writer; neither does she stick to one style in her works. (E) would not be a suggestion she would make.

PASSAGE IV

This sample passage may apply to these tests:
LSAT and MCAT

DIRECTIONS: Each passage below is followed by questions based on its content. Answer all questions following a passage on the basis of what is STATED or IMPLIED in that passage.

Today the role of business and government in solving social problems remains a controversial topic. Children no longer work in factories. Working hours for both men and women are regulated by government. Some observers feel that New Deal legislation sponsored by President Franklin D. Roosevelt provided the major thrust for governmental regulation of private sector personnel practices that were too long within the exclusive jurisdiction of industry and business management. At first the Supreme Court struck Roosevelt-initiated statutes. But the sentiment of the country and appointment of men politically sensitive to the political goals of the President led to judicial support of laws designed to deal with social ills in the country. In the 1930s and early 1940s, Congress followed the leadership of the top executive who proposed such legislation as Social Security, workers' compensation, and mandatory minimum wages. At that time a desire for change was ripe due to economic chaos caused by the Great Depression. Business and industry managers were suddenly cast into a different role when Congress and the Supreme Court became allies in authorizing governmental intrusion into the private sector's arena. Swift changes led to new professional expertise required for interpretation of law, additional paperwork, and implementation of personnel policies.

By the 1950s, long-standing racial discrimination was challenged. Congress had remained aloof too long and generally ignored problems associated with inequality. The NAACP bypassed the legislative branch and took its case to the judicial branch. By the 1960s, President Lyndon Johnson influenced Congress to take bold steps that eventually called for changes in the workplace. Title VII was passed, and a reduction of inequities was expected. However, NAACP director of labor, Joann Riggs, said in 1987 that racial discrimination remains, but federal legislation "does provide an avenue people can use to seek redress."

America has often been called a "melting pot" because of the variety of ethnic, cultural, and racial heritages of its citizens. With the exception of great flow of people from Africa before the early 1800s and the Chinese in the late 1880s, the majority of immigrants came from western Europe. The government set a national quota system. By the 1960s, laws changed and so did the national origin of immigrants, with the majority entering the country from Asia and Latin

America. The number of immigrants has grown to around nine million people coming into the country during a 10 year span. When employers hire immigrants, citizens whose ancestors could be traced back to more than one generation feel threatened when jobs are scarce. Competition for jobs is a major issue. Congressional response placed a large paperwork burden on the personnel departments of business and industry. The Immigration Reform and Control Act of 1986 penalizes employers who hire illegal aliens. Today, personnel offices must be accountable to the government with regard to the legal status of their employees. Documents must show that non-citizens have acquired authorization to work in this country. Some observers feel that governmental rules may drive illegal aliens from the workplace and that no one else will want to perform the low-level tasks required in some of the jobs.

1.   Where was political leadership lodged in the mid-twentieth century?

   (A)   It is evident that the author felt that President Roosevelt as chief executive should have stayed out of the legislative process and relied more on the judicial process.

   (B)   The author explained how President Roosevelt changed the direction of the government by showing a stronger social orientation than national leaders of judicial and executive branches in earlier years.

   (C)   Although new legislation was passed, the laws more or less left business and industry personnel policies intact by the 1940s.

   (D)   At first President Roosevelt had to rely more on the courts than on stubborn legislators in order to pass laws designed to deal with social problems.

   (E)   The above paragraphs show that personnel practices of business and industry have little impact on social problems in the country.

2.   What kinds of changes occurred due to strong leadership from the Oval Office?

   (A)   One can gather that bills sponsored by Roosevelt were successful in Congress because they were supported by the effective lobbying influence of business and industry.

   (B)   The reader can assume that when the Roosevelt administration enforced new laws described above, the manufacturing and business labor expenditures increased accordingly.

   (C)   Organizations representing the interests of business most likely welcomed changes in Supreme Court personnel appointed by Roosevelt.

(D)　Roosevelt's keen interest lay in ending racial discrimination through passage of the Special Security Act.

(E)　President Roosevelt was elected. He immediately appointed new justices on the Supreme Court. Then he submitted to Congress proposed legislation. The Supreme Court approved the bills, and then Congress passed the laws.

3.　Although observers may argue about what really happened during Roosevelt's term of office, interpret the factual information presented by the author by selecting the best description below.

(A)　New Deal legislation received its name from the deals the President made with business and industry for the purpose of pulling the rug out from under Congress, so to speak.

(B)　Evolution and transformation of labor policies increased at a rapid pace during the Roosevelt administration.

(C)　The author has inferred that historically the name "Great Depression" was a phrase that caught on after the press disclosed Roosevelt's mood when the Supreme Court struck the first three social welfare bills passed by Congress.

(D)　Strange alliances are often formed in the political arena. Unorganized labor and their representatives in the legislature were seldom impressed with promises of reforms which would lead to a welfare state.

(E)　During Roosevelt's term of office, racial discrimination was addressed vigorously, ending with the passage of the Civil Rights Act of 1964.

4.　Below are several statements that deal with discrimination in the workplace. Choose the sentence that conforms the author's analysis.

(A)　The recent immigration act is possibly the best example of affirmative action in recent years.

(B)　Illegal aliens are part of the establishment.

(C)　When business and industry employers ignored social problems associated with hiring illegal aliens, the government eventually stepped into the vacuum created by private sector negligence and mandated constructive activities.

(D)   Private sector and public sector policy makers by and large have the same goals when trying to solve social problems of employees.

(E)   The author implies that the statement made by Joann Riggs shows how the ruling elite often fails to be responsive to public opinion through institutional mechanisms.

5.   What is the major problem that stems from the way problems of non-Caucasians are handled by government?

(A)   Conflict among job applicants competing for scarce jobs has heightened friction among citizens whose differences are based on cultural, racial, or ethnic factors.

(B)   The term "melting pot" reflects the resolution of problems through direct representation.

(C)   The author maintains that political socialization, in the long run, must be the major responsibility of each ethnic and racial group living in the United States.

(D)   The author refused to deal with the problem of income distribution for illegal aliens.

(E)   One of the most interesting disclosures is the under-the-table wheeling and dealing of President Johnson who sought to undermine the NAACP's goals when he proposed separate-but-equal policies in schools and the factories.

6.   How did the federal government respond to evidence of widely practiced discrimination during other presidential administrations that followed the Roosevelt years?

(A)   Legislative leadership in eradicating racial discrimination was apparent, especially after special interests effectively pressured individual members of Congress immediately after World War II.

(B)   At first the judicial branch was the pathfinder in approving policies for eliminating racial discriminatory practices, but the administrative chief of the federal executive branch eventually prodded the legislative branch to pass major civil rights laws.

(C)   During the 10 to 15 years following President Roosevelt's death, the legislative branch moved speedily in the policymaking arena and protected black citizens more than the judicial and executive branches combined.

(D)   President Roosevelt, had he lived another 30 years, would have been ashamed of the executive and judicial branches when they over-turned strong civil rights laws that he managed to push through Congress.

(E)   President Johnson was too busy with domestic and foreign policies to provide leadership in the civil rights movement. Besides, everyone knows that he was from Texas.

DETAILED EXPLANATIONS
OF PASSAGE IV

1.   **(B)**   Answer (B) is correct. Although President Roosevelt was powerless when the Supreme Court made void several new laws, he persisted. Under other presidents Congress had earlier passed laws to protect the safety and health of children. It is the proper conclusion that Roosevelt's record showed that he was indeed more social welfare oriented while in the Oval Office than earlier presidents. Answer (A) tries to figure out the author's preferences. His analyses of the judicial process does not indicate that he favored the judicial over the executive. Answer (C) is wrong. The pre-1950 laws initiated tremendous change in governmental regulation of management practices previously left to the private sector. Answer (D) deals with chronology. Reviewing the text above, the reader will find that the judicial branch resisted change wanted by both Congress and the President. Answer (E) deals with sociological inferences. Consider the fate of young Dagenhart who as a young uneducated man was penalized by personnel practices of his boss when he was a child laborer.

2.   **(B)**   Answer (B) correctly assumes that such benefits as higher wages and fewer working hours would increase expenditures of manufacturing and business. Answer (A) requires review of how federal legislation attempted to change management/labor relations and improve the lot of the workers. Executive-sponsored bills described by the author were challenged in courts of law by business and industry. Answer (C) does not consider how new justices whose legal philosophy would radically increase the amount of government regulation, much to the detriment of freedom, to make decisions in the private sector. Answer (D) is wrong. Check the paragraphs again, and note that the author correctly gave no credit to Roosevelt for aggressive leadership in civil rights. There is no such act. Answer (E) is chronologically and factually incorrect. Note that the author discusses how the Supreme Court voided social legislation supported by Roosevelt. Later, he nominated justices to the Supreme Court. Nowhere does the author suggest that the Supreme Court acted in an advisory capacity before Congress passed social legislation.

3.   **(B)**   Answer (B) correctly concludes that although Congress had tried in earlier years to make great differences in labor policies, it was not until the Supreme Court interpretation changed during Roosevelt's term of office that new labor laws were rapidly passed and enforced. Answer (A) is wrong. The author does not imply that the term New Deal originated from such bizarre circumstances. Answer (C) is wrong. The Great Depression dealt with the economic situation; the author did not suggest any other definition. Rather he writes of economic problems. Answer (D) has misinterpreted the author's analysis. Since the welfare state seeks to assure minimum standards of all people, both workers and their representatives agreed that labor

conditions and wages should be improved. Answer (E) is incorrect. Note the dates cited by the author. Roosevelt was President during the 1930s and early 1940s. The Civil Rights Act was passed in 1964.

4.   **(C)**   Answer (C) correctly illustrates how governmental intrusion expands when leaders in the private sector fail to make fair policies. Answer (A) does not consider how the act works to the detriment of illegal aliens trying to find jobs rather than protecting them against discrimination. Answer (B) improperly assessed the status of illegal aliens. Their political weakness lies in the fact that they have very few links with those who are in power. Answer (D) is erroneous, as proved by the author as he traces tensions between the two sectors. Answer (E) misconstrues the statement, for she affirms that laws have provided ways to grieve unfair policies and behavior.

5.   **(A)**   Answer (A) is certainly well illustrated in the author's passage. As nine million people of foreign birth enter the United States when jobs are at a premium, friction will most likely develop. Answer (B) is incorrect in defining "melting pot" and introducing the term "direct representation," which was not suggested by the author. Answer (C) is wrong. In fact, the author carefully outlines how government has addressed several issues that affect political socialization of immigrants. Answer (D) is in error. The author examined the problem of inequalities that blacks experienced and how laws should help overcome inequality in the workplace — an important factor in income distribution. Answer (E) has misread the description of Johnson's role in fostering civil rights.

6.   **(B)**   (B) is the correct answer. Note how the NAACP successfully filed action in the federal court. Finally, President Johnson worked with Congress in fashioning civil rights laws. Answer (A) is incorrect. The record shows, as the author relates, that Congress was insensitive to the needs of black citizens during the years immediately following Roosevelt's administration. Answer (C) is wrong. Both the legislative and executive branches took little action in erasing inequality. Answer (D) wrongly assigns aggressive executive leadership in the civil rights movement to President Roosevelt. President Johnson's civil rights activities far exceeded Roosevelt's influence in passing laws, such as Title VII. Answer (E) is only partially correct. President Johnson was a Texan. Although Title VII was a giant step in enforcing equality, the author pointed out that pockets of prejudice remains.

CHAPTER 5

Critical Reading

➤ Critical Reading Review
➤ Sample Passages
➤ Attacking the Critical Reading Section
➤ Practice Test

CRITICAL READING
REVIEW

Study this chapter for the following tests:

PSAT and SAT I

The critical reading sections of the SAT are indeed critical, for they comprise 50 percent of the entire verbal section content and 75 percent of its allotted time. "Why," you must wonder, "would this much importance be attached to reading?" The reason is simple. Your ability to read at a strong pace while grasping a solid understanding of the material is a key factor in your high school performance and your potential college success, and the college admission boards know it. But "critical" can be taken in another sense, for the SAT will ask you to be a reading critic. You'll need not only to be able to summarize the material but analyze it, make judgments about it, and make educated guesses about what the writer implies and infers. Even your ability to understand vocabulary in context will come under scrutiny. "Can I," you ask yourself, "meet the challenge?" Yes, and preparation is the means!

THE DIRECTIONS

Make sure to study and learn the directions to save yourself time during the actual test. You should simply skim them when beginning the section. The directions will read similar to the following.

DIRECTIONS: Read each passage and answer the questions that follow. Each question will be based on the information stated or implied in the passage or its introduction.

A variation of these directions will be presented as follows for the double passage.

DIRECTIONS: Read the passage and answer the questions that follow. Each question will be based on the information stated or implied in the selection or its introduction, and may be based on the relationship between the passages.

CRITICAL READING PASSAGES AND QUESTIONS

Within the SAT verbal section you will be given four critical reading passages, one of 400–550 words, one of 550–700 words, one of 700–850 words, and two reading selections of 700–850 words combined referred to as a double passage. The double passage will be composed of two separate works which can be related to one another. The reading content of the passages will cover:

- the humanities (philosophy, the fine arts)

- the social sciences (psychology, archaeology, anthropology, economics political science, sociology, history)

- the natural sciences (biology, geology, astronomy, chemistry, physics)

- narration (fiction, non-fiction)

Following each passage are about 5–13 questions, totaling 38–40 in all. These questions are in four types:

1. Synthesis/Analysis

2. Evaluation

3. Vocabulary in Context

4. Interpretation

Through this review, you'll learn not only how to identify these types of questions but how to successfully attack each one. Familiarity with the test format and solid reading strategies will prove invaluable in getting you into the material quickly and through it unscathed and victorious.

THE PASSAGES

You may encounter any of a number of passage types in the Critical Reading section. These passages may consist of straight text, dialogue and text, or narration. A passage may appear by itself or as part of a pair in a double passage. A brief introduction will be provided for each passage to set the scene for the text being presented.

To familiarize yourself with the types of passages you will encounter, review the examples which follow. Remember that one passage in the section will be 400–550 words, one will be 550–700 words, one will be 700–850 words, and that the two passages in the double passage will consist of 700–850 words combined.

The content of the passages will include the humanities, social sciences, natural sciences, and also narrative text.

A humanities passage may discuss such topics as philosophy, the fine arts, and language. The following is an example of such a passage. It falls into the 550 to 700 word range.

Throughout his pursuit of knowledge and enlightenment, the philosopher Socrates made many enemies among the Greek citizens. The following passage is an account of the trial resulting from their accusations.

1   The great philosopher Socrates was put on trial in Athens in 400 B.C. on charges of corrupting the youth and of impiety. As recorded in Plato's dialogue *The Apology,* Socrates began his defense by saying he was going to "speak plainly and honestly," unlike the eloquent sophists the Athenian
5   jury was accustomed to hearing. His appeal to unadorned language offended the jurors, who were expecting to be entertained.

Socrates identified the two sets of accusers that he had to face: the past and the present. The former had filled the jurors' heads with lies about him when they were young, and was considered by Socrates to be the most
10   dangerous. The accusers from the past could not be cross-examined, and they had already influenced the jurors when they were both naive and impressionable. This offended the jury because it called into question their ability to be objective and render a fair judgment.

The philosopher addressed the charges himself, and dismissed them as
15   mere covers for the deeper attack on his philosophical activity. That activity, which involved questioning others until they revealed contradictions in their beliefs, had given rise to Socrates' motto, "The unexamined life is not worth living," and the "Socratic Method," which is still employed in many law schools today. This critical questioning of leading Athenians had made
20   Socrates very unpopular with those in power and, he insisted, was what led to his trial. This challenge to the legitimacy of the legal system itself further alienated his judges.

Socrates tried to explain that his philosophical life came about by accident. He had been content to be a humble stone mason until the day that
25   a friend informed him that the Oracle of Delphi had said that "Socrates is the wisest man in Greece." Socrates had been so surprised by this statement, and so sure of its inaccuracy, that he set about disproving it by talking to the reputed wise men of Athens and showing how much more knowledge they possessed. Unfortunately, as he told the jury, those citizens reputed to be
30   wise (politicians, businessmen, artists) turned out to be ignorant, either by knowing absolutely nothing, or by having limited knowledge in their fields of expertise and assuming knowledge of everything else. Of these, Socrates had to admit, "I am wiser, because although all of us have little knowledge, I am aware of my ignorance, while they are not." But this practice of

35   revealing prominent citizens' ignorance and arrogance did not earn Socrates their affection, especially when the bright young men of Athens began following him around and delighting in the disgracing of their elders. Hence, in his view, the formal charges of "corrupting the youth" and "impiety" were a pretext to retaliate for the deeper offense of challenging

40   the pretensions of the establishment.

       Although Socrates viewed the whole trial as a sham, he cleverly refuted the charges by using the same method of questioning that got him in trouble in the first place. Against the charges of corrupting the youth, Socrates asked his chief accuser, Meletus, if any wanted to arm himself, to which

45   Meletus answered, "no." Then, Socrates asked if one's associates had an effect on one: Good people for good, and evil people for evil, to which Meletus answered, "yes." Next, Socrates asked if corrupting one's companions makes them better or worse, to which Meletus responded, "worse." Finally Socrates set the trap by asking Meletus if Socrates had corrupted the

50   youth intentionally or unintentionally. Meletus, wanting to make the charges as bad as possible, answered, "intentionally." Socrates showed the contradictory nature of the charge, since by intentionally corrupting his companions he made them worse, thereby bringing harm on himself. He also refuted the second charge of impiety in the same manner, by showing

55   that its two components (teaching about strange gods and atheism) were inconsistent.

       Although Socrates had logically refuted the charges against him, the Athenian jury found him guilty, and Meletus proposed the death penalty. The defendant Socrates was allowed to propose an alternative penalty and

60   Socrates proposed a state pension, so he could continue his philosophical activity to the benefit of Athens. He stated that this is what he deserved. The Athenian jury, furious over his presumption, voted the death penalty and, thus, one of the great philosophers of the Western heritage was executed.

The social science passage may discuss such topics as psychology, archaeology, anthropology, economics, political science, sociology, and history. The following is an example of such a passage. It falls into the 400 to 550 word range.

Not only does music have the ability to entertain and enthrall, but it also has the capacity to heal. The following passage illustrates the recent indoctrination of music therapy.

1   Music's power to affect moods and stir emotions has been well known for as long as music has existed. Stories about the music of ancient Greece tell of the healing powers of Greek music. Leopold Mozart, the father of Wolfgang, wrote that if the Greeks' music could heal the sick, then our

5   music should be able to bring the dead back to life. Unfortunately, today's music cannot do quite that much.

The healing power of music, taken for granted by ancient man and by many primitive societies, is only recently becoming accepted by medical professionals as a new way of healing the emotionally ill.

10 Using musical activities involving patients, the music therapist seeks to restore mental and physical health. Music therapists usually work with emotionally disturbed patients as part of a team of therapists and doctors. Music therapists work together with physicians, psychiatrists, psychologists, physical therapists, nurses, teachers, recreation leaders, and families 15 of patients.

The rehabilitation that a music therapist gives to patients can be in the form of listening, performing, lessons on an instrument or even composing. A therapist may help a patient regain lost coordination by teaching the patient how to play an instrument. Speech defects can sometimes be helped 20 by singing activities. Some patients need the social awareness of group activities, but others may need individual attention to build self-confidence. The music therapist must learn what kinds of activities are best for each patient.

In addition to working with patients, the music therapist has to attend 25 meetings with other therapists and doctors that work with the same patients to discuss progress and plan new activities. Written reports to doctors about patients' responses to treatment are another facet of the music therapist's work.

Hospitals, schools, retirement homes, and community agencies and 30 clinics are some of the sites where music therapists work. Some music therapists work in private studies with patients that are sent to them by medical doctors, psychologists, and psychiatrists. Music therapy can be done in studios, recreation rooms, hospital wards, or classrooms depending on the type of activity and needs of the patients.

35 Qualified music therapists have followed a four-year course with a major emphasis in music plus courses in biological science, anthropology, sociology, psychology, and music therapy. General studies in English, history, speech, and government complete the requirements for a Bachelor of Music Therapy. After college training, a music therapist must participate 40 in a six-month training internship under the guidance of a registered music therapist.

Students who have completed college courses and have demonstrated their ability during the six-month internship can become registered music therapists by applying to the National Association for Music Therapy, Inc. 45 New methods and techniques of music therapy are always being developed, so the trained therapist must continue to study new articles, books, and reports throughout his/her career.

The natural science passage may discuss such topics as biology, geology, astronomy, chemistry, and physics. The following is an example of such a passage. It falls into the 550 to 700 word range.

The following article was written by a physical chemist and recounts the conflict between volcanic matter in the atmosphere and airplane windows. It was published in a scientific periodical in 1989. (Reprinted by permission of American Heritage Magazine, *a division of Forbes Inc., Forbes Inc., 1989.)*

1   Several years ago the airlines discovered a new kind of problem — a window problem. The acrylic windows on some of their 747s were getting hazy and dirty-looking. Suspicious travelers thought the airlines might have stopped cleaning them, but the windows were not dirty; they were inexpli-
5   cably deteriorating within as little as 390 hours of flight time, even though they were supposed to last for five to ten years. Boeing looked into it.

At first the company thought the culprit might be one well known in modern technology, the component supplier who changes materials without telling the customer. Boeing quickly learned this was not the case, so there
10   followed an extensive investigation that eventually brought in the Air Transport Association, geologists, and specialists in upper-atmosphere chemistry, and the explanation turned out to be not nearly so mundane. Indeed, it began to look like a grand reenactment of an ancient Aztec myth: the struggle between the eagle and the serpent, which is depicted on the
15   Mexican flag.

The serpent in this case is an angry Mexican volcano, El Chichon. Like its reptilian counterpart, it knows how to spit venom at the eyes of its adversary. In March and April of 1982 the volcano, in an unusual eruption pattern, ejected millions of tons of sulfur-rich material directly into the
20   stratosphere. In less than a year, a stratospheric cloud had blanketed the entire Northern Hemisphere. Soon the photochemistry of the upper atmosphere converted much of the sulfur into tiny droplets of concentrated sulfuric acid.

The eagle in the story is the 747, poking occasionally into the lower
25   part of the stratosphere in hundreds of passenger flights daily. Its two hundred windows are made from an acrylic polymer, which makes beautifully clear, strong windows but was never intended to withstand attack by strong acids.

The stratosphere is very different from our familiar troposphere envi-
30   ronment. Down here the air is humid, with a lot of vertical convection to carry things up and down; the stratosphere is bone-dry, home to the continent-striding jet stream, with unceasing horizontal winds at an average of 120 miles per hour. A mist of acid droplets accumulated gradually near the lower edge of the stratosphere, settling there at a thickness of about a mile a
35   year, was able to wait for planes to come along.

As for sulfuric acid, most people know only the relatively benign liquid in a car battery: 80 percent water and 20 percent acid. The stratosphere dehydrated the sulfuric acid into a persistent, corrosive mist 75 percent pure acid, an extremely aggressive liquid. Every time the 747 poked into the
40 stratosphere — on almost every long flight — acid droplets struck the windows and began to react with their outer surface, causing it to swell. This built up stresses between the softened outer layer and the underlying material. Finally, parallel hairline cracks developed, creating the hazy appearance. The crazing was sped up by the mechanical stresses always
45 present in the windows of a pressurized cabin.

The airlines suffered through more than a year of window replacements before the acid cloud finally dissipated. Ultimately the drops reached the lower edge of the stratosphere, were carried away into the lower atmosphere, and finally came down in the rain. In the meantime, more resistant window materials and coatings were developed. (As for the man-made
50 sulfur dioxide that causes acid rain, it never gets concentrated enough to attack the window material. El Chichon was unusual in its ejection of sulfur directly into the stratosphere, and the 747 is unusual in its frequent entrance into the stratosphere.)

As for the designers of those windows, it is hard to avoid the conclusion
55 that a perfectly adequate engineering design was defeated by bad luck. After all, this was the only time since the invention of the airplane that there were acid droplets of this concentration in the upper atmosphere. But reliability engineers, an eminently rational breed, are very uncomfortable when asked to talk about luck. In principle it should be possible to antici-
60 pate events, and the failure to do so somehow seems like a professional failure. The cosmos of the engineer has no room for poltergeists, demons, or other mystic elements. But might it accommodate the inexorable scenario of an ancient Aztec myth?

A narrative passage dealing with fictional material may be in the form of dialogue between characters, or one character speaking to the reader. The following is an example of the latter. It falls into the 700 to 850 word range.

In this passage, the narrator discovers that he has been transported to King Arthur's court in the year 528 A.D.

1 The moment I got a chance I slipped aside privately and touched an ancient common-looking man on the shoulder and said, in an insinuating, confidential way —

"Friend, do me a kindness. Do you belong to the asylum, or are you just
5 here on a visit or something like that?"

He looked me over stupidly, and said —

"Marry, fair sir, me seemeth —"

"That will do," I said; "I reckon you are a patient."

I moved away, cogitating, and at the same time keeping an eye out for
any chance passenger in his right mind that might come along and give me
some light. I judged I had found one, presently; so I drew him aside and
said in his ear —

"If I could see the head keeper a minute — only just a minute —"

"Prithee do not let me."

"Let you *what?*"

"*Hinder* me, then, if the word please thee better." Then he went on to
say he was an under-cook and could not stop to gossip, though he would
like it another time; for it would comfort his very liver to know where I got
my clothes. As he started away he pointed and said yonder was one who
was idle enough for my purpose, and was seeking me besides, no doubt.
This was an airy slim boy in shrimp-colored tights that made him look like
a forked carrot; the rest of his gear was blue silk and dainty laces and
ruffles; and he had long yellow curls, and wore a plumed pink satin cap
tilted complacently over his ear. By his look, he was good-natured; by his
gait, he was satisfied with himself. He was pretty enough to frame. He
arrived, looked me over with a smiling and impudent curiosity; said he had
come for me, and informed me that he was a page.

"Go 'long," I said; "you ain't more than a paragraph."

It was pretty severe, but I was nettled. However, it never phazed him;
he didn't appear to know he was hurt. He began to talk and laugh, in happy,
thoughtless, boyish fashion, as we walked along, and made himself old
friends with me at once; asked me all sorts of questions about myself and
about my clothes, but never waited for an answer — always chattered
straight ahead, as if he didn't know he had asked a question and wasn't
expecting any reply, until at last he happened to mention that he was born in
the beginning of the year 513.

It made the cold chills creep over me! I stopped, and said, a little
faintly:

"Maybe I didn't hear you just right. Say it again — and say it slow. What
year was it?"

"513."

"513! You don't look it! Come, my boy, I am a stranger and friendless:
be honest and honorable with me. Are you in your right mind?"

He said he was.

45   "Are these other people in their right minds?"

He said they were.

"And this isn't an asylum? I mean, it isn't a place where they cure crazy people?"

He said it wasn't.

50   "Well, then," I said, "either I am a lunatic, or something just as awful has happened. Now tell me, honest and true, where am I?"

"IN KING ARTHUR'S COURT."

I waited a minute, to let that idea shudder its way home, and then said:

"And according to your notions, what year is it now?"

55   "528 — nineteenth of June."

I felt a mournful sinking at the heart, and muttered: "I shall never see my friends again — never, never again. They will not be born for more than thirteen hundred years yet."

I seemed to believe the boy, I didn't know why. *Something* in me
60   seemed to believe him — my consciousness, as you may say; but my reason didn't. My reason straightway began to clamor; that was natural. I didn't know how to go about satisfying it, because I knew that the testimony of men wouldn't serve — my reason would say they were lunatics, and throw out their evidence. But all of a sudden I stumbled on the very thing, just by
65   luck. I knew that the only total eclipse of the sun in the first half of the sixth century occurred on the 21st of June, A. D. 528, o. s., and began at 3 minutes after 12 noon. I also knew that no total eclipse of the sun was due in what to *me* was the present year — *i. e.*, 1879. So, if I could keep my anxiety and curiosity from eating the heart out of me for forty-eight hours, I should then
70   find out for certain whether this boy was telling me the truth or not.

A narrative passage dealing with non-fiction material may appear in the form of a speech or any such discourse in which one person speaks to a group of people or to the reader. The following two selections are examples of non-fiction narratives. Together, they are also an example of a double passage, in which the subject matter in the selections can be either compared or contrasted. As you will recall, the two selections will total 700 to 850 words to form the double passage.

The following passages are excerpts from two different Presidential Inaugural Addresses. Passage 1 was given by President Franklin D. Roosevelt on March 4, 1933. Passage 2 comes from President John F. Kennedy's Inaugural Address, given on January 20, 1961.

Passage 1

1   Let every nation know, whether it wishes us well or ill, that we shall pay any price, bear any burden, meet any hardship, support any friend, oppose any foe to assure the survival and the success of liberty.

This much we pledge — and more.

5   To those old allies whose cultural and spiritual origins we share, we pledge the loyalty of faithful friends. United, there is little we cannot do in a host of co-operative ventures. Divided, there is little we can do, for we dare not meet a powerful challenge at odds and split asunder.

To those new states whom we welcome to the ranks of the free, we
10   pledge our word that one form of colonial control shall not have passed away merely to be replaced by a far more iron tyranny. We shall not always expect to find them supporting our view. But we shall always hope to find them strongly supporting their own freedom, and to remember that, in the past, those who foolishly sought power by riding the back of the tiger ended
15   up inside.

To those peoples in the huts and villages of half the globe struggling to break the bonds of mass misery, we pledge our best efforts to help them help themselves, for whatever period is required, not because the Communists may be doing it, not because we seek their votes, but because it is
20   right. If a free society cannot help the many who are poor, it cannot save the few who are rich.

Passage 2

This is pre-eminently the time to speak the truth, the whole truth, frankly and boldly. Nor need we shrink from honestly facing conditions in our country today. This great nation will endure as it has endured, will
25   revive, and will prosper.

So first of all let me assert my firm belief that the only thing we have to fear is fear itself — nameless, unreasoning, unjustified terror, which paralyzes needed efforts to convert retreat into advance.

In every dark hour of our national life a leadership of frankness and
30   vigor has met with that understanding and support of the people themselves which is essential to victory. I am convinced that you will again give that support to leadership in these critical days.

In such a spirit on my part and yours we face our common difficulties. They concern, thank God, only material things. Values have shrunken to
35   fantastic levels; taxes have risen; our ability to pay has fallen; government of all kinds is faced by serious curtailment of income; the means of exchange are frozen in the currents of trade; the withered leaves of industrial enterprise lie on every side; farmers find no markets for their produce; the savings of many years in thousands of families are gone.

40   More important, a host of unemployed citizens face the grim problem of existence, and an equally great number toil with little return. Only a foolish optimist can deny the dark realities of the moment.

    Yet our distress comes from no failure of substance. We are stricken by no plague of locusts. Compared with the perils which our forefathers
45 conquered because they believed and were not afraid, we have still much to be thankful for. Nature still offers her bounty, and human efforts have multiplied it. Plenty is at our doorstep, but a generous use of it languishes in the very sight of the supply.

    Primarily, this is because the rulers of the exchange of mankind's goods
50 have failed through their own stubbornness and their own incompetence, have admitted their failure and abdicated. Practices of the unscrupulous money-changers stand indicted in the court of public opinion, rejected by the hearts and minds of men.

THE QUESTIONS

As previously mentioned, there are four major question types which appear in the Critical Reading section. The following explains what these questions will cover.

1. *Synthesis/analysis* questions deal with the structure of the passage and how one part relates to another part or to the text as a whole. These questions may ask you to look at passage details and from them, point out general themes or concepts. They might ask you to trace problems, causes, effects, and solutions or to understand the points of an argument or persuasive passage. They might ask you to compare or contrast different aspects of the passage. Synthesis/analysis questions may also involve inferences, asking you to decide what the details of the passage imply about the author's general tone or attitude. Key terms in synthesis/analysis questions are example, difference, general, compare, contrast, cause, effect, and result.

2. *Evaluation* questions involve judgments about the worth of the essay as a whole. You may be asked to consider concepts the author assumes rather than factually proves and to judge whether or not the author presents a logically consistent case. Does he/she prove the points through generalization, citing an authority, use of example, implication, personal experience, or factual data? You'll need to be able to distinguish the supportive bases for the argumentative theme. Almost as a book reviewer, you'll also be asked to pinpoint the author's writing techniques. What is the style, the tone? Who is the intended audience? How might the author's points relate to information outside the essay, itself? Key terms you'll often see in evaluation questions and answer choices are generalization, implication, and support.

3. *Vocabulary in context* questions occur in several formats. You'll be given easy words with challenging choices or the reverse. You'll need to know multiple meanings of words. You'll encounter difficult words and difficult choices. In some cases, your knowledge of prefixes-roots-suffixes will gain you clear advantage. In addition, connotations will be the means of deciding, in some cases, which answer is the best. Of course, how the term works in the textual context is the key to the issue.

4. *Interpretation* questions ask you to decide on a valid explanation or clarification of the author's points. Based on the text, you'll be asked to distinguish probable motivations and effects or actions not stated outright in the essay. Furthermore, you'll need to be familiar with clichés, euphemisms, catch phrases, colloquialisms, metaphors, and similes, and be able to explain them in straightforward language. Interpretation question stems usually have a word or phrase enclosed in quotation marks.

Keep in mind that being able to categorize accurately is not of prime importance. What is important, however, is that you are familiar with all the types of information you will be asked and that you have a set of basic strategies to use when answering questions. The remainder of this review will give you these skills.

ATTACKING THE CRITICAL READING SECTION

You should follow these steps as you begin each critical reading passage. They will act as a guide when answering the questions.

Step 1

Before you address the critical reading, answer all analogies and sentence completions within the given verbal section. You can answer more questions per minute in these short sections than in the reading, and since all answers are credited equally, you'll get the most for your time here.

Now, find the critical reading passage(s). If more than one passage appears, give each a brief overview. Attack the easiest and most interesting passages first. Critical reading passages are not automatically presented in the order of least-to-most difficult. The difficulty or ease of a reading selection is an individual matter, determined by the reader's own specific interests and past experience, so what you might consider easy, someone else might consider hard, and *vice-versa*. Again, time is an issue, so you need to begin with something you can quickly understand in order to get to the questions, where the pay-off lies.

Step 2

First, read the question stems following the passage, making sure to block out the answer choices with your free hand. (You don't want to be misled by incorrect choices.)

In question stems, underline key words, phrases, and dates. For example:

1. In line 27, "<u>stand</u>" means:

2. From <u>1776 to 1812, King George</u> did:

3. <u>Lincoln</u> was <u>similar</u> to <u>Pericles</u> in that:

The act of underlining takes little time and will force you to focus first on the main ideas in the questions, then in the essays.

You will notice that questions often note a line number for reference. Place a small mark by the appropriate lines in the essay itself to remind yourself to read those parts very carefully. You'll still have to refer to these lines upon answering the questions, but you'll be able to find them quickly.

Step 3

If the passage is not divided into paragraphs, read the first ten lines. If the passage is divided into manageable paragraphs, read the first paragraph. Make sure to read at a moderate pace, as fast skimming will not be sufficient for comprehension, while slow, forced reading will take too much time and yield too little understanding of the overall passage.

In the margin of your test booklet, using two or three words, note the main point of the paragraph/section. Don't labor long over the exact wording. Underline key terms, phrases, or ideas when you notice them. If a sentence is particularly difficult, don't spend too much time trying to figure it out. Bracket it, though, for easy reference in the remote instance that it might serve as the basis for a question.

You should proceed through each paragraph/section in a similar manner. Don't read the whole passage with the intention of going back and filling in the main points. Read carefully and consistently, annotating and underlining to keep your mind on the context.

Upon finishing the entire passage, quickly review your notes in the margin. They should give you main ideas and passage structure (chronological, cause and effect, process, comparison-contrast). Ask yourself what the author's attitude is toward his/her subject. What might you infer from the selection? What might the author say next? Some of these questions may appear, and you'll be immediately prepared to answer.

Step 4

Start with the first question and work through to the last question. The order in which the questions are presented follows the order of the passage, so going for the "easy" questions first rather than answering the questions consecutively will cost you valuable time in searching and backtracking.

Be sure to block the answer choices for each question before you read the question, itself. Again, you don't want to be misled.

If a line number is mentioned, quickly re-read that section. In addition, circle your own answer to the question *before* viewing the choices. Then, carefully examine each answer choice, eliminating those which are obviously incorrect. If you find a close match to your own answer, don't assume that it is the best answer, as an even better one may be among the last choices. Remember, in the SAT, only one answer is correct, and it is the *best* one, not simply one that will work.

Once you've proceeded through all the choices, eliminating incorrect answers as you go, choose fromamong those remaining. If the choice is not clear, reread the question stem and the referenced passage lines to seek tone or content you might have missed. If the answer now is not readily obvious and you have reduced your choices by eliminating at least one, then simply choose one of the remaining and proceed to the next question. Place a small mark in your test booklet to remind you, should you have time at the end of this test section, to review the question and seek a more accurate answer.

TECHNIQUES AND STRATEGIES

➤ Do not spend too much time answering any one question.

➤ Vocabulary plays a large part in successful critical reading. As a long-term approach to improving your ability and therefore your test scores, read as much as you can of any type of material. Your speed, comprehension, and vocabulary will grow.

➤ Be an engaged reader. Don't let your mind wander. Focus through annotation and key terms.

➤ Time is an important factor on the SAT. Therefore, the rate at which you are reading is very important. If you are concerned

that you may be reading too slow, try to compete with yourself.
For example, if you are reading at 120 words per minute, try to
improve your speed to 250 words per minute (without decreasing your understanding). Remember that improving reading
speed is not a means in itself. Improved comprehension with
fewer regressions must accompany this speed increase. Make
sure to read, read, read. The more you read, the more you will
sharpen your skills.

Now, let's go back to our natural sciences passage. Read the passage, and
then answer the questions which follow using the skills gained through this
review.

*The following article was written by a physical chemist and recounts the
conflict between volcanic matter in the atmosphere and airplane windows. It was
published in a scientific periodical in 1989. (Reprinted by permission of* American Heritage Magazine, *a division of Forbes Inc., Forbes Inc., 1989.)*

1　　Several years ago the airlines discovered a new kind of problem—a
window problem. The acrylic windows on some of their 747s were getting
hazy and dirty-looking. Suspicious travelers thought the airlines might have
stopped cleaning them, but the windows were not dirty; they were inexpli-
5　cably deteriorating within as little as 390 hours of flight time, even though
they were supposed to last for five to ten years. Boeing looked into it.

　　At first the company thought the culprit might be one well known in
modern technology, the component supplier who changes materials without
telling the customer. Boeing quickly learned this was not the case, so there
10　followed an extensive investigation that eventually brought in the Air
Transport Association, geologists, and specialists in upper-atmosphere
chemistry, and the explanation turned out to be not nearly so mundane.
Indeed, it began to look like a grand reenactment of an ancient Aztec myth:
the struggle between the eagle and the serpent, which is depicted on the
15　Mexican flag.

　　The serpent in this case is an angry Mexican volcano, El Chichon. Like
its reptilian counterpart, it knows how to spit venom at the eyes of its
adversary. In March and April of 1982 the volcano, in an unusual eruption
pattern, ejected millions of tons of sulfur-rich material directly into the
20　stratosphere. In less than a year, a stratospheric cloud had blanketed the
entire Northern Hemisphere. Soon the photochemistry of the upper atmosphere converted much of the sulfur into tiny droplets of concentrated
sulfuric acid.

　　The eagle in the story is the 747, poking occasionally into the lower
25　part of the stratosphere in hundreds of passenger flights daily. Its two

hundred windows are made from an acrylic polymer, which makes beautifully clear, strong windows but was never intended to withstand attack by strong acids.

30 The stratosphere is very different from our familiar troposphere environment. Down here the air is humid, with a lot of vertical convection to carry things up and down; the stratosphere is bone-dry, home to the continent-striding jet stream, with unceasing horizontal winds at an average of 120 miles per hour. A mist of acid droplets accumulated gradually near the lower edge of the stratosphere, settling there at a thickness of about a mile a 35 year, was able to wait for planes to come along.

As for sulfuric acid, most people know only the relatively benign liquid in a car battery: 80 percent water and 20 percent acid. The stratosphere dehydrated the sulfuric acid into a persistent, corrosive mist 75 percent pure acid, an extremely aggressive liquid. Every time the 747 poked into the 40 stratosphere — on almost every long flight — acid droplets struck the windows and began to react with their outer surface, causing it to swell. This built up stresses between the softened outer layer and the underlying material. Finally, parallel hairline cracks developed, creating the hazy appearance. The crazing was sped up by the mechanical stresses always 45 present in the windows of a pressurized cabin.

The airlines suffered through more than a year of window replacements before the acid cloud finally dissipated. Ultimately the drops reached the lower edge of the stratosphere, were carried away into the lower atmosphere, and finally came down in the rain. In the meantime, more resistant 50 window materials and coatings were developed. (As for the man-made sulfur dioxide that causes acid rain, it never gets concentrated enough to attack the window material. El Chichon was unusual in its ejection of sulfur directly into the stratosphere, and the 747 is unusual in its frequent entrance into the stratosphere.)

55 As for the designers of those windows, it is hard to avoid the conclusion that a perfectly adequate engineering design was defeated by bad luck. After all, this was the only time since the invention of the airplane that there were acid droplets of this concentration in the upper atmosphere. But reliability engineers, an eminently rational breed, are very uncomfortable 60 when asked to talk about luck. In principle it should be possible to anticipate events, and the failure to do so somehow seems like a professional failure. The cosmos of the engineer has no room for poltergeists, demons, or other mystic elements. But might it accommodate the inexorable scenario of an ancient Aztec myth?

1. Initially the hazy windows were thought by the company to be a result of

    (A) small particles of volcanic glass abrading their surfaces.

    (B) substandard window material substituted by the parts supplier.

    (C) ineffectual cleaning products used by the maintenance crew.

    (D) a build-up of the man-made sulfur dioxide that also causes acid rain.

    (E) the humidity.

2. When first seeking a reason for the abraded windows, both the passengers and Boeing management exhibited attitudes of

    (A) disbelief.   (D) pacifism.

    (B) optimism.   (E) disregard.

    (C) cynicism.

3. In line 12, "mundane" means

    (A) simple.   (D) ordinary.

    (B) complicated.   (E) important.

    (C) far-reaching.

4. In what ways is El Chichon like the serpent on the Mexican flag, knowing how to "spit venom at the eyes of its adversary" (lines 17–18)?

    (A) It seeks to poison its adversary with its bite.

    (B) It carefully plans its attack on an awaited intruder.

    (C) It ejects tons of destructive sulfuric acid to damage jet windows.

    (D) It angrily blankets the Northern Hemisphere with sulfuric acid.

    (E) It protects itself with the acid rain it produces.

5. The term "photochemistry" in line 21 refers to a chemical change caused by

    (A) the proximity of the sun.

    (B) the drop in temperature at stratospheric altitudes.

    (C) the jet stream's "unceasing horizontal winds."

    (D) the vertical convection of the troposphere.

    (E) the amount of sulfur present in the atmosphere.

6. Unlike the troposphere, the stratosphere

   (A) is extremely humid as it is home to the jet stream.

   (B) contains primarily vertical convections to cause air particles to rise and fall rapidly.

   (C) is approximately one mile thick.

   (D) contains powerful horizontal winds resulting in an excessively dry atmosphere.

   (E) contains very little wind activity.

7. In line 39, "aggressive" means

   (A) exasperating.   (D) assertive.

   (B) enterprising.   (E) surprising.

   (C) prone to attack.

8. As the eagle triumphed over the serpent in the Mexican flag,

   (A) El Chichon triumphed over the plane as the 747s had to change their flight altitudes.

   (B) the newly designed window material deflected the damaging acid droplets.

   (C) the 747 was able to fly unchallenged by acid droplets a year later as they drifted away to the lower atmosphere.

   (D) the reliability engineers are now prepared for any run of "bad luck" which may approach their aircraft.

   (E) the component supplier of windows changed materials without telling the customers.

9. The reliability engineers are typified as people who

   (A) are uncomfortable considering natural disasters.

   (B) believe that all events are predictable through scientific methodology.

   (C) accept luck as an inevitable and unpredictable part of life.

   (D) easily accept their failure to predict and protect against nature's surprises.

   (E) are extremely irrational and are comfortable speaking about luck.

The questions following the passage which you just read are typical of those in the Critical Reading section. After carefully reading the passage, you can begin to answer these questions. Let's look again at the questions.

1.   Initially the hazy windows were thought by the company to be a result of

    (A)   small particles of volcanic glass abrading their surfaces.

    (B)   substandard window material substituted by the parts supplier.

    (C)   ineffectual cleaning products used by the maintenance crew.

    (D)   a build-up of the man-made sulfur dioxide that also causes acid rain.

    (E)   the humidity.

As you read the question stem, blocking the answer choices, you'll note the key term "result" which should alert you to the question category *synthesis/analysis*. Argument structure is the focus here. Ask yourself what part of the argument is being questioned: cause, problem, result, or solution. Careful reading of the stem and perhaps mental rewording to "_____ caused hazy windows" reveals cause is the issue. Once you're clear on the stem, proceed to the choices.

The word "initially" clues you in to the fact that the correct answer should be the first cause considered. Answer choice (B) is the correct response, as "substandard window material" was the *company's* first (initial) culprit, as explained in the first sentence of the second paragraph. They had no hint of (A) a volcanic eruption's ability to cause such damage. In addition, they were not concerned, as were the *passengers,* that (C) the windows were not properly cleaned. Answer (D) is not correct since scientists had yet to consider testing the atmosphere. Along the same lines, answer choice (E) is incorrect.

2.   When first seeking a reason for the abraded windows, both the passengers and Boeing management exhibited attitudes of

    (A)   disbelief.   (D)   pacifism.

    (B)   optimism.   (E)   disregard.

    (C)   cynicism.

As you read the stem before viewing the choices, you'll know you're being asked to judge or *evaluate* the tone of a passage. The tone is not stated outright, so you'll need to rely on your perception as you re-read that section, if necessary. Remember, questions follow the order of the passage, so you know to look after the initial company reaction to the windows, but not far after, as many more questions are to follow. Now, formulate your own word for the attitude of the passengers and employees. "Skepticism" or "criticism" work well. If you can't come up with a term, at least note if the tone is negative or positive. In this case, negative is clearly indicated as the passengers are distrustful of the maintenance crew and the company mistrusts the window supplier. Proceed to each choice, seeking the closest match to your term and/or eliminating words with positive connotations.

Choice (C) is correct because "cynicism" best describes the skepticism and distrust with which the passengers view the cleaning company and the parts suppliers. Choice (A) is not correct because both Boeing and the passengers believed the windows were hazy, they just didn't know why. Choice (B) is not correct because people were somewhat agitated that the windows were hazy — certainly not "optimistic." Choice (D), "pacifism," has a rather positive connotation, which the tone of the section does not. Choice (E) is incorrect because the people involved took notice of the situation and did not disregard it. In addition to the ability to discern tone, of course, your vocabulary knowledge is being tested. "Cynicism," should you be unsure of the term, can be viewed in its root, "cynic," which may trigger you to remember that it is negative, and therefore, appropriate in tone.

3.   In line 12, "mundane" means

   (A)   simple.   (D)   ordinary.

   (B)   complicated.   (E)   important.

   (C)   far-reaching.

This question obviously tests *vocabulary-in-context.* Your strategy here should be quickly to view line 12 to confirm usage, block answer choices while devising your own synonym for "mundane," perhaps "common," and then viewing each choice separately, looking for the closest match. Although you might not be familiar with "mundane," the choices are all relatively simple terms. Look for contextual clues in the passage if you can't define the term outright. While the "component supplies" explanation is "mundane," the Aztec myth is not. Perhaps, you could then look for an opposite of mythical; "real" or "down-to-earth" comes to mind.

Choice (D) "ordinary" fits best as it is clearly the opposite of the extraordinary Aztec myth of the serpent and the eagle, which is not as common as a supplier switching materials. Choice (A), "simple," works contextually, but not as an accurate synonym for the word "mundane"; it does not deal with "mundane's" "down-to-earth" definition. Choice (B), "complicated," is inaccurate because the parts switch is anything but complicated. Choice (C), "far-reaching," is not better as it would apply to the myth rather than the common, everyday action of switching parts. Choice (E), "important," does not work either, because the explanation was an integral part of solving the problem. Had you eliminated (B), (C), and (E) due to contextual inappropriateness, you were left with "ordinary" and "simple." A quick re-reading of the section, then, should clarify the better choice. But, if the re-reading did not clarify the better choice, your strategy would be to choose one answer, place a small mark in the booklet, and proceed to the next question. If time is left at the end of the test, you can then review your answer choice.

4. In what ways is El Chichon like the serpent on the Mexican flag, knowing how to "spit venom at the eyes of its adversary" (lines 17-18)?

    (A) It seeks to poison its adversary with its bite.

    (B) It carefully plans its attack on an awaited intruder.

    (C) It ejects tons of destructive sulfuric acid to damage jet windows.

    (D) It angrily blankets the Northern Hemisphere with sulfuric acid.

    (E) It protects itself with the acid rain it produces.

As you view the question, note the word "like" indicates a comparison is being made. The quoted simile forms the comparative basis of the question, and you must *interpret* that phrase with respect to the actual process. You must carefully seek to duplicate the tenor of the terms, coming close to the spitting action in which a harmful substance is expelled in the direction of an object similar to the eyes of an opponent. Look for key words when comparing images. "Spit," "venom," "eyes," and "adversary" are these keys.

In choice (C), the verb that is most similar to the serpent's "spitting" venom is the sulfuric acid "ejected" from the Mexican volcano, El Chichon. Also, the jet windows most closely resemble the "eyes of the adversary" that are struck by El Chichon. Being a volcano, El Chichon is certainly incapable of injecting poison into an adversary, as in choice (A), or planning an attack on an intruder, as in choice (B). In choice (D), although the volcano does indeed "blanket the Northern Hemisphere" with sulfuric acid, this image does not coincide with the "spitting" image of the serpent. Finally, in choice (E), although a volcano can indirectly cause acid rain, it cannot produce acid rain on its own and then spew it out into the atmosphere.

5. The term "photochemistry" in line 21 refers to a chemical change caused by

    (A) the proximity of the sun.

    (B) the drop in temperature at stratopheric altitudes.

    (C) the jet stream's "unceasing horizontal winds."

    (D) the vertical convection of the troposphere.

    (E) the amount of sulfur present in the atmosphere.

Even if you are unfamiliar with the term "photochemistry," you probably know its root or its prefix. Clearly, this question fits in the *vocabulary-in-context* mode. Your first step may be a quick reference to line 21. If you don't know the term, context may provide you a clue. The conversion of sulfur-rich *upper* atmosphere into droplets may help. If context does not yield information, look at the term "photochemistry," itself. "Photo" has to do with light or sun, as in photosynthesis. Chemistry deals with substance composition and change. Knowing these two parts can take you a long way toward a correct answer.

Answer choice (A) is the correct response, as the light of the sun closely compares with the prefix "photo." Although choice (B), "the drop in temperature," might lead you to associate the droplet formation with condensation, light is not a factor here, nor is it in choice (C), "the jet stream's winds"; choice (D) "the vertical convection"; or choice (E), "the amount of sulfur present."

6.   Unlike the troposphere, the stratosphere

    (A)   is extremely humid as it is home to the jet stream.

    (B)   contains primarily vertical convections to cause air particles to rise and fall rapidly.

    (C)   is approximately one mile thick.

    (D)   contains powerful horizontal winds resulting in an excessively dry atmosphere.

    (E)   contains very little wind activity.

"Unlike" should immediately alert you to a *synthesis/analysis* question asking you to contrast specific parts of the text. Your margin notes should take you right to the section contrasting the atmospheres. Quickly scan it before considering the answers. Usually you won't remember this broad type of comparison from your first passage reading. Don't spend much time, though, on the scan before beginning to answer, as time is still a factor.

This question is tricky because all the answer choices contain key elements/phrases in the passage, but again, a quick, careful scan will yield results. Answer (D) proves best as the "horizontal winds" dry the air of the stratosphere. Choices (A), (B), (C), and (E) are all characteristic of the troposphere, while only the acid droplets accumulate at the rate of one mile per year within the much larger stratosphere. As you answer such questions, remember to eliminate incorrect choices as you go; don't be misled by what seems familiar, yet isn't accurate — read all the answer choices.

7. In line 39, "aggressive" means

    (A) exasperating.   (D) assertive.

    (B) enterprising.   (E) surprising.

    (C) prone to attack.

Another *vocabulary-in-context* surfaces here; yet, this time, the word is probably familiar to you. Again, before forming a synonym, quickly refer to the line number, aware that perhaps a secondary meaning is appropriate as the term already is a familiar one. Upon reading the line, you'll note "persistent" and "corrosive," both strong terms, the latter being quite negative in its destruction. Now, form an appropriate synonym for aggressive, one that has a negative connotation. "Hostile" might come to mind. You are ready at this point to view all choices for a match.

Using your vocabulary knowledge, you can answer this question. "Hostile" most closely resembles choice (C), "prone to attack," and is therefore the correct response. Choice (A), "exasperating," or irritating, is too weak a term, while choice (B), "enterprising," and (D), "assertive," are too positive. Choice (E), "surprising," is not a synonym for "aggressive."

8. As the eagle triumphed over the serpent in the Mexican flag,

    (A) El Chichon triumphed over the plane as the 747s had to change their flight altitudes.

    (B) the newly designed window material deflected the damaging acid droplets.

    (C) the 747 was able to fly unchallenged by acid droplets a year later as they drifted away to the lower atmosphere.

    (D) the reliability engineers are now prepared for any run of "bad luck" which may approach their aircraft.

    (E) the component supplier of the windows changed materials without telling the customer.

This question asks you to compare the eagle's triumph over the serpent to another part of the text. "As" often signals comparative relationships, so you are forewarned of the *synthesis/analysis* question. You are also dealing again with a simile, so, of course, the question can also be categorized as *interpretation*. The eagle-serpent issue is a major theme in the text. You are being asked, as you will soon discover in the answer choices, what this general theme is. Look at the stem keys: eagle, triumphed, and serpent. Ask yourself to what each corresponds. You'll arrive at the eagle and the 747, some sort of victory, and the volcano or its sulfur. Now that you've formed that corresponding image in your own mind, you're ready to view the choices.

Choice (C) is the correct choice because we know the statement, "the 747 was able to fly unchallenged..." to be true. Not only do the remaining choices fail to reflect the eagle-triumphs-over-serpent image, but choice (A) is inaccurate because the 747 did not "change its flight altitudes." In choice (B), the windows did not deflect "the damaging acid droplets." Furthermore, in choice (D), "the reliability engineers" cannot be correct because they cannot possibly predict the future, and therefore, cannot anticipate what could go wrong in the future. Finally, we know that in (E) the window materials were never changed.

9.   The reliability engineers are typified as people who

   (A)   are uncomfortable considering natural disasters.

   (B)   believe that all events are predictable through scientific methodology.

   (C)   accept luck as an inevitable and unpredictable part of life.

   (D)   easily accept their failure to predict and protect against nature's surprises.

   (E)   are extremely irrational and are comfortable speaking about luck.

When the question involves such terms as type, kind, example, or typified, be aware of possible *synthesis/analysis* or *interpretation* issues. Here the question deals with implications: what the author means but doesn't state outright. Types can also lead you to situations which ask you to make an unstated generalization based on specifically stated details. In fact, this question could even be categorized as *evaluation* because specific detail to generalization is a type of argument/ essay structure. In any case, before viewing the answer choices, ask yourself what general traits the reliability engineers portray. You may need to check back in the text for typical characteristics. You'll find the engineers to be rational unbelievers in luck. These key characteristics will help you to make a step toward a correct answer.

Choice (B) is the correct answer because the passage specifically states that the reliability engineers "are very uncomfortable when asked to talk about luck" and believe "it should be possible to anticipate events" scientifically. The engineers might be uncomfortable, as in choice (A), but this is not a main concern in the passage. Choice (C) is obviously incorrect, because the engineers do not believe in luck at all, and choice (D) is not correct because "professional failure" is certainly unacceptable to these scientists. There is no indication in the passage that (E) the scientists are "irrational and are comfortable speaking about luck."

CRITICAL READING PRACTICE TEST

1. Ⓐ Ⓑ Ⓒ Ⓓ Ⓔ
2. Ⓐ Ⓑ Ⓒ Ⓓ Ⓔ
3. Ⓐ Ⓑ Ⓒ Ⓓ Ⓔ
4. Ⓐ Ⓑ Ⓒ Ⓓ Ⓔ
5. Ⓐ Ⓑ Ⓒ Ⓓ Ⓔ
6. Ⓐ Ⓑ Ⓒ Ⓓ Ⓔ
7. Ⓐ Ⓑ Ⓒ Ⓓ Ⓔ
8. Ⓐ Ⓑ Ⓒ Ⓓ Ⓔ
9. Ⓐ Ⓑ Ⓒ Ⓓ Ⓔ
10. Ⓐ Ⓑ Ⓒ Ⓓ Ⓔ
11. Ⓐ Ⓑ Ⓒ Ⓓ Ⓔ
12. Ⓐ Ⓑ Ⓒ Ⓓ Ⓔ
13. Ⓐ Ⓑ Ⓒ Ⓓ Ⓔ
14. Ⓐ Ⓑ Ⓒ Ⓓ Ⓔ
15. Ⓐ Ⓑ Ⓒ Ⓓ Ⓔ
16. Ⓐ Ⓑ Ⓒ Ⓓ Ⓔ
17. Ⓐ Ⓑ Ⓒ Ⓓ Ⓔ
18. Ⓐ Ⓑ Ⓒ Ⓓ Ⓔ
19. Ⓐ Ⓑ Ⓒ Ⓓ Ⓔ
20. Ⓐ Ⓑ Ⓒ Ⓓ Ⓔ
21. Ⓐ Ⓑ Ⓒ Ⓓ Ⓔ

22. Ⓐ Ⓑ Ⓒ Ⓓ Ⓔ
23. Ⓐ Ⓑ Ⓒ Ⓓ Ⓔ
24. Ⓐ Ⓑ Ⓒ Ⓓ Ⓔ
25. Ⓐ Ⓑ Ⓒ Ⓓ Ⓔ
26. Ⓐ Ⓑ Ⓒ Ⓓ Ⓔ
27. Ⓐ Ⓑ Ⓒ Ⓓ Ⓔ
28. Ⓐ Ⓑ Ⓒ Ⓓ Ⓔ
29. Ⓐ Ⓑ Ⓒ Ⓓ Ⓔ
30. Ⓐ Ⓑ Ⓒ Ⓓ Ⓔ
31. Ⓐ Ⓑ Ⓒ Ⓓ Ⓔ
32. Ⓐ Ⓑ Ⓒ Ⓓ Ⓔ
33. Ⓐ Ⓑ Ⓒ Ⓓ Ⓔ
34. Ⓐ Ⓑ Ⓒ Ⓓ Ⓔ
35. Ⓐ Ⓑ Ⓒ Ⓓ Ⓔ
36. Ⓐ Ⓑ Ⓒ Ⓓ Ⓔ
37. Ⓐ Ⓑ Ⓒ Ⓓ Ⓔ
38. Ⓐ Ⓑ Ⓒ Ⓓ Ⓔ
39. Ⓐ Ⓑ Ⓒ Ⓓ Ⓔ
40. Ⓐ Ⓑ Ⓒ Ⓓ Ⓔ
41. Ⓐ Ⓑ Ⓒ Ⓓ Ⓔ

CRITICAL READING
PRACTICE TEST

DIRECTIONS: Read each passage and answer the questions that follow. Each question will be based on the information stated or implied in the passage or its introduction.

In this excerpt from Dickens's Oliver Twist, *we read the early account of Oliver's birth and the beginning of his impoverished life.*

1   Although I am not disposed to maintain that the being born in a workhouse, is in itself the most fortunate and enviable circumstance that can
possibly befall a human being, I do mean to say that in this particular
instance, it was the best thing for Oliver Twist that could by possibility
5   have occurred. The fact is, that there was considerable difficulty in inducing
Oliver to take upon himself the office of respiration, — a troublesome
practice, but one which custom has rendered necessary to our easy existence; and for some time he lay gasping on a little flock mattress, rather
unequally poised between this world and the next: the balance being
10   decidedly in favour of the latter. Now, if, during this brief period, Oliver
had been surrounded by careful grandmothers, anxious aunts, experienced
nurses, and doctors of profound wisdom, he would most inevitably and
indubitably have been killed in no time. There being nobody by, however,
but a pauper old woman, who was rendered rather misty by an unwonted
15   allowance of beer; and a parish surgeon who did such matters by contract;
Oliver and Nature fought out the point between them. The result was, that,
after a few struggles, Oliver breathed, sneezed, and proceeded to advertise
to the inmates of the workhouse the fact of a new burden having been
imposed upon the parish, by setting up as loud a cry as could reasonably
20   have been expected from a male infant who had not been possessed of that
very useful appendage, a voice, for a much longer space of time than three
mintues and a quarter....

For the next eight or ten months, Oliver was the victim of a systematic
course of treachery and deception. He was brought up by hand. The hungry
25   and destitute situation of the infant orphan was duly reported by the workhouse authorities to the parish authorities. The parish authorities inquired
with dignity of the workhouse authorities, whether there was no female then
domiciled in 'the house' who was in a situation to impart to Oliver Twist,
the consolation and nourishment of which he stood in need. The workhouse
30   authorities replied with humility, that there was not. Upon this, the parish
authorities magnanimously and humanely resolved, that Oliver should be
'farmed,' or, in other words, that he should be despatched to a branch-
workhouse some three miles off, where twenty or thirty other juvenile

offenders against the poor-laws, rolled about the floor all day, without the
35   inconvenience of too much food or too much clothing, under the parental
superintendence of an elderly female, who received the culprits at and for
the consideration of sevenpence-halfpenny per small head per week.
Sevenpence-halfpenny's worth per week is a good round diet for a child; a
great deal may be got for sevenpence-halfpenny: quite enough to overload
40   its stomach, and make it uncomfortable. The elderly female was a woman
of wisdom and experience; she knew what was good for children; and she
had a very accurate perception of what was good for herself. So, she
appropriated the greater part of the weekly stipend to her own use, and
consigned the rising parochial generation to even a shorter allowance than
45   was originally provided for them. Thereby finding in the lowest depth a
deeper still; and proving herself a very great experimental philosopher.

Everybody knows the story of another experimental philosopher, who
had a great theory about a horse being able to live without eating, and who
demonstrated it so well, that he got his own horse down to a straw a day,
50   and would most unquestionably have rendered him a very spirited and
rampacious animal on nothing at all, if he had not died, just four-and-twenty
hours before he was to have had his first comfortable bait of air. Unfortunately for the experimental philosophy of the female to whose protecting
care Oliver Twist was delivered over, a similar result usually attended the
55   operation of *her* system...

It cannot be expected that this system of farming would produce any
very extraordinary or luxuriant crop. Oliver Twist's ninth birth-day found
him a pale thin child, somewhat diminutive in stature, and decidedly small
in circumference. But nature or inheritance had implanted a good sturdy
60   spirit in Oliver's breast. It had had plenty of room to expand, thanks to the
spare diet of the establishment; and perhaps to this circumstance may be
attributed his having any ninth birth-day at all.

1.   After Oliver was born, he had an immediate problem with his

(A)   heart rate.   (D)   hearing.

(B)   breathing.   (E)   memory.

(C)   vision.

2.   What are the two worlds that Oliver stands unequally poised between in
lines 8-10?

(A)   Poverty and riches

(B)   Infancy and childhood

(C)   Childhood and adolescence

(D) Love and hatred

(E) Life and death

3. What does the author imply about "careful grandmothers, anxious aunts, experienced nurses, and doctors of profound wisdom" in lines 10-13?

(A) They can help nurse sick children back to health.

(B) They are necessary for every being's survival.

(C) They are the pride of the human race.

(D) They tend to adversely affect the early years of children.

(E) Their involvement in Oliver's birth would have had no outcome on his survival.

4. What is the outcome of Oliver's bout with Nature?

(A) He is unable to overcome Nature's fierceness.

(B) He loses, but gains some dignity from his will to fight.

(C) It initially appears that Oliver has won, but moments later he cries out in crushing defeat.

(D) Oliver cries out with the breath of life in his lungs.

(E) There is no way of knowing who won the struggle.

5. What is the "systematic course of treachery and deception" that Oliver falls victim to in the early months of his life?

(A) He is thrown out into the streets.

(B) His inheritance is stolen by caretakers of the workhouse.

(C) He is relocated by the uncaring authorities of the workhouse and the parish.

(D) The records of his birth are either lost or destroyed.

(E) He is publicly humiliated by the parish authorities.

6. What is meant when the residents of the branch-workhouse are referred to by the phrase "juvenile offenders against the poor-laws" (line 34)?

(A) They are children who have learned to steal early in life.

(B) They are adolescents who work on probation.

(C)   They are infants who have no money to support them.

(D)   They are infants whose parents were law offenders.

(E)   They are adults who have continuously broken the law.

7. What is the author's tone when he writes that the elderly caretaker "knew what was good for children" (lines 41-42)?

(A)   Sarcastic   (D)   Astonished

(B)   Complimentary   (E)   Outraged

(C)   Impressed

8. What does the author imply when he further writes that the elderly caretaker "had a very accurate perception of what was good for herself" (lines 42-43)?

(A)   She knew how to keep herself groomed and clean.

(B)   She knew how to revenge herself on her enemies.

(C)   She had a sense of confidence that inspired others.

(D)   She really had no idea how to take care of herself.

(E)   She knew how to selfishly benefit herself despite the cost to others.

9. Why is the elderly caretaker considered "a very great experimental philosopher" (line 46)?

(A)   She was scientifically weaning the children off of food trying to create stronger humans.

(B)   She experimented with the survival of the children in her care.

(C)   She thought children were the key to a meaningful life.

(D)   She made sure that the children received adequate training in philosophy.

(E)   She often engaged in parochial and philosophical discussions.

10. In line 52, "bait" most nearly means

(A)   worms.   (D)   a trap.

(B)   a hook.   (E)   a meal.

(C)   a breeze.

11. To what does the author attribute Oliver's survival to his ninth year?

    (A) A strong, healthy diet

    (B) Money from an anonymous donor.

    (C) Sheer luck

    (D) His diminutive stature

    (E) His sturdy spirit

12. Based upon the passage, what is the author's overall attitude concerning the city where Oliver lives?

    (A) It is the best of all possible worlds.

    (B) It should be the prototype for future cities.

    (C) It is a dark place filled with greedy, selfish people.

    (D) Although impoverished, most of its citizens are kind.

    (E) It is a flawed place, but many good things often happen there.

The following passage analyzes the legal and political philosophy of John Marshall, a chief justice of the Supreme Court in the nineteenth century.

1   As chief justice of thc Supreme Court from 1801 until his death in
    1835, John Marshall was a staunch nationalist and upholder of property
    rights. He was not, however, as the folklore of Arnerican politics would
    have it, the lonely and embattled Federalist defending these values against
5   the hostile forces of Jeffersonian democracy. On the contrary, Marshall's
    opinions dealing with federalism, property rights, and national economic
    development were consistent with the policies of the Republican Party in its
    mercantilist phase from 1815 to 1828. Never an extreme Federalist,
    Marshall opposed his party's reactionary wing in the crisis of 1798-1800.
10 Like almost all Americans of his day, Marshall was a Lockean republican
    who valued property not as an economic end in itself, but rather as the
    foundation of civil liberty and a free society. Property was the source both
    of individual happiness and social stability and progress.

    Marshall evinced strong centralizing tendencies in his theory of federal-
15 ism and completely rejected the compact theory of the Union expressed in
    the Virginia and Kentucky Resolutions. Yet his outlook was compatible
    with the Unionism that formed the basis of the post-1815 American System
    of the Republican Party. Not that Marshall shared the democratic sensibili-
    ties of the Republicans; like his fellow Federalists, he tended to distrust the
20 common people and saw in legislative majoritarianism a force that was
    potentially hostile to constutionalism and the rule of law. But aversion to

democracy was not the hallmark of Marshall's constitutional jurisprudence. Its central features rather were a commitment to federal authority versus states' rights and a socially productive and economically dynamic concep-
25 tion of property rights. Marshall's support of these principles placed him near the mainstream of American politics in the years between the War of 1812 and the conquest of Jacksonian Democracy.

In the long run, the most important decisions of the Marshall Court were those upholding the authority of the federal government against the
30 states. *Marbury v. Madison* provided a jurisprudential basis for this undertaking, but the practical significance of judicial review in the Marshall era concerned the state legislatures rather than Congress. The most serious challenge to national authority resulted from state attempts to administer their judicial systems independent of the Supreme Court's appellate super-
35 visions as directed by the Judiciary Act of 1789. In successfully resisting this challenge, the Marshall Court not only averted a practical disruption of the federal system, but it also evolved doctrines of national supremacy which helped preserve the Union during the Civil War.

13. The primary purpose of this passage is to

(A) describe Marshall's political jurisprudence.

(B) discuss the importance of centralization to the preservation of the Union.

(C) criticize Marshall for being disloyal to his party.

(D) examine the role of the Supreme Court in national politics.

(E) chronicle Marshall's tenure on the Supreme Court.

14. According to the author, Marshall viewed property as

(A) an investment.

(B) irrelevant to constitutional liberties.

(C) the basis of a stable society.

(D) inherent to the upper class.

(E) an important centralizing incentive.

15. In line 15, the *compact theory* was most likely a theory

(A) supporting states' rights.

(B) of the extreme Federalists.

(C) of the Marshall Court's approach to the Civil War.

(D)   supporting centralization.

(E)   advocating jurisprudential activism.

16.   According to the author, Marshall's attitude toward mass democratic politics can best be described as

(A)   hostile.   (D)   nurturing.

(B)   supportive.   (E)   distrustful.

(C)   indifferent.

17.   In line 21 the word "aversion" means

(A)   loathing.   (D)   forbidding.

(B)   acceptance.   (E)   misdirection.

(C)   fondness.

18.   The author argues the Marshall Court

(A)   failed to achieve its centralizing policies.

(B)   failed to achieve its decentralizing policies.

(C)   helped to bring on the Civil War.

(D)   supported federalism via judicial review.

(E)   had its greatest impact on Congress.

19.   According to the author, Marshall's politics were

(A)   extremist.   (D)   moderate.

(B)   right-wing.   (E)   majoritarian.

(C)   democratic.

In this passage, the author discusses the properties and uses of selenium cells, which convert sunlight to energy, creating solar power.

1   The physical phenomenon responsible for converting light to electricity—the photovoltaic effect—was first observed in 1839 by the renowned French physicist, Edmund Becquerel. Becquerel noted that a voltage appeared when one of two identical electrodes in a weak conducting
5   solution was illuminated. The PV effect was first studied in solids, such as selenium, in the 1870s. In the 1880s, selenium photovoltaic cells were built that exhibited 1%-2% efficiency in converting light to electricity. Selenium

converts light in the visible part of the sun's spectrum; for this reason, it was quickly adopted by the then merging field of photography for photo-
10   metric (light-measuring) devices. Even today, the light-sensitive cells on cameras used for adjusting shutter speed to match illumination are made of selenium.

Selenium cells have never become practical as energy converters because their cost is too high relative to the tiny amount of power they
15   produce (at 1% efficiency). Meanwhile, work on the physics of PV phe-nomena has expanded. In the 1920s and 1930s, quantum mechanics laid the theoretical foundation for our present understanding of PV. A major step forward in solar-cell technology came in the 1940s and early 1950s when a new method (called the Czochralski method) was developed for producing
20   highly pure crystalline silicon. In 1954, work at Bell Telephone Laborato-ries resulted in a silicon photovoltaic cell with a 4% efficiency. Bell Labs soon bettered this to a 6% and then 11% efficiency, heralding an entirely new era of power-producing cells.

A few schemes were tried in the 1950s to use silicon PV cells commer-
25   cially. Most were for cells in regions geographically isolated from electric utility lines. But an unexepected boom in PV technology came from a different quarter. In 1958, the U.S. Vanguard space satellite used a small (less than one-watt) array of cells to power its radio. The cells worked so well that space scientists soon realized the PV could be an effective power
30   source for many space missions. Technology development of the solar cell has been a part of the space program ever since.

Today, photovoltaic systems are capable of transforming one kilowatt of solar energy falling on one square meter into about a hundred watts of electricity. One hundred watts can power most household appliances: a
35   television, a stereo, an electric typewriter, or a lamp. In fact, standard solar cells covering the sun-facing roof space of a typical home can provide about 8,500-kilowatt-hours of electricity annually, which is about the average household's yearly electric consumption. By comparison, a modern, 200-ton electric-arc steel furnace, demanding 50,000 kilowatts of electricity,
40   would require about a square kilometer of land for a PV power supply.

Certain factors make capturing solar energy difficult. Besides the sun's low illuminating power per square meter, sunlight is intermittent, affected by time of day, climate, pollution, and season. Power sources based on photovoltaics require either back-up from other sources or storage for times
45   when the sun is obscured.

In addition, the cost of a photovoltaic system is far from negligible (electricity from PV systems in 1980 cost about 20 times more than that from conventional fossil-fuel-powered systems).

Thus, solar energy for photovoltaic conversion into electricity is
50   abundant, inexhaustible, and clean; yet, it also requires special techniques to gather enough of it effectively.

20. To the author, Edmund Becquerel's research was

    (A)   unimportant.

    (B)   of some significance.

    (C)   not recognized in its time.

    (D)   weak.

    (E)   an important breakthrough.

21. In the first paragraph, it can be concluded that the photovoltaic effect is the result of

    (A)   two identical negative electrodes.

    (B)   one weak solution and two negative electrodes.

    (C)   two positive electrodes of different qualities.

    (D)   positive electrodes interacting in a weak environment.

    (E)   one negative electrode and one weak solution.

22. The author establishes that selenium was used for photometric devices because

    (A)   selenium was the first solid to be observed to have the PV effect.

    (B)   selenium is inexpensive.

    (C)   selenium converts the visible part of the sun's spectrum.

    (D)   selenium can adjust shutter speeds on cameras.

    (E)   selenium is abundant.

23. Which of the following can be concluded from the passage?

    (A)   Solar energy is still limited by problems of technological efficiency.

    (B)   Solar energy is the most efficient source of heat for most families.

    (C)   Solar energy represents the PV effect in its most complicated form.

    (D)   Solar energy is 20 percent cheaper than fossil-fuel-powered systems.

    (E)   Solar energy is 40 percent more expensive than fossil-fuel-powered systems.

24. In line 21, the word "heralding" most nearly means

    (A) celebrating.   (D) anticipating.

    (B) observing.   (E) introducing.

    (C) commemorating.

25. According to the passage, commercially used PV cells have powered

    (A) car radios.   (D) electric utility lines.

    (B) space satellite radios. (E) space stations.

    (C) telephones.

26. Through the information in lines 31-33, it can be inferred that two kilowatts of solar energy transformed by a PV system equal

    (A) 200 watts of electricity.

    (B) 100 watts of electricity.

    (C) no electricity.

    (D) two square meters.

    (E) 2,000 watts of electricity.

27. Sunlight is difficult to procure for transformation into solar energy. Which of the following statements most accurately supports this belief derived from the passage?

    (A) Sunlight is erratic and subject to variables.

    (B) Sunlight is steady but never available.

    (C) Sunlight is not visible because of pollution.

    (D) Sunlight would have to be artificially produced.

    (E) Sunlight is never erratic.

28. The author's concluding paragraph would be best supported with additional information regarding

    (A) specific benefits of solar energy for photovoltaic conversion into electricity.

    (B) the negative effects of solar energy for photovoltaic conversion into electricity.

(C)   the negative effects of photovoltaic conversion.

(D)   why solar energy is clean.

(E)   why solar energy is abundant.

In Passage 1, the author writes a general summary about the nature of comedy. In Passage 2, the author sums up the essentials of tragedy.

Passage 1

1   　　　The primary aim of comedy is to amuse us with a happy ending, although comedies can vary according to the attitudes they project, which can be broadly identified as either **high** or **low**, terms having nothing to do with an evaluation of the play's merit. Generally, the amusement found in
5   comedy comes from an eventual victory over threats or ill fortune. Much of the dialogue and plot development might be laughable, yet a play need not be funny to be comic. In fact, some critics in the Renaissance era thought that the highest form of comedy should elicit no laughter at all from its audience. A comedy that forced its audience into laughter failed in the
10   highest comic endeavor, whose purpose was to amuse as subtly as possible. Note that Shakespeare's comedies themselves were often under attack for their appeal to laughter.

　　　Farce is low comedy intended to make us laugh by means of a series of exaggerated, unlikely situations that depend less on plot and character than
15   on gross absurdities, sight gags, and coarse dialogue. The "higher" a comedy goes, the more natural the characters seem and the less boisterous their behavior. The plots become more sustained, and the dialogue shows more weighty thought. As with all dramas, comedies are about things that go wrong. Accordingly, comedies create deviations from accepted nor-
20   malcy, presenting problems which we might or might not see as harmless. If these problems make us judgmental about the involved characters and events, the play takes on the features of **satire**, a rather high comic form implying that humanity and human institutions are in need of reform. If the action triggers our sympathy for the characters, we feel even less protected
25   from the incongruities as the play tilts more in the direction of **tragi-comedy**. In other words, the action determines a figurative distance between the audience and the play. Such factors as characters' personalities and the plot's predictability influence this distance. The farther away we sit, the more protected we feel and usually the funnier the play becomes. Closer
30   proximity to believability in the script draws us nearer to the conflict, making us feel more involved in the action and less safe in its presence.

Passage 2

　　　The term "tragedy" when used to define a play has historically meant something very precise, not simply a drama which ends with unfortunate consequences. This definition originated with Aristotle, who insisted that

35   the play be an imitation of complex actions which should arouse an emotional response combining fear and pity. Aristotle believed that only a certain kind of plot could generate such a powerful reaction. Comedy shows us a progression from adversity to prosperity. Tragedy must show the reverse; moreover, this progression must be experienced by a certain kind

40   of character, says Aristotle, someone whom we can designate as the tragic hero. This central figure must be basically good and noble: "good" because we will not be aroused to fear and pity over the misfortunes of a villain, and "noble" both by social position and moral stature because the fall to misfortune would not otherwise be great enough for tragic impact. These virtues

45   do not make the tragic hero perfect, however, for he must also possess hamartia — a tragic flaw — the weakness which leads him to make an error in judgment which initiates the reversal in his fortunes, causing his death or the death of others or both. These dire consequences become the hero's catastrophe. The most common tragic flaw is hubris; an excessive pride that

50   adversely influences the protagonist's judgment.

       Often the catastrophic consequences involve an entire nation because the tragic hero's social rank carries great responsibilities. Witnessing these events produces the emotional reaction Aristotle believed the audience should experience, the catharsis. Although tragedy must arouse our pity for

55   the tragic hero as he endures his catastrophe and must frighten us as we witness the consequences of a flawed behavior which anyone could exhibit, there must also be a purgation, "a cleansing," of these emotions which should leave the audience feeling not depressed but relieved and almost elated. The assumption is that while the tragic hero endures a crushing

60   reversal, somehow he is not thoroughly defeated as he gains new stature through suffering and the knowledge that comes with suffering. Classical tragedy insists that the universe is ordered. If truth or universal law is ignored, the results are devastating, causing the audience to react emotionally; simultaneously, the tragic results prove the existence of truth, thereby

65   reassuring our faith that existence is sensible.

29. In Passage 1, the term "laughable" (line 6) suggests that on occasion comic dialogue and plot development can be

    (A)   senselessly ridiculous.

    (B)   foolishly stupid.

    (C)   amusingly droll.

    (D)   theoretically depressing.

    (E)   critically unsavory.

30. The author of Passage 1 makes an example of Shakespeare (lines 11-12) in order to

    (A) make the playwright look much poorer in our eyes.

    (B) emphasize that he wrote the highest form of comedy.

    (C) degrade higher forms of comedy.

    (D) suggest the foolishness of Renaissance critics.

    (E) show that even great authors do not always use high comedy.

31. The protagonist in a play discovers he has won the lottery, only to misplace the winning ticket. According to the author's definition, this situation would be an example of which type of comedy?

    (A) Satire   (D) Sarcasm

    (B) Farce   (E) Slapstick

    (C) Tragi-comedy

32. In line 26, the phrase "figurative distance" suggests

    (A) the distance between the seats in the theater and the stage.

    (B) the lengths the comedy will go to elicit laughter.

    (C) the years separating the composition of the play and the time of its performance.

    (D) the degree to which an audience relates with the play's action.

    (E) that the play's matter is too high for the audience to grasp.

33. What is the author trying to espouse in lines 28-31?

    (A) He warns us not to get too involved with the action of the drama.

    (B) He wants the audience to immerse itself in the world of the drama.

    (C) He wants us to feel safe in the presence of the drama.

    (D) He wants us to be critical of the drama's integrity.

    (E) He feels that we should not enjoy the drama overly much.

34. In Passage 2, the author introduces Aristotle as a leading source for the definition of tragedy. He does this

    (A) to emphasize how outdated the tragedy is for the modern audience.

(B)   because Greek philosophy is the only way to truly understand the world of the theater.

(C)   because Aristotle was one of Greece's greatest actors.

(D)   because Aristotle instituted the definition of tragedy still used widely today.

(E)   in order to prove that Aristotle's sense of tragedy was based on false conclusions.

35.   In line 41, "noble" most nearly means

(A)   of high degree and superior virtue.

(B)   of great wealth and self-esteem.

(C)   of quick wit and high intelligence.

(D)   of manly courage and great strength.

(E)   of handsome features and social charm.

36.   Which of the following is an example of *harmatia* (line 47)?

(A)   Courtesy to the lower class

(B)   The ability to communicate freely with others

(C)   A refusal to acknowledge the power of the gods

(D)   A weak, miserly peasant

(E)   A desire to do penance for one's crimes

37.   Which of the following best summarizes the idea of *catharsis* explained in lines 51-54?

(A)   All of the tragic consequences are reversed at the last moment; the hero is rescued from certain doom and is allowed to live happily for the rest of his life.

(B)   The audience gains a perverse pleasure from watching another's suffering.

(C)   The play's action ends immediately, unresolved, and the audience is left in a state of blissful confusion.

(D)   When the play ends, the audience is happy to escape the drudgery of the tragedy's depressing conclusion.

(E)   The audience lifts itself from a state of fear and pity for the tragic hero to a sense of renewal and absolution for the hero's endurance of great suffering.

38. The authors of both passages make an attempt to

    (A) ridicule their subject matter.

    (B) outline the general terms and guidelines of a particular aspect of drama.

    (C) thrill their readers with sensational information.

    (D) draw upon Shakespeare as an authority to back up their work.

    (E) persuade their readers to study only one or the other type of drama (i.e., comedy or tragedy).

39. Which of the following best describes the differences between the structure of both passages?

    (A) Passage 1 is concerned primarily with the Renaissance era. Passage 2 is concerned primarily with Classical Greece.

    (B) Passage 1 is concerned with dividing its subject into subcategories. Passage 2 is concerned with extracting its subject's individual elements.

    (C) Passage 1 makes fun of its subject matter. Passage 2 treats its subject matter very solemnly.

    (D) Passage 1 draws upon a series of plays that serve as examples. Passage 2 draws upon no outside sources.

    (E) Passage 1 introduces special vocabulary to illuminate the subject matter; Passage 2 fails to do this.

40. What assumption do both passages seem to draw upon?

    (A) Tragedy is a higher form of drama than comedy.

    (B) Tragedy is on the decline in modern society; comedy, however, is on the rise.

    (C) *Catharsis* is an integral part of both comedy and tragedy.

    (D) An audience's role in the performance of either comedy or tragedy is a vital one.

    (E) The tragi-comedy is a form that is considered greater than drama that is merely comic or tragic.

41. Based upon both passages, which of the following best sums up the distinction between comedy and tragedy?

    (A) In a comedy, the protagonists successfully overcome all conflicts. In a tragedy, the hero is destroyed by them.

    (B) The best comedies elicit laughter from their audiences. Tragedies that elicit laughter are doomed to failure.

    (C) A comedy requires a minimal number of actors and sets. Tragedies usually require large casts and extravagant sets.

    (D) While a tragedy's main protagonist is the tragic hero, a comedy does not have a main character; its parts are usually equally distributed.

    (E) The purpose of comedy is to leave the audience in hysterical laughter. The purpose of tragedy is to leave the audience gloomy and depressed.

CRITICAL READING PRACTICE TEST

ANSWER KEY

1.	(B)	12.	(C)	23.	(A)	34.	(D)
2.	(E)	13.	(A)	24.	(E)	35.	(A)
3.	(D)	14.	(C)	25.	(B)	36.	(C)
4.	(D)	15.	(A)	26.	(A)	37.	(E)
5.	(C)	16.	(E)	27.	(A)	38.	(B)
6.	(C)	17.	(A)	28.	(A)	39.	(B)
7.	(A)	18.	(D)	29.	(C)	40.	(D)
8.	(E)	19.	(D)	30.	(E)	41.	(A)
9.	(B)	20.	(E)	31.	(C)		
10.	(E)	21.	(D)	32.	(D)		
11.	(E)	22.	(C)	33.	(B)		

DETAILED EXPLANATIONS
OF ANSWERS

1.   **(B)**   In line 6, the author refers to Oliver's difficulty with "respiration," which is a synonym for "breathing." Choices (A), (C), (D), and (E) are therefore incorrect, because they refer to other life functions which are not mentioned.

2.   **(E)**   Because of his breathing problem, Oliver's life is threatened; he is poised between the two worlds of life and death. Nowhere is poverty and riches (A) mentioned. (B) and (C) are incorrect because at this point, Oliver is still in his early infancy. No mention is made of love and hatred (D).

3.   **(D)**   The author states that if "Oliver had been surrounded by careful grandmothers, anxious aunts, experienced nurses, and doctors of profound wisdom, he would most inevitably and indubitably have been killed in no time." Dickens clearly feels the influence of this group is a harmful one. Therefore, (A), which states the opposite, must be incorrect. Similarly, (B) cannot be true. Dickens obviously does not think that these people are the pride of the human race (C); in fact, he feels contempt towards them. Choice (E) is incorrect because it makes a neutral statement about the effect of this group on Oliver.

4.   **(D)**   The outcome of Oliver's struggle against death is a positive one; he cries out in as strong a voice as he can muster. Choices (A), (B), and (C) are all incorrect because they indicate that Oliver dies. Choice (E) is wrong because we clearly see how the struggle is resolved.

5.   **(C)**   In lines 32 and 33, we are told that Oliver is "despatched to a branch-workhouse some three miles off." Nowhere is it said that Oliver is thrown into the streets (A). The money that the elderly woman steals is not Oliver's; it is that of the workhouse he was born in (B). No mention is made of his birth records (D) or any public humiliation by parish authorities (E).

6.   **(C)**   Dickens's overwhelming sense of irony is reflected in his commenting that infants were jailed simply because they have no money. Since Dickens mentions Oliver Twist being sent to the workhouse during infancy, these children are clearly not adolescents (B) or adults (E). The description of Twist's age and poor health further demonstrate that few of these children can walk, let alone steal (A). Since the children are called "juvenile offenders," (lines 33 and 34), Dickens indicates that they are in the workhouse for their own offenses, not those of their parents, so (D) is wrong.

7.   **(A)**   "Sarcastic" is the best description, since the woman does not act in the best interest of the children, even if she knew "what was good for them."

"Complimentary" (B) implies a positive tone, and such a tone is unlikely for a character who steals from children. "Impressed" (C), "astonished" (D), and "outraged" (E) are reactionary words; they usually describe a person's feelings in response to a new statement or action. Since Dickens used this phrase to describe the woman's general conduct, it is unlikely that the tone would be reactionary.

8. **(E)** There is no mention of cleanliness or good hygiene in the passage; on the contrary, any reference to health is poor, so choice (A) is wrong. Nowhere do we read of the elderly woman's friends or relations, and there is no mention of her enemies (B). Since the elderly female's character is not explained in-depth, we never read of her self-respect and confidence (C). Any sense of irony in the passage supports the woman's ability to "take care of herself," especially line 43, where it is mentioned that she "appropriated...the weekly stipend to her own use." This line does not support choice (D), since the woman acts in a selfish way by taking money from children.

9. **(B)** Dickens feels that by not providing properly for the children the elderly caretaker is experimenting with their lives. She was not, however, weaning the children off food to create stronger humans, but in order to embezzle money (A). Choice (C) is clearly incorrect. If the women felt that children were so important, she would have treated them better. Choices (D) and (E) are wrong, since they assume a literal translation of the word "philosopher." Dickens is not using the word "philosophy" as a subject of study.

10. **(E)** The passage describes the great philosopher's attempt to prove a horse needs no food to survive. Unfortunately, just as the philosopher had the horse down to eating only one straw a day, the horse died before being able to receive his first "bait of air," or, rather, his first meal which would consist of nothing but air. Therefore, "worms" (A), "a hook" (B), and "a trap" (D), although appropriate synonyms for "bait," are not correct when considered in context. Choice (C), "a breeze," although synonymous with "air," has little to do with the horse's first meal of nothingness.

11. **(E)** In lines 59 and 60, the author writes of Oliver's "good, sturdy spirit..." Since all indications are that Oliver was undernourished, (A) cannot be correct. Choice (B) is wrong because no mention is made of a donation to Oliver. (C) "sheer luck," contradicts Dickens's comment on Oliver's sturdy spirit. (D) Oliver's diminutive stature is a factor working against him.

12. **(C)** Dicken's attitude toward the city where Oliver lives is one of pure contempt. Therefore, choices (A), (B), (D) and (E) cannot be correct.

13. **(A)** The first paragraph tells us Marshall was a Federalist, but not an extreme one, and a nationalist. The second and third paragraphs elaborate on these facts and discuss their results in the form of the decisions made by the

Marshall Court. The author does suggest in the final paragraph that doctrines evolved under Marshall's centralizing tendencies helped to preserve the Union, but this is only one result of the overall theme of the passage. Thus, (B) is incorrect. (C) is incorrect because there is no indication in the passage that Marshall was disloyal to the Federalists (disagreement does not equal disloyalty), nor that the author is criticizing Marshall for his politics. The passage does, incidentally, concern the role of the Supreme Court in national politics. It must if it is to discuss the politics of Marshall while he was chief justice of the Court. The focus of the passage, however, is narrowly concentrated on Marshall, rather than on the broader topic of the Supreme Court in general. Thus, (D) is incorrect. (E) is incorrect because the passage is too short to be considered much of a *chronicle* of Marshall's time as chief justice (a position we are told he held for 34 years). In addition, the passage only focuses on one aspect of Marshall's politics; too narrow a focus to be considered a chronicle.

14. **(C)** We are told this in the last two sentences of the first paragraph. From these sentences, in particular where we are told Marshall believed property to be the "foundation of civil liberty," (B) is clearly wrong. In these same sentences Marshall is described as Lockean. We are then told this means he viewed property "not as an economic end in itself," making (A) incorrect. (D) is incorrect because there is no indication in the passage that property should only be held by the upper class. We are told Marshall distrusted the common people, but this is in relation to majoritarian politics, not property. Similarly, (E) is incorrect because the author does not make a connection between Marshall's view of property and his desire for a centralized government.

15. **(A)** In the first sentence of the second paragraph, we are told Marshall strongly supported centralization and "completely rejected the compact theory." Later in the paragraph the author tells us Marshall was committed to "federal authority versus states' rights." From these comments we can conclude that the compact theory supported states' rights, which also makes (D) incorrect. (In addition, though a minor point, the resolutions the author associates with the compact theory are named for two states, Virginia and Kentucky.) (C) must be incorrect if Marshall rejected the compact theory. In addition, we are told Marshall died in 1835, well before the start of the Civil War. Although we are told Marshall was not an extreme Federalist, it should still be clear that the Federalists, extreme or otherwise, were in favor of a strong central (federal) government. Thus, the compact theory cannot be a theory of the extreme Federalists, making (B) incorrect. (E) is incorrect because the passage makes no mention of jurisprudential activism or what that means.

16. **(E)** We are told this in the second paragraph when the author says Marshall "tended to distrust the common people." The author continues by indicating Marshall also saw legislative democracy as a threat to his (Marshall's) view of constitutionalism. Given this distrust, Marshall cannot be said to have

been either supportive or nurturing toward mass democratic politics, making both (B) and (D) incorrect. Similarly, (C) is incorrect because by distrusting the common people and seeing a threat to constitutionalism Marshall is not being indifferent. (A) is incorrect because the author uses the word *hostile* to refer to Marshall's perceived conflict between legislative majoritarianism and constitutionalism.

17.   **(A)**   Choice (A) is correct because "loathing," which means "a strong dislike of," is a synonym for "aversion." Choices (B) and (C) are too positive, and convey an endorsement of something, rather than dislike. "Forbidding" (D) means "menacing or sinister" and "misdirection" means "wrongly guided," and therefore, are not synonyms for "aversion."

18.   **(D)**   From the passage we can conclude that *federalism* is related to the policies of the Federalists, and we know that they supported a centralized government. In the third paragraph, the author discusses the significance of judicial review under the Marshall Court. We are also told how Marshall's doctrines (which we were previously told had strong centralizing tendencies) supported national supremacy. From all of these pieces we can conclude judicial review was a mechanism used by the Marshall Court to support federalism. (A) is incorrect because we can conclude from the last sentence of the passage that the author believes Marshall was successful in his centralizing policies. (B) is nonsensical because it is clear from the passage that the Marshall Court did not have *decentralizing* policies. (C) is incorrect because there is no mention in the passage of the causes of the Civil War. The author only notes that doctrines developed by the Marshall Court later helped to preserve the Union. (E) is incorrect because the author tells us in the third paragraph that the practical effects of Marshall's policies were felt most strongly on "state legislatures rather than Congress."

19.   **(D)**   This can be concluded from the author's comments in the last sentence of the second paragraph where he says that Marshall's "principles placed him near the mainstream of American politics." This comment also makes (A) incorrect. (A) is also incorrect because we are told in the first paragraph that Marshall did not agree with the extremist ("reactionary") wing of his own party. (B) is incorrect because there is no mention of what constitutes right- or left-wing politics. Given *current* definitions, Marshall might be considered nearer to the right than the left, but this neither obviates the fact that we are told his politics were "mainstream," nor is it sufficient to characterize Marshall as right-wing. (C) and (E) are incorrect because we are told in the second paragraph that Marshall distrusted the common people and saw legislative majoritarianism as a threat to constitutionalism.

20.   **(E)**   The correct answer is (E) which can be seen in the first sentence with the use of the word "renowned." Since Becquerel's reputation was built

through his research, the conclusion can be drawn that his work represented "an important breakthrough." Answers (A) through (D) portray his research as insignificant.

21. **(D)** The correct answer is (D) because it cites the correct interaction of electrodes in the correct solution, as stated in the second sentence. Choices (A), (B), (C), and (E) incorrectly identify the electrodes or do not stipulate the correct kind of environment.

22. **(C)** Although (A) is a true statement, it does not reflect why selenium is used for photometric devices. Choice (B) is false. Choice (D) is a misreading of the sentence, "Even today, light sensitive cells on cameras for adjusting shutter speed to match illumination are made of selenium." Choice (E) is not correct, because regardless of the abundance of selenium, it must be capable of converting the visible part of the sun's spectrum. Therefore, answer (C) is correct.

23. **(A)** Solar energy is not the most efficient source of heat (B). Solar energy is relatively simple but difficult to capture (C). Solar energy is not cheaper than fossil-fuel powered energy (D).

24. **(E)** "Heralding" in line 21 most nearly means (E), "introducing," as it denotes the beginning of a "new era." Although the remaining answer choices are close, they do not accurately represent the meaning of "heralding."

25. **(B)** Choice (B) is the correct answer based on the part of the passage that states, "In 1958, the U.S. Vanguard satellite used a small...amount of cells (solar) to power its radio." Choice (A) is not addressed. Choices (C) and (D) might be inferred from the passage, but telephones and electric utility lines are discussed in conjunction with potential effects of solar energy and not in the context of actual use.

26. **(A)** This answer is arrived at by doubling the amounts in the sentence, "Today, photovoltaic systems are capable of transforming one kilowatt of solar energy falling on one square meter into about a hundred watts of electricity."

27. **(A)** Answer (A) captures the sense of both the difficulty and the availability of sunlight as a source of solar energy. Choice (B) negates any availability of the sun. Choice (C) reflects only one of the variables that impairs the visibility of the sun. Choice (D) does not address the question. Choice (E) is not true.

28. **(A)** Choice (A) is correct because the benefits of solar energy for photovoltaic conversion into electricity must be explained in order to justify using special techniques to gather the solar energy. The remaining answer choices do not provide this support.

29. **(C)** The sentence tells us that a comedy need not be funny or "laughable" (i.e., able to be laughed at). Choice (C), "amusingly droll," is therefore the word that is most synonymous with laughable. While comic dialogue can be "senselessly ridiculous" (A) or "foolishly stupid" (B), the sentence in question is only concerned with the general laughableness of comedy. Passage 1 does not indicate that comedy might be "theoretically depressing" (D) or "critically unsavory" (E).

30. **(E)** The author implies that Shakespeare was the subject of criticism for engaging in comedy that elicited laughter. However, this certainly does not make Shakespeare look poorer in our eyes; modern comedies may be laughable without receiving such criticism (A). However, the laughableness of some of Shakespeare's comedies indicated that they were not technically of the "highest form" of comedy (B). The passage does not imply that higher forms of comedy should be degraded simply because Shakespeare did not always engage in them (C), nor does it criticize the Renaissance tradition of comedy without laughter (D).

31. **(C)** The correct answer is "tragi-comedy." The situation, while being humorous, also triggers our sympathy for the character involved, since we can all relate to losing something important. Choice (A) is incorrect because the situation does not contain the elements of satire, which implies "humanity and human institutions are in need of reform." (B) This situation does not rely on absurdity, sight gags, or other elements of farce, for its humor. (D) Sarcasm is a comedic device employing irony, often used in satire. Finally (E) "slapstick" is a particularly boisterous form of farce, which does not apply in this scenario.

32. **(D)** The close of Passage 1 is very much concerned with the interaction of the audience and the action on stage. There is no mention in the passage about theater seating (A), forced comedy (B), the contemporaneousness of the play and its audience (C), or the complexity of the play's matter (E).

33. **(B)** The passage calls for us to believe in the script and thereby draw "nearer to the conflict." The author clearly expects the play's audience to become one with the material they are observing. There is certainly no warning against over-involvement (A) or over-enjoyment (E) on the audience's part, nor is there a call to stand critically apart from the drama (D). The author specifically wants us to feel "less safe" in the presence of the drama (C).

34. **(D)** The passage notes that the definition of tragedy "originated with Aristotle." There is no indication in the passage that tragedy is now outdated (A), nor that Greek philosophy is the sole code to theater (B). The passage nowhere mentions Aristotle as an actor (D), nor that his sense of tragedy was based on false conclusions (E).

35. **(A)**   The passage describes the "noble" aspect of the tragic hero as his "social position and moral stature"; therefore, degree and virtue are appropriate synonyms. Great wealth is not always a mark of social rank, nor is self-esteem always a measure of morality (B). Wit and intelligence are not cited in the passage as elements of tragic nobility (C), nor are courage and strength (D). Handsome features and social charm also belong to a different mode of nobility than the tragic (E).

36. **(C)**   A strong-willed character whose pride, or "hubris," exceeds that of the gods is a typical example of a tragic hero; his pride is his *harmatia,* or tragic flaw. Courtesy to the lower class (A) and good communication skills (B) are hardly character flaws. A weak, miserly peasant is not material for a tragic hero (a tragic hero requires good social standing). In addition, a person himself cannot *be* a flaw; this choice reflects a misunderstanding of the term *harmatia* (D). If a tragic hero has committed crimes, a desire to do penance for them could hardly be considered a character flaw (E).

37. **(E)**   The passage describes at great length the "relieved and almost elated" feeling that the audience should feel at the conclusion of a tragedy, despite the pity and fear they felt for the tragic hero during the drama. The hero's new stature comes after his consummated suffering; he is not rescued from it (A). The passage does not imply that the audience is deriving a "perverse pleasure" from the hero's suffering, but a sense of cleansing from the release of the hero's anguish (B). *Catharsis* does not denote an inconclusive ending to a tragedy, nor an audience's response to such an ending (C). The passage states clearly that audience members should not feel depressed when they experience *catharsis*; they should instead feel purged from the experience (D).

38. **(B)**   Both passages run through the basic terminology and general information surrounding their particular aspects of drama. While the author of Passage 1 seems a bit judgmental concerning certain forms of "low" comedy, there is neither an attempt on his part, nor on the part of the author of Passage 2, to ridicule the aspects of drama they are analyzing (A). There is no sensational information provided in either passage (C). Shakespeare is not used as an authority in Passage 1; he is merely an example. Passage 2 does not even mention Shakespeare (D). Neither author seeks to persuade his readers to read only one type of drama (E).

39. **(B)**   Passage 1 primarily distinguishes between the different types of comedy (farce, satire, etc.). Passage 2, on the other hand, does not explore different types of tragedies, but rather discloses the various elements that create the tragedy in general. Although Passage 1 makes a reference to the Renaissance era and Passage 2 cites an author from Classical Greece, neither passage is concerned "primarily" with these eras when discussing their subject matter (A). Neither passage pokes fun at its subject matter, nor do they treat their discussions

with any undue solemnity (C). Passage 1 does not draw upon any specific plays as examples. Passage 2 draws upon Aristotle as a source of information (D). Passage 2, like Passage 1, introduces special vocabulary *(catharsis, hamartia,* etc.) to illuminate its subject matter.

40. **(D)** Both passages make several mentions of the audience's key element of participation in the drama. Tragedy is never mentioned as being a "higher form of drama" than comedy (A), nor is tragedy considered "on the decline" in either passage (B). *Catharsis* is mentioned only in respect to tragedy (C). Tragi-comedy, although mentioned briefly, is not mentioned as having any greater worth than a pure tragedy or comedy (E).

41. **(A)** Passage 1 is careful to specify that it is merely the victory over conflict that defines a comedy. The hero's fall is necessitated in a tragedy. Passage 1 warns us that a comedy need not be laughable to have merit; on the other hand, there is nothing to stop a good tragedy from having an occasional break in the mood (B). There is no mention in either passage of the number of actors or sets required for a particular aspect of drama (C), nor is there any mention of role distribution (D). To reiterate, a comedy's sole purpose is not necessarily to elicit laughter. According to Aristotle, a tragedy should not leave its audience "gloomy and depressed" (E).

CHAPTER 6

Essay Writing

- ➤ Essay Writing Review
- ➤ Writing Samples
- ➤ Writing Your Application Essay

ESSAY WRITING
REVIEW

Preparing to Write for Your Tests

These writing strategies can be used for the essays for these tests:
LSAT, MCAT, CLEP, CLAST, CBEST, GMAT, and PPST

Before you begin to write an answer to an essay question, you will want to complete certain preparatory steps.

➤ Read the Statement/Question Carefully

You may re-read the question/statement several times before and during the writing of the essay. You may want to underline key words or phrases of the statement/question in the test booklet.

➤ Consider the Audience

Successful writers determine which of the three types of audiences they will be addressing and address their writing to that audience. An audience might be

1) a general audience,

2) a mixed audience, or

3) a specialized audience.

A general audience consists of people who may not be experts on a subject but who are willing to read the material. This is usually not the group that will mark your essay. A mixed audience may consist of both specialists and general readers; again, this is not likely to be the group that will score your essay. It is the third group — a specialized audience — that will likely score the essay; they have considerable knowledge of the subject and will be looking for certain things. A savvy test-taker will be aware of the concerns of the specialized audience. These concerns include:

➤ correct grammar,

➤ correct spelling,

➤ logical organization,

➤ generalizations supported by specific details, and

➤ an objective tone that is not too personal or too informal.

➤ Study the Writing Tasks That Follow the Statement

In order to receive full credit for your essay, you must address each writing task. It is helpful, in writing the essay, to use wording similar to that of the question so that the scorer can see immediately which task is being addressed, or that the question is being addressed.

Writing the Introductory Paragraph

The first paragraph (the introductory paragraph) keeps the question(s) in focus for the writer and restates the question(s) for the reader. The introductory paragraph contains a thesis statement that should do two things:

1) Give the main idea(s) of the essay

2) Provide the organization for the reader

Developing the Paragraphs in the Body of the Essay

Ideally, each paragraph should contain a topic sentence to which all the sentences in the paragraph will relate. Each of these paragraphs will relate to the thesis sentence as stated in the introductory paragraph.

Preparing the Concluding Paragraph of the Essay

The successful examinee includes a concluding paragraph in the essay. This paragraph should review the main points of the answer(s), sum up the answer(s), and restate the thesis sentence. This concluding paragraph is an important part of a well-written essay.

Proofreading and Revising the Essay

You should allow a few minutes at the end of the assigned period as a time to proofread and (if necessary) revise the essay. The specialized audience scoring the essay reads the essay as a first draft; a perfect copy is not expected. Nevertheless, you should make sure of the following:

- All writing is clear and legible

- All sentences have a subject and a verb and express a clear thought

- Run-on sentences have been avoided

- The antecedent of each pronoun is clear

- Each pronoun agrees with its antecedent in number

- Each subject and verb agree in number

- The same tense is used throughout the essay

- Words are spelled correctly

- Items in a series have been separated by commas

- All proper nouns and the first word of each sentence have been capitalized

- Each sentence ends with its proper mark of punctuation

- Apostrophes have been used correctly for possession. (Contractions are avoided in formal writing.)

  — Singular nouns are made to show possession by adding *'s*

  — Plural nouns ending in *s* are made to show possession by adding *'*; plural nouns not ending in *s* are made to show possession by adding *'s*

- *It's* is a contraction meaning "it is" and should be avoided since contractions should be avoided in formal writing

- *Its* is a possessive pronoun and requires no apostrophe (')

- To add a word, use the caret (^); to add a whole section, make a note in the paper where the insertion is to be made and write the section at the end

- To delete a word or a section, a line through the word or a large *X* through a paragraph is quicker and neater than scratching out each word

General Essay Writing Strategies

The following is a list of general essay writing strategies for both the test essay and the application essay.

➤ Avoid Using Slang and Clichès

Slang makes you sound unintelligent, while clichès are unoriginal. For example, do not end your essay with, "All's well that ends well." While this may *seem* to conclude your essay nicely, it really shows a lack of originality and indicates that you may be unsure of your writing ability.

➤ Do Not Overuse Contractions

Since this will be a formal piece of writing, you should write in a knowledgeable manner. It is customary to spell out words. *Occasional* contractions are fine and perfectly acceptable. You may even find that a contraction works better in a particular sentence. In most cases, however, you should write out "do not," "will not," and "would not," instead of don't," "won't," and "wouldn't."

➤ Use Pronouns Sparingly

Using pronouns may tend to confuse the reader. If you use "she" often, for example, the reader may begin to wonder who "she" is, even though you mentioned in the first paragraph that "she" is your sister. Be sure to indicate the specific person, instead of using "she" or "he," whenever possible.

➤ Smoother Sentences Are Better than Choppy Ones

For example, writing, "After hearing both arguments, it was clear that Jeff knew more about the subject," is smoother than "Both arguments were heard. It was clear Jeff knew more."

➤ State Your Position Clearly and Effectively

Write: "I believe that the educational process would work much more effectively if students attended school twelve months a year," if that's how you feel. Don't assume that the reader will figure out your point before getting to the end of the essay.

➤ **Avoid Using Words Incorrectly or Misspelling Them**

You should carefully study the grammar and vocabulary reviews. Even though your essay may be excellent, misspelled and incorrectly used words may cost you points.

➤ **Indent Your Paragraphs Clearly and Write Legibly**

You are sure to receive a more favorable response if the reader doesn't have to decipher your essay.

➤ **Keep Your Essay Points Organized and Logical**

Don't discuss your success on the debating team and then jump to why you want to study medicine. If there is no clear transition from idea to idea, the reader will have a hard time understanding your main point.

Scoring the Essay

Readers of the Writing Samples most often use a holistic method of scoring the essays. Each essay is regarded as a unit and is assigned a single score based on what is considered to be its total quality. Some mistakes are expected on the timed essays, so an occasional mistake will not affect the evaluation of the essay. Readers of the papers are trained. Retraining is given at intervals to assure that accurate scoring is continued.

Each paper is scored by two readers using a zero-four or a one-six-point scale, with the highest numbers representing the highest scores. If the paper receives two scores that are more than one point apart, a third reader will determine the total score for the paper. Clarity, depth, and unity are used to determine the score. Papers may be reported as "Not scorable" or given a score of 0 if they are blank, not written in English, illegible, or totally disregard the assigned topic.

Listed below are some general points that may be taken into consideration by the readers of your essay:

1) Grammar, usage, and spelling should be accurate. Since this is a first-draft, timed essay, an error or two will not affect your grade. An essay reads more easily, though, when it is relatively error-free.

2) The topic has been completely addressed.

3) The essay is cohesive and the point of view is consistent. There are supporting details to the main theme.

WRITING FOR THE GMAT

You will be given 30 minutes to write on each assigned topic.

The AWA Section of the GMAT consists of two essay questions. The essay responses will be used to inform score recipients of their prospective applicants' writing skills.

The two essays differ in nature. For the first essay, "Analysis of an Issue," the essayist must analyze a particular issue, whether business-related or otherwise. He or she must take a position based upon a particular topic and support that position with logical reasons, examples, and observations.

In the "Analysis of an Argument" essay, the essayist must explore a thesis already made by another writer; he or she must then intelligently support or contend with the provided argument. The essayist must examine each idea presented in the argument, judge the merit of its conclusion, and make suggestions that would improve the argument.

Sample Analysis of an Issue Essay Topic

Many new businesses are finding it difficult to survive in modern times without an enormous amount of financial backing. Many people recall "the good old days," when a person with a smart head, an ambitious heart, and a pocketful of change could start a potentially prosperous business. Today, however, larger companies continually swallow up smaller companies, or offer the type of competition against which no small business could ever hope to survive. However, larger corporations provide the country with a certain economic stability that would be lost if the nation were overrun solely with tiny businesses struggling to keep themselves alive.

Which type of business described above, the small business or the large corporation, do you feel is most beneficial to both consumers and the business community at large? Explain your position, using relevant reasons and/or examples drawn from your own experience, observations, or reading.

Sample Essay

Despite the illusion of financial security offered by large corporations, this country's economy will crumble unless small businesses are given a chance. The fundamental flaw of large corporations' advocates is that they ignore the overwhelmingly negative consequences of the demise of small businesses. The formulating principle of this nation and all capitalistic societies is that every man and woman can pursue a prosperous life without bounds or limitations. However, the rise of the large corporation is turning this country into a place where ambition is discouraged, and competition unthinkable.

Advocates of large corporations ignore the fact that these businesses did not simply spring out of nowhere. Most of them began as small businesses that, through initiative and sweat, built themselves up into something far beyond their original expectations. Enterprising individuals, in an attempt to better themselves, found in this nation avenues for financial improvement.

America was famous for being a land of opportunity. For the first time, immigrants from countries with restrictive caste systems could choose their social standing for themselves; they were no longer forced to adopt a role imposed upon them at birth. Now, however, freedom for personal expansion and growth has become extremely limited by the presence of larger corporations. It is much more financially stable and lucrative to become an employee in a large company, and next to impossible to strike out on one's own. The very premises of this country's existence have been undermined by its own successes.

Let us imagine that an enterprising individual, Mr. Smith, is very ambitious and eager to make a comfortable living. He lives in a remote neighborhood where there is a need for a grocery store. Years ago, he might have simply found a backer to help him get started or borrowed enough capital from the bank to start a prosperous business. Now, however, in order to start a business with any chance of competing with the larger food store chains, Smith would have to pay a considerably larger fee to become part of a grocery store chain. If he were to strike out on his own, his business would always be jeopardized by the possibility that a Foodtown or an A&P would open up in his area. The only way he could compete with such a store would be to drastically reduce his prices, and this would turn his enterprising skills into a mere struggle for survival.

Of course, there are also advantages to large corporations. Job security and market stability are two important factors that they offer. However, a chain reaction has begun that will certainly end in disaster for this country. If the most ambitious individuals in this country are forced to be underlings in larger corporations, or, at best, buy into large corporations for the sake of competition, then more and more of our nation's outstanding individuals will vanish in the system. The successful ones will be those without initiative, those only willing to take the smooth road laid out by large corporations. Because of this, these corporations will suffer. Top executives will be those "smart" enough to play the game by the rules and squelch ambition in the process.

It is therefore imperative that small businesses be given a fairer chance. We have seen how large corporations stifle ambition and initiative, and how they are on the way to creating a society where conformity is the key to success. Perhaps the government can step in and create charters that will lend more advantages to people starting businesses. State budgets should devote portions of tax money to aid small businesses in peril. If not, our country will be sold to corporate giants that will turn our land of promise and dreams into a living nightmare.

Analysis of Sample Essay

This essay scores highly because of several factors. The writer shows a willingness to take a bold stand and support his or her position with concrete reasons and examples. There is a serious attempt on the writer's part to use descriptive phrases and vary sentence structure to avoid monotony. While his or her views are sometimes generalized and could use some additional support or evidence, they are presented clearly and consistently. There is an overall flow and direction to the essay; each paragraph follows the next in a specific order.

The first paragraph states the writer's perspective and suggests some of his or her reasons for maintaining that position. The second paragraph introduces the premise that large corporations owe their success to having been able to begin as small businesses. The third paragraph provides a reason why smaller businesses are having difficulty surviving in a world filled with large corporations. The fourth paragraph provides a hypothetical example, using "Mr. Smith" to illustrate that ambitious individuals were in a much greater environment in previous years than they are now. The fifth paragraph admits the advantages provided by large corporations but expresses the overwhelming penalties that they impose on society. The sixth paragraph reiterates the writer's position and suggests possible solutions to avert a potential catastrophe.

Sample Analysis of an Argument Essay Topic

Television is about to become one of the most important resources of Americans today. With new cellular technology, hundreds of stations from around the world will be available at a user's fingertips. In addition, cellular television users will be able to call specific programs (movies, documentaries, etc.) onto their screens at the touch of a button. An entire world of information will be available to the modern television viewer, who will no longer be a passive "couch potato," but an active student of a global society.

Discuss how logically convincing you find this argument. In explaining your point of view, be sure to analyze the line of reasoning and the use of evidence in the argument. Also discuss what, if anything, would make the argument more sound and persuasive or would help you to better evaluate its conclusion.

Sample Essay

This passage makes a number of interesting points about the future of video technology in America. The author anticipates a vast array of resources available "at the touch of a button" for future users of cellular television. There are, however, a few assumptions made by the writer that require additional support. He or she assumes first of all that cellular technology will be marketed as an

educational tool, and not solely commercialized as a supreme entertainment center. Even granting the assumption that a significant amount of cellular technology
users will pool their new resources for the sake of research, we must question
whether there is enough activity involved in the process to free these television
viewers from the title of "couch potato."

The author identifies two principal uses for cellular television. He or she
notes primarily that users will be able to access "hundreds of [television] stations
from around the world." There is little doubt that this could indeed be a significant source of educational research. However, it would be ridiculous to assume
that this is the avenue that will be pursued by most television viewers. This is
clear to anyone with seventy cable stations filled with mindless drivel. The writer
might have suggested that some sort of selection process be employed to choose
a substantial percentage of research-oriented programming. Without this selection process, there would be "hundreds of stations from around the world" that
provided the same commercialistic, mind-wasting rubbish.

Users will also be able to call up "specific programs (movies, documentaries,
etc.)"; in effect, they will be able to view any known program at any time. This,
on the surface, certainly seems to conform to the idea that cellular television
users will become "active student[s] of a global society." It would be pointless to
once again drill the point that such resources could be abused by those with no
educational purposes in mind. A more serious concern involves those who would
indeed be using this technology for proper research needs. What frightens me is
that an unlimited supply of research "at the touch of a button" is not really
"research" at all.

This can only be explained by redefining the connotations of the word "research." There is a certain quality of initiative and ambition that builds itself
around the "research" conducted by an archaeologist in ancient Egypt as opposed
to a high school student examining an encyclopedia to write a history report. It is
for this reason that instructors send students to the library to quest for data rather
than simply photocopy all the data their students could possibly require. The very
act of searching for resources is a significant exercise in our mental development.
If all we need do is punch in a few keys, there will be no challenge to the affair.

Seen in this way, we realize that something of the backbone of humanity will
be lost if the connotations of "research" change this drastically. Faced with a
seemingly infinite array of information before them, young students of the future
will no longer be motivated by that drive which would compel them to seek out
and find what humanity has yet to even imagine. Students of the next generation
will be blinded by the illusion that all things are already known. Untold discoveries will be lost because that primal urge to explore and discover will be perma-
nently extinguished by this cellular technology.

It would therefore be imperative that this technology be carefully utilized.
The writer of this passage should have stressed the potential dangers of cellular

television, as well as its benefits. For there is no denying that this will indeed be a supreme source of information. But it must be regarded solely as a tool, a way to rediscover that which has already been discovered. Its chief purpose should be to help those in the midst of researching matters unknown to humanity, not simply to appear as a source of infinite knowledge. For there will never be a time that we will know all. Unfortunately, with the rise of cellular technology, there may be a tragic time when we *think* we know all.

Analysis of Sample Essay

This essay scores strongly for a number of reasons. Its main strength is that it directly interacts with the passage. The essay shows a distinct understanding of the points made by the author, and reveals a lack of support in the author's assertions that: 1) cellular technology will be used primarily for educational reasons; 2) cellular research will be an active, not a passive, enterprise. The essay is clear, structurally sound, and easy to follow. Its various criticisms of the main passage are also clearly and firmly supported.

The introductory paragraph clearly states the two assertions with which the essay will contend. The second paragraph explores the first premise (entertainment vs. research) with regard to the author's mention of the many television stations that will be available to users of cellular technology. The third paragraph introduces the second premise (active vs. passive) with regard to cellular television's ability to call up "any known program at any time." The fourth paragraph continues this premise by defining some connotations of the word "research." The fifth paragraph continues this point even further by projecting the dark future that will result if cellular technology is abused in this manner. The sixth paragraph concludes by suggesting that cellular technology can indeed be an excellent source of productive research, as long as it is clearly labelled as a "tool" and not "as a source of infinite knowledge." This conclusion is weakened by the fact that the essayist has lost track of that other, less significant premise (entertainment vs. research). However, the depth of interaction between the essay and the passage more than makes up for this minor flaw.

WRITING FOR THE LSAT

You will be given 30 minutes to write on an assigned topic.

Organize your writing sample so it will contain approximately five paragraphs. Your first paragraph should state your theme. The middle three or four paragraphs should present an argument, and the final paragraph should sum up the argument.

The middle paragraphs should clearly reflect your argument. When choosing a position, you will probably be better off choosing the one with more "pro" arguments (if you can find one) since it will provide substantial material on which to base your argument. Keep in mind, however, that the given facts are presented in such a balanced way that any argument you choose will have enough supporting evidence to write a good essay. Do not, however, ignore the negative facts. An effective essay demonstrates that opposing arguments have been considered.

The closing paragraph should be used as your summary. It should restate the position you took in your opening paragraph and tie up any loose ends. It is important to have a strong final paragraph, since it is the last portion of the writing sample read and remembered.

LSAT WRITING SAMPLE

DIRECTIONS: You will write a short essay about the topic which is provided below. You will have 30 minutes in which you must organize your thoughts and complete the essay. BE CERTAIN THAT YOU STICK TO THE ASSIGNED TOPIC – OTHERWISE, YOU WILL NOT RECEIVE CREDIT.

You are a career counselor at a local state college and must argue in favor of a student, John Rock, entering one of the two fields presented below. The student does equally well in both disciplines, but has no interest in being a double major. Since John Rock has made an appointment with you to discuss his career plans, your recommendation of a major must take into account:

- the major which will yield the best job opportunities in the future

- the interests and talents of the student

Rock is a sophomore and has taken five courses in philosophy, in each of which he has earned "A's." Rock tells you that his greater interest is in philosophy and that he knows he can use a philosophy background as a preparation for a legal career which he has frequently considered. John knows that the only job opportunities available in philosophy per se are in college teaching. Rock, however, is not enthusiastic about the idea of going to graduate school. John enjoys reading, writing, and debating and can argue both logically and persuasively. John is also aware that philosophy is an impractical field which pays little.

John Rock has also taken six courses in physics and received all "B+'s." John tells you that although he finds physics more difficult than philosophy, he also finds it more challenging, but less enjoyable. John is unsure if he wants to spend the rest of his life in a scientific career, but is happy that a career in physics would be both profitable and prestigious. Rock is also happy that even with a bachelor's degree he could find a well-paying job. Rock's father has consistently encouraged his son John to major in physics, so the choice of physics would also please his father.

LSAT SAMPLE ESSAY

Given the tight job market for humanities graduates, and given Mr. Rock's solid competence in physics, I must recommend that John Rock pursue a degree in physics. This recommendation is based on the fact that science and technology majors are in greater demand and better paid than liberal arts majors.

John is a mature individual and a good student. He is aware that choosing to pursue a degree in physics will mean more work and more difficult assignments. He has demonstrated by his grades that he has the talent and willingness to succeed as a physics major. I note that although John receives higher grades in philosophy than in physics, this is undoubtedly due to the more difficult nature of scientific disciplines in general.

If Rock majors in philosophy, he will have to go to graduate school to obtain a doctorate degree and prepare himself for an academic life of teaching and research at low pay. If, however, he chooses physics as a major, he will not only have more job opportunities, but also better paying ones.

Despite these advantages, it should be noted that John will have to work harder in a field that he does not like as much as philosophy. Mr. Rock will also have to put aside his interest in reading and writing and debating. Choosing physics as a major would mean that Rock cannot exercise his mind as broadly as he could studying philosophy. It is certainly fair to say that John's heart is more in philosophy than in physics. It is also fair to say that enjoying one's work is extremely important, especially in the long run.

All in all, I would recommend that John Rock major in physics. While he may be more interested in philosophy, it is more important that he choose a major that offers the opportunity of securing a practical and profitable job. I would note that choosing physics also enables John to avoid going to graduate school and leads to a career that is stable, secure, and prestigious. In short, the financial and social rewards for John in pursuing a career in physics outweigh the benefits of majoring in philosophy simply because it is easier and he likes it more.

COMMENTARY ON LSAT
SAMPLE ESSAY

This essay is well written because it is concise and well organized. In the first paragraph, the author clearly and effectively states his position. The reason stated for the recommendation is also indirectly linked to one of the two required considerations in the topic statement.

The second paragraph is linked to the second required consideration in the topic statement. John Rock's ability to successfully major in physics is assessed. The difference in grades Rock received in physics and philosophy is explained, and it demonstrated that Rock should not necessarily major in philosophy simply because he receives higher grades in that field than in physics.

In the fourth paragraph, the author considers arguments against his position. The author also states in the following paragraph why those reasons are unpersuasive challenges to his position.

Sentence length and structure are varied in the essay to avoid it sounding monotonous. The essay is also properly punctuated and the spelling is correct.

The last paragraph summarizes the author's position and restates the justification for taking that position.

WRITING FOR THE MCAT

Composing a Well-Written Essay

Physicians must be able to communicate with their patients, clientele, staff, and colleagues. Not only must they be able to convey facts, findings, their thoughts and feelings, but they must be able to respond to the important questions asked by those with whom they come into contact. Doctors must be able to receive information efficiently in both oral and written form. They must be able to organize this information, give directives, and provide clear, relevant answers to questions, particularly those asked by their patients. Even factual information can confuse and frighten patients—who may already be anxious, uninformed, or misinformed—if this information is carelessly presented.

Patients expect satisfactory verbal skills from their physicians. Tabulations from surveys done by the National Research Corporation (NRC) show that a physician's ability to communicate effectively is of prime concern to the general public. Those surveyed deem this "bedside manner" to be of greater importance than any other factor, including cost and location. *Social Science and Medicine* reports a finding that the physician's behavior (including communication) had more of an impact on patient outcome than did the patient's own behavior. The best physicians encourage the understanding and participation of their patients. Clearly, effective communication is vital.

Most medical schools consider the writing ability and analytical synthesizing skills of their applicants as part of their required admission criteria. One important part of the MCAT focuses on demonstrating these skills.

The MCAT Writing Sample

Each MCAT Writing Sample consists of a statement—often a direct quotation from a well-known figure or from a work of literature. The selected reading is not, however, directly related to the biological or physical sciences, religious issues, topics that tend to generate strong emotions in the readers, the application process for medical schools, or to the rationale/motives for the examinee's decision to pursue medical school admission.

Following the quotation or statement are three specific tasks for the reader to complete in a 30-minute period. There are usually two Writing Samples (each with a quotation/statement and three writing tasks) on the MCAT. During a one hour testing session, the examinee normally is expected to complete both MCAT Writing Samples.

Purpose of the MCAT Writing Samples

The MCAT Writing Samples require the examinee to demonstrate expository writing, a type of writing that focuses the reader's attention on objects, people, events, or ideas, rather than on one's feelings or attitudes about them. Expository writing must contain information or cover important points. This is the usual type of writing demanded on standardized exams requiring essay writing. Expository writing differs from expressive writing (which places its emphasis on the writer's feelings and reactions to the world, people, objects, events, and ideas) and from writing which is done strictly for the pleasure of the reader/writer. The expository writing called for on the MCAT differs from persuasive writing, which is often called for on the Law School Admission Test (LSAT). The purpose of persuasive writing is to influence the reader's attitudes and actions by arguing for or against a position. Consider how this differs from expository writing.

The Writing Samples included on the MCAT test many levels of knowledge. The reader is required to read at the literal level; for instance, in order to answer the question(s) asked, the writer must be able to demonstrate an understanding of what is asked. The writer is also required to comprehend; for example, the writer must be able to explain unusual terms. The writer must analyze (break into parts) what is expected of him/her and synthesize (put together) concepts and ideas. The examinee must develop a central idea and present ideas logically, using correct grammar, sentence and paragraph structure, punctuation, capitalization, and spelling.

Certain steps are necessary in preparing a good answer to the MCAT Writing Sample and in meeting these goals.

WRITING FOR THE CBEST and PPST

Both the CBEST and PPST require you to write two essays as part of the examination. You will have 60 minutes to write on the two assigned topics — 30 minutes for each topic.

Each test will be scored holistically. This means that the test will be graded as a whole, and not by parts. In other words, spelling, grammar, subject, and style will be combined to receive one grade.

Typical topics on the CBEST and PPST ask you to analyze a particular situation or to relate a personal experience using the guidelines listed in the question. An essay question might ask you to relate a significant event in your life to your career decision to teach.

WRITING FOR THE CLEP

Examinees will be asked to prepare and write an essay on the topic presented within a 45-minute time frame. Read the topic carefully and organize your approach before you put pen to paper. Write clearly and concisely, and in a way that will interest the reader. Keep to the topic, and support you thoughts with concrete examples. And remember, the essay will be scored on how well, not how much you write.

WRITING FOR THE CLAST

The first part of the CLAST consists of a free-response essay question. You will have 60 minutes to write on one of two assigned topics.

As with the CBEST and PPST, the test will be graded as a whole and not by parts. Two readers will assign a score of between 1 and 6. These scores will be combined to produce a final score of between 2 and 12.

The CLAST essay section is intended to draw upon your writing skills: your ability to develop a thesis relevant to the topic, to support or refute this thesis with sophisticated ideas, and to organize those ideas in a logical fashion. MCAT, CBEST, PPST, CLEP, and CLAST examinees can read the following essay for an example of a well-written essay.

MCAT, CBEST, PPST, CLEP, and CLAST WRITING SAMPLE

DIRECTIONS: This section tests your writing skills by asking you to write an essay. The MCAT writing sample requires you to write two essays based on similar topic statements such as the one presented below.

Read the assigned topic carefully. Make sure your essay responds to the topic. You may use blank space below the assignment to organize and outline your thoughts.

Make sure your essay is written in complete sentences and paragraphs, and is as clear as you can make it. Make any corrections or additions between the lines of your essay. Do not write in the margins.

Consider this statement:

"That government is best which governs least."

From *On the Duty of Civil Disobedience,* by Henry David Thoreau.

Write a comprehensive essay in which you accomplish the following objectives. Explain what you think the above statement means. Describe one or two specific situations in which the powers of government should be increased. Discuss what you think should be the basis for increasing or decreasing a government's powers.

MCAT, CBEST, PPST, CLEP, and CLAST SAMPLE ESSAY

This statement reflects the suspicion of government, which has been so common throughout the history of the United States. The statement suggests that government is essentially in opposition to the interests of the free individual, and that, at best, a government's use of power is a necessary evil. Ideally, each individual would take care of his or her own affairs, without interference from anyone. In reality, however, individuals need to be protected from others who attempt to violate their rights. Government, then, has the right to protect individuals from interference but no right to extend its powers and activities beyond this function. In other words, government should not interfere in the lives of individuals, except to prevent them from infringing upon the rights of one another. Any other exercise of power, the statement implies, would be excessive.

Since the beginnings of this nation, citizens of the United States have been on the lookout for government interference in their lives. The Revolutionary War was fought to gain independence from excessive governmental power. With this experience behind them, the framers of the Constitution of the United States sought to limit the power of government. The Bill of Rights lists ways in which individual freedom is guaranteed against such interference. The legislative, judicial, and executive branches of government were separated so that each might prevent the others from becoming too powerful. More recently, the tenure in office of a president was limited to two consecutive terms, to prevent any individual from gaining too much personal power over the government of its citizens. Since government can overpower individual interests, it has been treated with the same caution and constraint which one might use when handling a dangerous animal.

This attitude toward government is not always healthy, for there are circumstances in which the powers of government should be enhanced, rather than limited. In periods of national emergency, such as in time of war, or after a natural disaster, the federal government must assume extraordinary powers for the good of citizens who otherwise would not be able to help themselves. During a war, for the good of everyone in the nation, the government must be able to conscript troops for battle, and to impose severe penalties on individuals who, without very good reason, refuse to obey. After a community has been devastated by a flood, the federal government should provide aid to those who would not be able to recover without it. In such instances, it seems clear that government should do more than just protect individuals from one another. It must, in addition, use its power to provide aid and to compel individuals to engage in activities required for the good of everyone.

The quote above, then, expresses a view of government that is too extreme. While we can sympathize with a desire to restrain government from becoming too powerful, we can still agree that there are circumstances in which individuals can only be helped by an increase in governmental power. No simple formula can decide what the correct amount of governmental power should be. The statement could be revised in the following manner, to express a more reasonable understanding of government: "That government is best which governs for the well-being of the governed." This statement subordinates government to "the governed," without suggesting that government would ideally not exist. Whether the power of government in any specific circumstance should be great, or small, would depend upon the circumstances in which its power is to be exercised.

COMMENTARY ON THE MCAT, CBEST, PPST, CLEP, and CLAST SAMPLE ESSAY

This essay directly addresses the issue of the statement, and accomplishes the required tasks. Paragraphs 1 and 2 explain clearly the fundamental meaning of the statement, indicated as the first task ("Explain what you think the above statement means"). The second task ("Describe one or two specific situations in which the powers of government should be increased") is accomplished in the third paragraph. Finally, the third task ("Discuss what you think should be the basis for increasing or decreasing a government's powers") is accomplished in the fourth paragraph.

The essay develops the theme of the statement with insight, explaining not only the fundamental meaning of the statement, but exploring other important implications as well. The first three sentences indicate the attitude of rugged individualism which is the basis for distrusting governmental power. The fourth sentence indicates a basis for properly coercing individuals, and thus provides a basis, made explicit in the fifth sentence, for the coercive power of government. The final two sentences of the first paragraph return to the topic of distrust of governmental power, basing this, again, on the right of individuals to independence. The second paragraph provides historical examples of the attitude toward individuality and government, expressed in the first paragraph. The third paragraph looks at governmental power in a more positive light, thus, apparently contradicting the almost purely negative attitude toward it, expressed in the first two paragraphs. This sets the stage for a criticism, in the fourth paragraph of the statement, and allows for a reasonable correction of the statement.

The ideas in this essay are clearly and logically developed. Each paragraph leads naturally into the next, such that the ideas developed in each seem spontaneously to call forth the ideas that follow. The idea of government interference, for example, expressed in sentence 1 of paragraph 2, is anticipated by sentence 6 of the first paragraph. The basic attitude toward government, expressed in the statement, is expressed again in the last sentence of paragraph 2, setting the stage for the criticism of the statement expressed in paragraph 3. The essay thus acquires structural unity.

The essay uses correct grammar and, while using sentences which are clearly organized, it varies their length and cadence to provide an interesting flow. For example, the final sentence of paragraph 1 is short and to the point, driving home the ideas developed through the longer and more complex sentences that precede it. The vocabulary employed is appropriate for expressing the ideas clearly and accurately, neither drawing attention to itself by being pretentious, nor giving the impression of talking down to the reader by being too stinted or simplistic (for example, in sentence 1 of paragraph 3: "the powers of government should be enhanced …"; and in sentence 4 of paragraph 3: "After a community has been devastated …").

Writing Your Application Essay

➤ Undergraduate Application
Essay Writing

➤ Graduate Application Essay Writing

GENERAL STRATEGIES FOR WRITING YOUR APPLICATION ESSAY

➤ Stick to the assigned topic. If you are asked to write about a significant experience in college, for example, don't start off with a significant experience from high school, even if you find that particular experience more amusing. You may receive no credit because you moved away from the assigned topic. No matter how creative your idea is, make sure it applies to the assigned topic!

➤ Normally, undergraduate schools are looking to discover something unique about you. For instance, they may want you to relate an experience that significantly changed your views on an important issue. Another popular essay topic asks you to write about what you hope to gain from a college education.

➤ Graduate schools assign a different type of topic. The schools' admissions officers want to know what you plan to do with the course of study you have chosen to pursue. If you are applying for candidacy to an MBA program, you can probably expect to write about what you plan to do with an MBA. Admissions officers not only observe how well you put your thoughts into words, but also whether or not the program of study you have chosen correlates with your career interests.

ESSAY FOR THE UNDERGRADUATE APPLICATION

Writing Your Essay

Your essay will be one of the most important elements of your application. Not only will this be an opportunity for you to talk about yourself, but it will also show the admissions officers how well you express yourself in written words. It is important to them to accept students who can write clearly and intelligently. The content of your essay and how well you write may also increase your chances of being accepted.

The most common topics colleges ask you to write about involve the reason you want to go to college and the reason you want to go to the particular college for which you are applying. They also want to know a little bit about you and your interests. Follow these hints to create a winning essay:

BE UNIQUE

Admissions officers read thousands of essays and yours will have to stick in their minds. You might discuss an interesting hobby you have or a situation you experienced which you think is unique. Perhaps you might explain the time you tried skiing to overcome your fear of heights. You might discuss the time you saved someone in a restaurant from choking. If you want to discuss your experience on a trip, write about something specific which happened on the trip. Explain something specific about your hobby. The more specific you are about the topic, the more interesting and unique you will be. The more general you are about a topic, the more commonplace your essay will seem to the admissions board.

BE HONEST

Instead of writing what you think the college is looking for, write what you think is interesting about yourself. Do not say that you are "looking forward to the challenge of the academic world" when you are really more excited about living away from home or making new friends. What your honesty reveals will be more important to the admissions board than what you think they want to hear. Remember that admissions officers read thousands of essays and can usually detect which statements are contrived and which ones are honest and truthful.

BE CLEAR, SIMPLE, AND CONCISE

Most colleges place a limit to the amount of words your essay should contain. Thus, you will want to say as much as you can without being too flowery or wordy. Use simple and concise sentences and words. Make sure your grammar is correct and that your thoughts are well organized. It is strongly suggested that you ask a friend, a teacher, or a parent to proofread and edit your essay before you submit the final work to the college. You might know what you are trying to say in your essay, but a reader may not. It is easier to have an objective person spot the mistakes you may miss. Consult an English grammar handbook, such as REA's Handbook of English Grammar, Style, and Writing or William Strunk, Jr. and E.B. White's The Elements of Style, as you write the essay.

BE PRESENTABLE

If you could imagine yourself being interviewed by the admissions officer who will read your essay, you would want to look your best. Your essay should represent the way you would want to physically present yourself. Make sure you type the essay neatly or write legibly if handwriting is allowed. Your paper should not be crumpled, wrinkled, or folded numerous times. You should create a few draft copies before submitting your final copy on good paper. If using a word-processor or computer, be sure to spell-check your essay before submitting the final draft. A sloppy essay may force an admissions officer into a negative decision. You may want to have a friend, parent, or teacher read over your essay for you. Looks count.

BE CONFIDENT BUT NOT EGOTISTICAL

You will want to show the admissions officers that you will be able to handle the pressures and stresses of your college years. If you can express your confidence and intention of studying hard, you will gain the respect of the admissions board. Do not center your essay around yourself. *Show,* rather than tell about, your best attributes. For example, rather than simply stating that you are a responsible person, describe a situation where you may have overcome difficult times and thereby showed your responsibility. It is important to appear self-confident without appearing obnoxious and egotistical.

BE HUMOROUS BUT NOT SILLY

If you can succeed in telling a joke or relating a humorous situation in written words, go ahead. If your essay makes the admissions officer smile or even chuckle, he may remember your name when it comes down to making the admission decision. However, keep in mind that it is difficult to be humorous without coming across as peculiar or clumsy, especially when the words are written and your audience is not known. You cannot be sure whether the admissions officer will relate to your humor or read your essay in the same manner in which you intended. We suggest that you stay away from using a tone which is humorous unless you are absolutely certain the reader will understand the humor.

STAY AWAY FROM POLITICS

If you have ever had a discussion concerning politics, chances are the person in the discussion expressed a different viewpoint or opinion from your own. The discussion may have even developed into a heated battle. If you feel strongly about a political issue, it may be best not to mention it since you do not know how the reader will react. Remember that an admissions officer is an individual who will have his or her own beliefs and opinions. You do not want to threaten or patronize his or her beliefs in any way. It is also best to stay away from discussing religion unless you are applying to a college with a strong religious affiliation.

ESSAY FOR THE
GRADUATE APPLICATION

Writing Your Essay

Generally, the fact that you plan to attend graduate school for a particular course of study suggests that you have an idea as to what career you might like to pursue with your degree. The schools are interested in what you plan to do with your graduate education. Often, this is the topic on which you will be asked to write your essay.

Do not be alarmed if you have not decided on your specific career goals. Some people choose graduate school in a particular area with the hopes that it will lead them to the right career choice. They may be confident about their ability in the subject they have chosen to study, but they may not know exactly where it will lead them.

Other people know exactly what they want to do, but feel that their motivation behind seeking a particular program of study will seem inappropriate to the admissions officers. For instance, many people seek MBA degrees to make themselves more marketable and to attract a better starting salary. These are perfectly good intentions. Admissions officers are aware that many candidates are seeking degrees to advance their business careers.

Be honest! Whatever your intentions are, writing the truth will be much easier than creating a story. The most important thing is that your writing portrays you as intelligent and interested in your chosen course of study.

The essay can mean the difference between being accepted and being rejected. A student who is slightly weak in one area, but who writes an excellent essay, might be accepted. Because an excellent essay signifies intelligence, creativity, and a logical mind (not to mention strong writing and verbal skills), it is important to learn to be a good writer.

ESSAY WRITING

Use this grid to practice writing your essay.

INSTALLING REA'S VERBAL BUILDER SOFTWARE

System Requirements

Macintosh: Any Macintosh with a 68020 or higher processor, or Power Macintosh, 4 MB of RAM minimum, System 7.1 or later. At least 5 MB of hard disk space available. CD-ROM drive.

Windows: Any PC with 4 MB of RAM minimum, Windows 3.1x, Windows 95, 98, or later. At least 5 MB of hard disk space available. CD-ROM drive.

MACINTOSH INSTALLATION

1. Insert REA's Verbal Builder CD into the CD-ROM drive.

2. Double-click on the REA Verbal Builder Installer icon. The installer will automatically place the program into a folder entitled "REA Verbal Builder." If the name and location are suitable, click the Install button. If you want to change this, type over the existing information, and then click Install.

3. Start the REA Verbal Builder application by double-clicking on its icon.

WINDOWS INSTALLATION

1. Insert REA's Verbal Builder CD into the CD-ROM drive.

2. From the Windows 9x Start Menu, choose the Run command. When the Run dialog box appears, type D:\setup (where D is the letter of your CD-ROM drive) at the prompt and click OK.

3. The installation process will begin. A dialog box proposing the directory "Verbal_Builder" will appear. If the name and location are suitable, click the Install button. If you wish to specify a different name or location, type it in and click OK.

4. Start Verbal Builder application by double-clicking on its icon.

TECHNICAL SUPPORT

For problems with installation or operation of your Verbal Builder software, contact REA at (732) 819-8880, Monday through Friday, between 8:30 A.M. and 5:00 P.M. ET, or on the Web at http://www.rea.com.